LEARN
ITALIAN
(ITALIANO)
THE FAST AND FUN WAY

SECOND EDITION

by Marcel Danesi, Ph.D.
Professor of Italian
Professor of Methodology
University of Toronto

Heywood Wald, Coordinating Editor
Chairman, Department of Foreign Languages
Martin Van Buren High School, New York

To help you pace your learning, we've included
stopwatches *like the one above* throughout
the book to mark each 15-minute interval.
You can read one of these units each day
or pace yourself according to your needs.

BARRON'S

CONTENTS

Cover and Book Design Milton Glaser, Inc.
Illustrations Juan Suarez

© Copyright 1997, 1985 by Barron's Educational Series, Inc.

All inquiries should be addressed to:
Barron's Educational Series, Inc.
250 Wireless Boulevard
Hauppauge, New York 11788

Library of Congress Catalog Card No. 97-8788

International Standard Book No. 0-7641-0210-9 (bk.)
                                0-7641-7025-2 (pkg.)

PRINTED IN THE UNITED STATES OF AMERICA
98765432

Library of Congress Cataloging-in-Publication Data

Danesi, Marcel, 1946–
    Learn Italian (Italiano) the fast and fun way / by Marcel
Danesi ; Heywood Wald, coordinating editor. — 2nd ed.
        p.   cm.
    ISBN 0-7641-0210-9. — ISBN 0-7641-7025-2
    1. Italian language—Conversation and phrase books—
English. I. Wald, Heywood. II. Title.
PC1121.D36   1997
458.3'421—dc21   97-8788
                                      CIP

The map is titled "POMPEII (EXCAVATIONS)" with a scale bar showing 0 to 200 m and a "Sightseeing route" legend. Labels on the map include: VILLA DEI MISTERI, Porta Vesuvio, Torre di Mercurio, Casa dell' Ara Massima, Casa degli Amorini Dorati, CASA DEI VETTII, Station (Pompei Scavi), Porta di Nola, Circumvesuviana, Nola, Porta di Sarno, Porta Ercolano, Via dei Sepolcri, Casa della Fontana Grande, Casa del Fauno, Casa di Pansa, Casa del Poeta Tragico, Casa di M. Fabius Rufus, Tempio della Fortuna Augusta, Pistrinum, Lupanare, Macellum, Tempio di Giove, Horreum, FORO, Tempio di Apollo, Tempio di Vespasiano, Edificio di Eumachia, Basilica, Porta Marina, Antiquarium, TERME STABIANE, Fullonica Stephani, Tempio di Iside, Teatro Grande, Odeon, Foro Triangolare, Caserma dei Gladiatori, Porta di Stabia, Casa di Trebio Valente, Casa di Iulius Polybius, Thermopolium, Casa del Criptoportico, Casa di L. Ceius Secundus, Casa di Menandro, Casa di Octavius Quartie, Abbondanza, Villa di Giulia Felice, Anfiteatro, Palestra, Porta Nuceria, Necropoli, Entrance, Via Plinio, Autostrada A 3, Station (Villa dei Misteri), NAPOLI, Circumvesuviana.

STABIAN BATHS
PALESTRA — A
SWIMMING POOL — B
DRESSING-ROOMS — C
CENTRAL HEATING — D
WOMEN'S BATHS
Dressing-rooms — e
Tepidarium — f
Caldarium — g
MEN'S BATHS
Dressing-rooms — h
Frigidarium — k
Tepidarium — l
Caldarium — m

(Courtesy of Michelin Guide, Italy, 10th Edition— reprinted with permission)

Italian is a ''Romance'' language, along with French, Spanish, Portuguese, and Rumanian, to mention the most widely spoken ones. This is because they all derive directly from the language of Rome—Latin. Most of the approximately 56 million inhabitants of Italy speak Italian. There are also many immigrants of Italian origin in North America who continue to speak Italian, especially in the home.

Italy is a peninsula in the shape of a "boot." There are also two islands on its western coast: Sardinia **(Sardegna)** and Sicily **(Sicilia)**. It is surrounded by the Mediterranean Sea **(Mar Mediterraneo)**, which takes on different names, as you can see on the map. The Alps **(le Alpi)** and the Apennines **(gli Appennini)** are the two main mountain chains in Italy. Politically, the country is divided into regions—each with its own dialect and local traditions. The capital of Italy is Rome **(Roma)**. You will enjoy visiting many interesting spots.

You might, for example, want to see Venice's famous San Marco church and square, Florence's breathtaking Piazza del Duomo, Rome's immortal Colosseum, Naples' famous San Carlo theater. You might also want to shop in Milan's world-famous Galleria. Or, you might want to enjoy the tranquil surroundings on the island of Capri. Other famous cities you might want to visit are Trieste, Turin **(Torino)**, Genoa **(Genova)**, Bologna, Pisa, and Palermo—to mention but a few.

Italian painting, sculpture, literature, and music are famous all over the world. Who has not heard of the great Renaissance artist Michelangelo or of the great scientist Galileo? The names Dante, Boccaccio, Petrarch **(Petrarca)**, Leonardo da Vinci, Verdi, Puccini, Rossini, Paganini, Marconi are forged into history, as, of course, is that of Christopher Columbus **(Cristoforo Colombo)**. Today, Italy is famous for its artisanship and design, especially in the fields of clothing, furniture, and automobiles. Its cinematography is internationally acclaimed. Italy's cuisine also enjoys a worldwide reputation, notably with spaghetti, ravioli, lasagna **(lasagne)**, gnocchi, and macaroni **(maccheroni)**.

By learning the language of Italy, you will acquire a valuable key to many of its cultural treasures. Just put in 15 minutes a day at a pace comfortable for you. Some days you'll cover many pages, some not so many. Now, let's get started.

PRONUNCIATION

It is thought by many that Italian is an easy language to speak, that it is written as it is spoken. This is generally true. The following charts will help you with the troublesome letters and sounds. First we give you the vowels, then the consonants. You'll need to familiarize yourself with these sounds, even though each time a new phrase is introduced in this book, the pronunciation is also shown.

VOWELS

ITALIAN VOWELS	ENGLISH EQUIVALENT	SYMBOL
casa (house)	f*a*ther	ah
bene (well)	b*e*t	eh
riso (rice)	*ea*se	ee
volo (flight)	b*o*ne	oh
scusi (excuse me)	r*u*le	oo

NOTE: Speakers in different parts of Italy will pronounce *e* and *o* slightly differently, but not enough to make a substantial difference. The *i* and *u* may stand for ''y'' and ''w'' sounds respectively. This has to do with syllable considerations. For your own practical purposes, just follow the pronunciation aids provided throughout the book.

CONSONANTS

ITALIAN LETTERS	SYMBOLS	PRONUNCIATION/EXAMPLES
c	k	Before *a, o, u,* and all consonants, pronounce with a hard "c." Example: *come* (KOH-meh) how.
c	ch	Before *e* and *i*, use the "ch" sound, as in "church." Example: *arrivederci* (ah-rree-veh-DEHR-chee) good-bye.
ch	k	Before *e* and *i*, pronounce with a hard "k" sound. Example: *che* (keh) what.
ci	ch	Before *a, o,* and *u,* use the "ch" sound, as in "church." Example: *ciao* (CHAH-oh) hi or bye.
g	g	Before *a, o, u,* and all consonants, pronounce with a hard "g" as in "gas." Example: *gatto* (GAH-ttoh) cat.
g	j	Before *e* and *i*, pronounce with a "j" sound as in "just." Example: *gita* (JEE-tah) trip.
gh	g	Before *e* and *i*, use the hard "g" sound. Example: *spaghetti* (spah-GEH-ttee).
gi	j	Before *a, o,* and *u*, pronounce with a "j" sound. Example: *giorno* (JOHR-noh) day.
gli	lly	Pronounce like the "lli" in "million." Example: *figlia* (FEE-llyah) daughter.
gn	ny	Pronounce like the "ny" in "canyon." Example: *gnocchi* (NYOH-kkee) dumplings.

CONSONANTS (continued)

ITALIAN LETTERS	SYMBOLS	PRONUNCIATION/EXAMPLES
qu	kw	Pronounce like the English "quick." Example: *quando* (KWAHN-doh) when.
s	s, z	Might be pronounced "s" as in "sit" or "z" as in "zoo." Examples: *sorella* (soh-REH-llah) sister and *sbaglio* (ZBAH-llyoh) mistake.
sc, sch	sk	**The letters "sc" before *a*, *o*, *u*, and consonants, and the letters "sch" before *e* and *i* are pronounced "sk" as in "ski." Examples: *scusi* (SKOO-see) excuse me and *scherzo* (SKEHR-tsoh) prank.**
sc	sh	Before *e* and *i*, use the English "sh" sound. Example: *scendere* (SHEHN-deh-reh) to get off.
z	ts, dz	Sometimes pronounced "ts" and sometimes "dz." Examples: *zio* (TSEE-oh) uncle and *zucchero* (DZOO-kkeh-roh) sugar.

Most consonants can be doubled, and these are represented by double letters. In this book, doubled consonants are indicated with double letters ("kk," "gg," and so on). Simply double, or lengthen, your articulation.

The remaining Italian sounds and letters correspond, more or less, to English ones. For example:

(boh-LOH-nyah) **Bologna**	(sahr-DEH-nyah) **Sardegna**	(fee-REHN-tseh) **Firenze**	(pah-LEHR-moh) **Palermo**	(MAH-reh) **mare**
(NAH-poh-lee) **Napoli**	(PEE-sah) **Pisa**	(ROH-mah) **Roma** (rolled)	(toh-REE-noh) **Torino** (touching the upper teeth)	(VEE-noh) **vino**

Now write these words, along with the English translation, and pronounce them, using the pronunciation rules just given.

arrivederci _____

figlia _____

figlio _____

valige _____

volo _____

HOW ENGLISH AND ITALIAN ARE SIMILAR

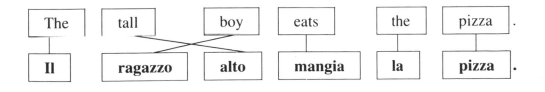

Many simple Italian sentences follow the same arrangement as English ones:

The	boy	eats	the	pizza	.
Il	ragazzo	mangia	la	pizza	.

The differences that exist between the two languages will come out as you study this book. For example, you will learn that adjectives usually follow nouns in Italian:

The	tall	boy	eats	the	pizza	.
Il	ragazzo	alto	mangia	la	pizza	.

Many Italian words can be learned simply by recognizing patterns such as the following:

ENGLISH WORDS ENDING IN: ITALIAN WORDS ENDING IN:

-ION	**-IONE**
correction	**correzione**
occasion	**occasione**
nation	**nazione**
station	**stazione**
function	**funzione**

-TY	**-TÀ**
city	**città**
ability	**abilità**
parity	**parità**
sociability	**sociabilità**
sincerity	**sincerità**

-IST	**-ISTA**
dentist	**dentista**
violinist	**violinista**
pianist	**pianista**
artist	**artista**

-OR	**-ORE**
actor	**attore**
sculptor	**scultore**
vigor	**vigore**
color	**colore**

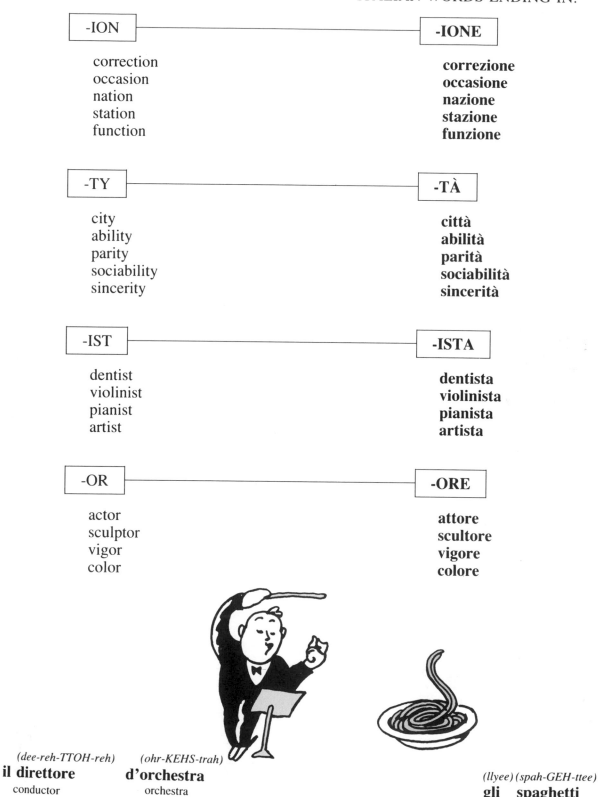

(dee-reh-TTOH-reh)   *(ohr-KEHS-trah)*
il direttore   **d'orchestra**
conductor   orchestra

(llyee) *(spah-GEH-ttee)*
gli spaghetti

As you learn the language, you will discover many other similar patterns.

This book will attempt to make it as easy and as enjoyable as possible for you to learn to speak and understand basic Italian. For your purposes, you will need a few important grammatical skills and a basic vocabulary of about one thousand words.

(mee-keh-LAHN-jeh-loh)
il "David" di Michelangelo
Michelangelo's David

(MAH-kkee-nah)
la macchina
car

You will learn only the present and imperative tenses, which is really all you will need in order to communicate your needs and intentions. Some of the dialogues may seem to be somewhat unrealistic—this is because they are deliberately written in the present tense. All dialogues have been written with a humorous touch, so that you can enjoy them more.

You will have opportunities to check your progress throughout the book. If you forget something, or feel that you need some reinforcement, go over the appropriate parts.

By working through this book for about 15 minutes a day, you will develop the ability to ask for a hotel room, to exchange money, to order food, and so on. Do not overdo it! In the 15 minutes you will spend each day on learning Italian, work only through the pages that you can cover comfortably. Have fun!

GETTING TO KNOW PEOPLE

(FAH-reh)   *(koh-noh-SHEHN-tsah)*   *(JEHN-teh)*
Fare la conoscenza della gente

1	*(KOH-meh)* *(see)* *(ee-NEE-tsee-ah)* *(kohn-vehr-sa-TSYOH-neh)* ## Come si inizia una conversazione Starting a Conversation

When you go to Italy, and we hope you will soon, one of the first things you will want to do is to meet people and strike up a friendly conversation. To do this you will need some handy expressions for conversation openers. You'll find several of them you can use in these easy conversations. Underline them so you can remember them better.

Read over the following dialogue several times, pronouncing each line carefully out loud. Try to "act out" each role. The dialogue contains some basic words and expressions that will be useful to you.

(Mark and Mary Smith, their daughter Anne, and their son John have just arrived at the Rome airport and are looking for their luggage. Mark approaches an airline employee.)

(BWOHN) (JOHR-noh) (see-NYOH-reh) MARK **Buon giorno, signore.**	Hello (or Good day/Good morning), sir.
(deh-SEE-deh-rah) IMPIEGATO **Buon giorno. Desidera** *(kwahl-KOH-sah)* **qualcosa?**	Hello. May I help you? (*literally*, do you want something)
(CHEHR-koh)(MEE-eh) (vah-LEE-jeh) MARK **Sì. Cerco le mie valige.**	Yes. I am looking for my suitcases.
(BEH-neh) *(KYAH-mah)* IMPIEGATO **Bene. Come si chiama,** *(LEH-ee)* **lei?**	Well (or Fine/Okay). What is your name? (*literally*, what do you call yourself)
(KYAH-moh) MARK **Mi chiamo Mark Smith.**	My name is (Mr.) Mark Smith.
(DOH-veh) (AH-bee-tah) IMPIEGATO **Dove abita?**	Where do you live?
(AH-bee-toh) (NEH-llyee) MARK **Abito negli Stati Uniti,** **a Chicago.**	I live in the United States, in Chicago.

8

	(NOO-meh-roh) (SOO-oh)	
COMMESSO	**Il numero del suo volo?**	Your flight number?
	(treh-chehn-toh-TREH)	
MARK	**Trecentotré da New York.**	303 from New York.
	(moh-MEHN-toh) (fah-VOH-reh)	
COMMESSO	**Un momento, per favore.**	One moment, please.

(joh-VAH-nnee)

(As the clerk looks through some papers on his desk, Giovanni, an Italian business friend, runs into Mark.)

	(CHAH-oh) (STAH-ee)	
GIOVANNI	**Ciao, Mark. Come stai?**	Hi, Mark. How are you?
MARK	**Giovanni! Sto bene, e tu?**	John! I am well, and you?
	(MOHL-toh) (SEH-ee) (kwee)	
GIOVANNI	**Molto bene. Sei qui per una**	Very well. Are you here for a holiday?
	(vah-KAHN-tsah)	
	vacanza?	
	(preh-ZEHN-toh) (MEE-ah)	
MARK	**Sì. Ti presento la mia**	Yes. Let me introduce my family to you. My
	(fah-MEE-llyah) (MOH-llyeh)	
	famiglia. Mia moglie Mary, mia	wife Mary, my daughter Anne, and my son John.
	(FEE-llyah) (FEE-llyoh)	
	figlia Anne, e mio figlio John.	
	(pyah-CHEH-reh)	
GIOVANNI	**Piacere.**	A pleasure.
	(SKOO-see)	
COMMESSO	**Scusi, signore, le valige**	Excuse me, sir, the suitcases are arriving with
	(ah-RREE-vah-noh) (PROH-ssee-moh)	
	arrivano con il prossimo volo.	the next flight.
	(ah-chee-DEHN-tee)	
MARK	**Accidenti!**	Darn it!
	(pah-TSYEHN-tsah)	
GIOVANNI	**Pazienza, Mark. Sei in Italia.**	Patience, Mark. You're in Italy.

(GRAH-tsee-eh)
MARK *(to the clerk)* **Grazie**   Thank you and good-bye *(polite)*.
     (ah-rree-veh-DEHR-lah)
   e arriverderla.
        (PREH-goh)
IMPIEGATO   **Prego, signore.**   You're welcome, sir.

MARK *(to Giovanni)* **Ciao.**   Good-bye *(familiar)*.
               (TOO-ttee)
GIOVANNI **Arrivederci a tutti.**   Good-bye to all.
          (ah-rree-veh-DEHR-chee)
TUTTI   **Arrivederci.**   Good-bye *(familiar)*.

Now without looking back try to fill in the missing dialogue parts. Check your answers from the dialogue only *after* attempting to fill in the parts from memory.

Buon giorno, signore.

B_uon_ g_iorno_. Desidera qualcosa?

Sì. Cerco le mie v_alige_.

Bene. Come si c_hiama_, lei?

M_i_ c_hiamo_ Mark Smith.

Il n_umero_ del suo v_olo_?

Trecentotré d_a_ New York.

Un momento, p_er_ f_avore_.

By rearranging the following words you will get sentences from the dialogue.

mia / la / presento / Ti / famiglia

Ti presento la mia famiglia

arrivano / valige / le / prossimo / volo / il / con / Scusi / signore

Scusi signore. Le valige arrivano con il prossimo volo

tutti / a / Arrivederci

Arrivederci a tutti

10

LE PERSONE E LE COSE

(pehr-SOH-neh) *(KOH-seh)*

People and Things

One of the first things you will need to know how to do in Italian is naming people and things. Look carefully at the following:

Singolare e plurale

(seen-goh-LAH-reh) *(ploo-RAH-leh)*

singular   plural

SINGULAR

(rah-GAH-tsoh)

ragazz o

boy

gatt o

cat

(PYEH-deh)

pied e

foot

(FYOH-reh)

fior e

flower

PLURAL

(rah-GAH-tsee)

ragazz i

boys

gatt i

cats

pied i

feet

fior i

flowers

These are called masculine nouns *(nomi maschili)*.

(mahs-KEE-lee)

Notice that they end in either o or e .

To form the plural, simply change the o

or the e to i . Got it? This diagram will help you remember.

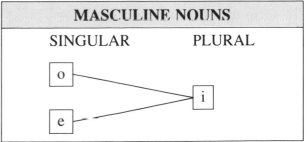

MASCULINE NOUNS	
SINGULAR	PLURAL
o	
	i
e	

11

Now look at the following additional nouns.

SINGULAR   PLURAL

cas a
house

(KAH-seh)
cas e
houses

(MEH-lah)
mel a
apple

mel e
apples

(ah-oo-toh-MOH-bee-leh)
automobil e
automobile

(ah-oo-toh-MOH-bee-lee)
automobil i
automobiles

(MAH-dreh)
madr e
mother

madr i
mothers

(feh-mmee-NEE-lee)

These are called feminine nouns (*nomi femminili*). Notice that they end in either a or e .

To form the plural of those ending in a , simply change the a to e .

To form the plural of those ending in e ,
change the e to i (as in the case
of masculine nouns). The chart at the
right will help you remember how to form
feminine plural nouns.

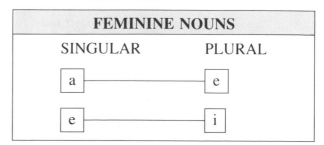

FEMININE NOUNS	
SINGULAR	PLURAL
a	e
e	i

An even easier way to remember how to form the plural of any noun is seen in this chart, which simply combines the previous two.

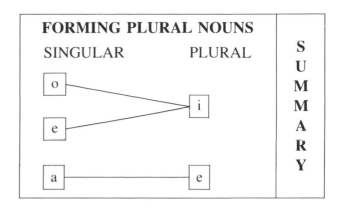

FORMING PLURAL NOUNS

SINGULAR   PLURAL

S U M M A R Y

Got it? Now test yourself by trying to put the following nouns into the plural.

(kwah-DEHR-noh)
quaderno
workbook

quaderni
workbooks

(PEH-nnah)
penna
pen

penne
pens

(PAH-dreh)
padre
father

padri
fathers

(rah-GAH-tsah)
ragazza
girl

ragazze
girls

madre
mother

madri
mothers

ragazzo
boy

ragazzi
boys

ANSWERS
Plurals quaderni penne padri ragazze madri ragazzi

13

Una, un', uno, un
A and *An*

When we name something (that is, use a noun) in English, we often precede the noun with "a" or "an." The same is true in Italian. Here is how we say these words, depending on whether the noun is masculine or feminine.

WITH FEMININE NOUNS

BEFORE ANY CONSONANT

(OO-nah)

una	*r*agazza

una	*m*adre

BEFORE ANY VOWEL

(ah-MEE-kah)

un'	**amica**

girl friend

un'	**automobile**

WITH MASCULINE NOUNS

BEFORE Z OR BEFORE S FOLLOWED BY A CONSONANT

(OO-noh)

uno	**zio**

uncle

(stoo-DEHN-teh)

uno	**studente**

male student

BEFORE ANY OTHER CONSONANT OR ANY VOWEL

un	*r*agazzo

un	*p*adre

un	**amico**

male friend

(AHL-beh-roh)

un	**albero**

tree

14

As you can see, in front of feminine nouns, "a" or "an" is [una] if the noun begins with a consonant, and [un'] if it begins with a vowel. In front of masculine nouns, [uno] is used if the noun begins with *z* or with *s* plus a consonant (*sp, st, sm, etc.*); otherwise [un] is used. Notice that [un] does not have an apostrophe in the masculine. The following chart is a handy summary to which you might refer if you run into any difficulties.

SUMMARY—HOW WE SAY "A" OR "AN"	
WITH FEMININE NOUNS	**WITH MASCULINE NOUNS**
una *(before any consonant)*	**uno** *(before z or before s plus a consonant)*
un' *(before any vowel)*	**un** *(before any other consonant or any vowel)*

Now give this a try. Fill in the appropriate form of "a" or "an" in the space provided for each of the following nouns.

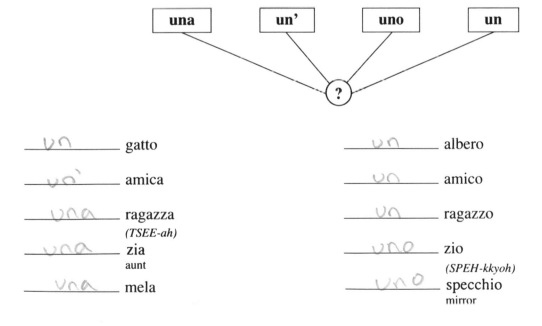

_____ un _____ gatto

_____ un' _____ amica

_____ una _____ ragazza
(TSEE-ah)

_____ una _____ zia
aunt

_____ una _____ mela

_____ un _____ albero

_____ un _____ amico

_____ un _____ ragazzo

_____ uno _____ zio
(SPEH-kkyoh)

_____ uno _____ specchio
mirror

15

How did you do? Let's try another, this time filling in both the "a" or "an" and the Italian word for what is shown.

(kee)
Chi è?
Who is it?

(keh)
Che cosa è?
What is it?

a boy

un ragazzo

a cat

un gatto

a foot

un piede

a flower

un fiore

a house

una casa

an apple

una mela

a car

un'automobile

a pen

una penna

a workbook

un quaderno

an uncle

uno zio

a tree

un albero

a mirror

uno specchio

16

Io, tu, lei e voi
I and You

In Italian, "I" is translated as _(EE-oh)_ | io |. This word is not capitalized as in English, unless it is the first word in a sentence.

"You" is represented in several ways:

| **tu** | —When addressing friends or family members in the singular (familiar address). |

| **lei** | —When addressing any stranger or superior in the singular (polite address). May also be capitalized when written (**Lei**). |

| **voi** | —As the plural of both | tu | and | lei | in current spoken Italian. |

(Although there is a more formal way of addressing more than one person (**loro**), it is seldom used in the spoken language.)

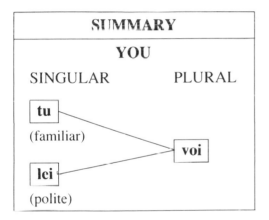

| SUMMARY |
| YOU |
SINGULAR	PLURAL
tu	
(familiar)	**voi**
lei	
(polite)	

The chart at the left will help you remember how to say "you" in Italian.

(pahr-LYAH-moh) _(pah-REHN-tee)_
PARLIAMO DEI PARENTI
Let's Talk About Relatives

Here is Giorgio's family.

And here is Giorgio's family tree. Fill in the blanks to practice the words that tell the different family relationships.

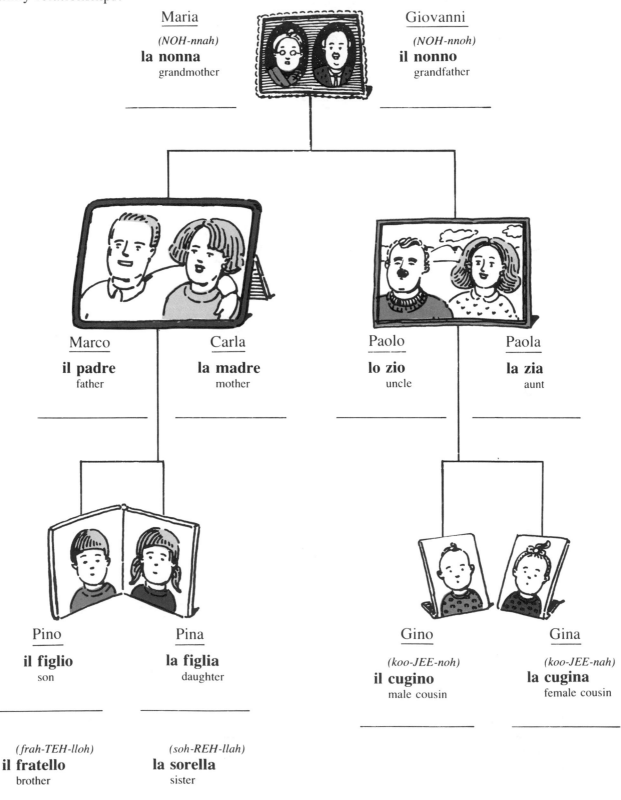

Maria

(NOH-nnah)
la nonna
grandmother

Giovanni

(NOH-nnoh)
il nonno
grandfather

_____

Marco

il padre
father

Carla

la madre
mother

Paolo

lo zio
uncle

Paola

la zia
aunt

_____

Pino

il figlio
son

Pina

la figlia
daughter

Gino

(koo-JEE-noh)
il cugino
male cousin

Gina

(koo-JEE-nah)
la cugina
female cousin

_____   _____

_____   _____

(frah-TEH-lloh)
il fratello
brother

(soh-REH-llah)
la sorella
sister

_____   _____

18

Look carefully at the family tree and then fill in the following blanks. We've done one as an example. *Be careful to copy the forms of "the"* (**il, la, lo**) *correctly.* You should know that **il marito** is the husband and **la moglie** is the wife. Good luck!

Model: Pino è _____*il figlio*_____ di Marco.

1. Gino è _____il fratello_____ di Gina.
2. Giovanni è _____il padre_____ di Carla.
3. Paola è _____la zia_____ di Pino.
4. Maria è _____la nonna_____ di Pina.
5. Pino è _____il cugino_____ di Gina.
6. Giovanni è _____il marito_____ di Maria.
7. Paola è _____la moglie_____ di Paolo.
8. Pina è _____la sorella_____ di Pino.
9. Giovanni è _____il nonno_____ di Pina.
10. Carla è _____la madre_____ di Pino.
11. Gino è _____il figlio_____ di Paola.
12. Paolo è _____lo zio_____ di Pina.
13. Pina è _____la cugina_____ di Gina.

Not so hard, right? Practice your knowledge of family names by finding the plurals of these nouns that are hidden in the puzzle, and then writing them out for additional practice.

cugino _____   sorella _____

cugina _____   figlio _____

zio _____   figlia _____

zia _____   madre _____

fratello _____   padre _____

nonna _____   nonno _____

c	u	g	i	n	i	x	x	x	x	x	x	x	x	x	x	x	x	x	z
x	x	x	x	x	x	x	c	u	g	i	n	e	x	x	x	x	x	x	i
x	x	x	x	z	x	x	x	x	x	x	x	x	f	r	a	t	e	l	l	i
x	x	x	x	i	x	n	x	x	x	x	x	x	x	x	x	x	x	x	x
x	x	x	x	e	x	x	o	x	x	x	x	x	x	x	x	x	x	x	x
x	x	x	x	x	x	x	x	n	o	n	n	e	x	x	x	x	x	x	x
m	a	d	r	i	x	x	x	x	n	x	x	x	p	a	d	r	i	x	x
x	x	x	x	x	x	x	x	x	f	i	g	l	i	x	x	x	x	x	x
f	i	g	l	i	e	x	x	x	x	x	x	s	o	r	e	l	l	e	x	x

ANSWERS

Plurals cugini cugine zii zie zio zii nonne sorelle figli figlie madri padri nonni

Fill-ins 1. il fratello **2.** il padre **3.** la zia **4.** la nonna **5.** il cugino **6.** il marito **7.** la moglie **8.** la sorella **9.** il nonno **10.** la madre **11.** il figlio **12.** lo zio **13.** la cugina

19

Now you're really moving! If you're a puzzle fan, give this a try—in Italian, of course.

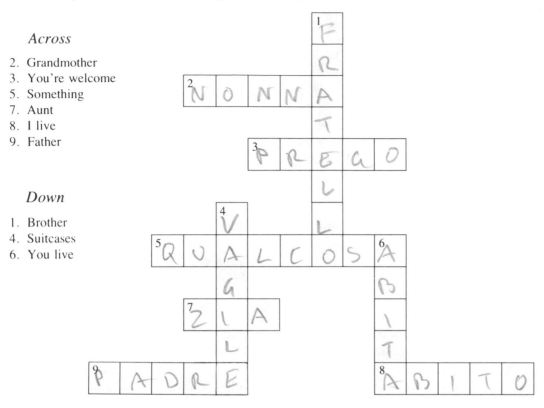

Across

2. Grandmother
3. You're welcome
5. Something
7. Aunt
8. I live
9. Father

Down

1. Brother
4. Suitcases
6. You live

It is time to return to the Smiths, just beginning their trip to Italy. See if you understand what the following paragraph is all about. Read the selection, then answer the questions that follow.

(fah-MEE-llyah)
La famiglia Smith arriva in Italia
    family
con il volo trecentotré da New York. Il signor
      (DEE-cheh)
Smith dice «Buon giorno» all'impiegato.
  says   clerk
Il signor Smith dice «Grazie» e l'impiegato.
        (een-FEE-neh)
dice «Prego». Infine, il signor Smith dice
        finally
«Arrivederla».

(kee)
Chi arriva da New York?
Who

☐ Il commesso arriva da New York.
☑ Il signor Smith e la sua famiglia arrivano da New York.

(keh)
Che dice il signor Smith?
What

☑ Il signor Smith dice «Buon giorno».
☐ Il signor Smith dice «Ciao».

Che dice l'impiegato?

☐ L'impiegato dice «Accidenti!"»
☑ L'impiegato dice «Prego».

Now study and say aloud these parts of Giorgio's house.

Una casa
home

(free-goh-REE-feh-roh)
il frigorifero
refrigerator

Il bagno
toilet

(eh-LEH-ttree-kah)
la cucina elettrica
stove

le scale
stairway

il lavandino
sink

(VAHS kah)
la vasca da bagno
bathtub

(koo-CHEE-nah)
la cucina
kitchen

(BAH-nyoh)
il bagno
bathroom

(dee-VAH-noh)
il divano
sofa

(ahr-MAH-dyoh)
l'armadio
closet

(LEH-ttoh)
il letto
bed

(soh-JJOHR-noh)
il soggiorno
living room

la camera da letto
bedroom

(SEH-dee-eh)
le sedie
chairs

(jahr-DEE-noh)
il giardino
garden

(fee-NEHS-trah)
la finestra
window

(TAH-voh-lah)
la tavola
table

(POHR-tah)
la porta
door

(koh-rree-DOH-yoh)
il corridoio
hallway

21

ARRIVAL
(ah-RREE-voh)
L' arrivo

2	*(CHEHR-kah)* **In cerca di un posto per la** *(NOH-teh)* **notte**

Finding a Place to Spend the Night

You'll probably book your hotel room from home—at least for your first night—but whether you have a reservation or not, you'll want to know some basic words that describe the services and facilities you expect to find at your hotel. Learn these words first, and notice how they are used in the dialogue you will read later.

(ahl-BEHR-goh)
l'albergo
hotel

(preh-noh-tah-TSYOH-neh)
la prenotazione
reservation

(PREH-tsoh)
il prezzo
price

(pah-ssah-POHR-toh)
il passaporto
passport

(KAH-meh-rah)
la camera
room

(BAH-nyoh)
il bagno
bathroom

(preh-noh-TAH-reh)
prenotare
to reserve

(eem-PEE-gah-tah)
l'impiegata
female clerk

(kah-meh-RYEH-rah)
la cameriera
maid/waitress

(POHR-tah)
la porta
door

(fee-NEHS-trah)
la finestra
window

22

I diversi modi di dire «the» in italiano

The Many Ways of Saying "The" in Italian

WITH FEMININE NOUNS

SINGULAR   PLURAL

Before Any Consonant

(lah)
la   *c*asa

(leh)
le   *c*ase

la   *r*agazza

le   *r*agazze

la   *m*adre

le   *m*adri

Before Any Vowel

(OH-rah)
l'   *o*ra
hour

le   *o*re

l'   *a*mica

(ah-MEE-keh)
le   *a*miche

23

WITH MASCULINE NOUNS

| SINGULAR | PLURAL |

Before z or Before s Plus a Consonant

(loh)

lo   *zio*

(llyee)

gli   *zii*

lo   *studente*

gli   *studenti*

Before Any Other Consonant

(eel)

il   *ragazzo*

(ee)

i   *ragazzi*

il   *padre*

i   *padri*

Before Any Vowel

l'   *albero*

(llyee)

gli   *alberi*

Got it? This chart will help you remember.

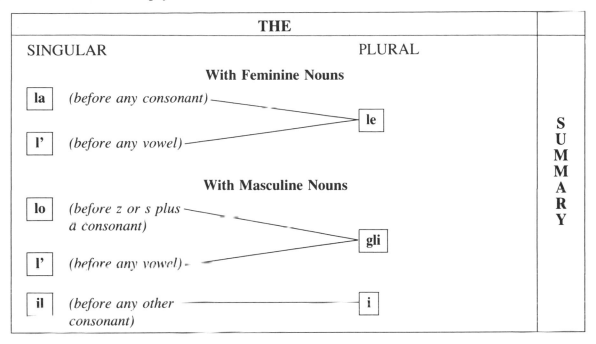

THE		
SINGULAR	PLURAL	S U M M A R Y

With Feminine Nouns

la	*(before any consonant)*	le
l'	*(before any vowel)*	

With Masculine Nouns

lo	*(before z or s plus a consonant)*	gli
l'	*(before any vowel)*	
il	*(before any other consonant)*	i

That's it! Now test your familiarity with "the." Choose the appropriate way of saying "the" in front of the following singular nouns.

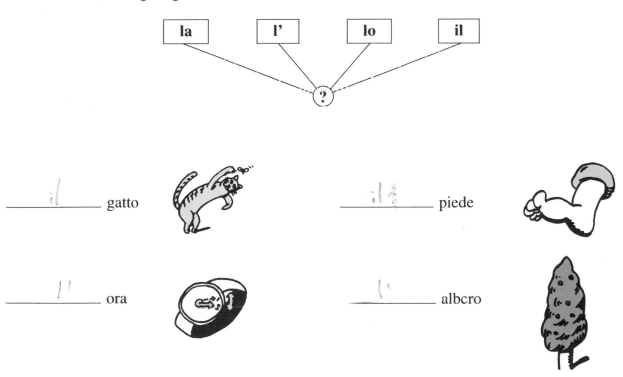

la	l'	lo	il

?

_____ gatto

_____ piede

_____ ora

_____ albcro

_____ il fiore

_____ l' amica

_____ la mela

_____ la penna

Magnifico! Now choose the correct form of "the" in Italian for the same nouns in the plural.

| le | gli | i |

?

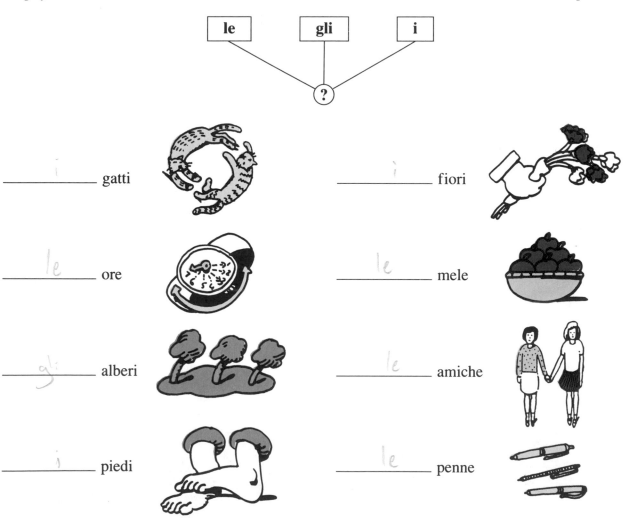

_____ i gatti

_____ i fiori

_____ le ore

_____ le mele

_____ gli alberi

_____ le amiche

_____ i piedi

_____ le penne

26

(seh) (VWOH-EE) (KYEH-deh-reh)   (kwal-KOH-zah)

SE VUOI CHIEDERE QUALCOSA...

If You Want To Ask For Something

You'll find yourself asking questions every day of your trip—of hotel clerks, tour guides, waiters, and taxi drivers. To form a question, become familiar with these key words.

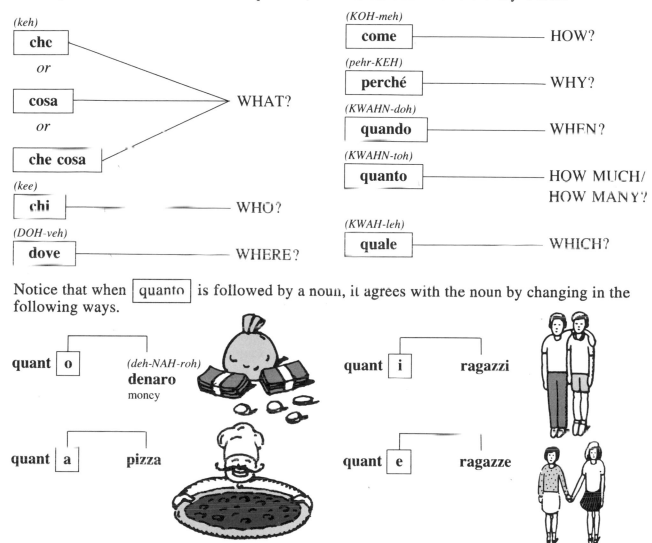

(keh)

che

or

cosa   ———— WHAT?

or

che cosa

(kee)

chi ———————— WHO?

(DOH-veh)

dove ——————— WHERE?

(KOH-meh)

come ——————— HOW?

(pehr-KEH)

perché —————— WHY?

(KWAHN-doh)

quando ————— WHEN?

(KWAHN-toh)

quanto ————— HOW MUCH/ HOW MANY?

(KWAH-leh)

quale ——————— WHICH?

Notice that when quanto is followed by a noun, it agrees with the noun by changing in the following ways.

quant o   *(deh-NAH-roh)* **denaro** money

quant a   **pizza**

quant i   **ragazzi**

quant e   **ragazze**

There are times when you don't even need to use these words to ask a question. Often you can turn a statement into a question by either of these two methods:

(1) raise your voice intonation in the normal way for questions:

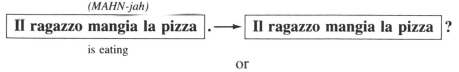

(MAHN-jah)

Il ragazzo mangia la pizza . ⟶ **Il ragazzo mangia la pizza** ?

is eating

or

(2) put the *subject* at the end of the sentence:

Il ragazzo   **mangia la pizza** . ⟶ **Mangia la pizza** , **il ragazzo** ?

27

Now match up each question with its answer.

1. **Che cosa mangia Maria?** *b.*

a. (EH-kkoh)
Ecco la penna.
Here is

2. **Parla italiano Giovanni?** *d.*
does speak

b. **Maria mangia la pizza.**

3. **Perché canti?** *e.*
do you sing

c. **È il padre di Maria.**
of

4. **Quando arrivano?** *f.*
do they arrive

d. **Sì, Giovanni parla italiano**
speaks

5. **Dove arrivano?** *g.*

e. (PYAH-cheh)
Canto perché mi piace.
I sing   because   I like it

6. **Dov'è la penna?** *a.*
is

f. **Arrivano domani.**
tomorrow

7. **Chi è?** *c.*
Who is it?

g. (ah-eh-roh-POHR-toh)
Arrivano all' aeroporto.
at the   airport

Now here are some more adventures of the Smith family. (We don't recommend that you go to a strange city without a reservation; but let's see how our friends make out.)

Read each line carefully several times out loud. *Role-play* the dialogue.

MARK
(chee) (pwoh)
Scusi, signore, ci   può dare una
(KAH-meh-rah)   (seh-ttee-MAH-nah)   (oh)
camera per una settimana? Non ho

una prenotazione.

Excuse me, sir, can

you give us a room for a

week? I do not have a reservation.

IMPIEGATO
(eem-poh-SSEE-bee-leh)
Impossibile, signore.

Impossible, sir.

MARK **Perché?**

Why?

IMPIEGATO
(ahl-BEHR-goh)
Perché l'albergo è molto
(PYEH-noh)
pieno.

Because the hotel is very full.

MARK	**Senta, io e la mia famiglia**	Listen, my family and I
	(ah-BBYAH-moh) (bee-ZOH-nyoh) (oor-JEHN-teh)	
	abbiamo bisogno urgente di	urgently need
	(SYAH-moh) (ah-meh-ree-KAH-nee)	
	una camera. Siamo americani.	a room. We are Americans.
	(cheh) (PEE-kkoh-lah)	
IMPIEGATO	**Va bene. C'è una piccola**	Okay. There is a small room on the third floor
	(TEHR-tsoh) (PYAH-noh)	(fourth floor in North American terms).
	camera al terzo piano.	
	(KOHS-tah)	
MARK	**Quanto costa?**	How much does it cost?
	(cheen-kwahn-tah-MEE-lah) (LEE-reh)	
IMPIEGATO	**Cinquantamila lire.**	50.000 lira. *(See unit 25 on banking for information on money.)*
MARK	**D'accordo.**	Okay.
IMPIEGATO	**Come si chiama?**	What's your name?
	(KWEHS-tah)	
MARK	**Sono Mark Smith. Questa è mia**	I am Mark Smith. This is my wife, Mrs. Mary
	(see-NYOH-rah)	
	moglie, la signora Mary Smith. Ecco	Smith. Here are our passports.
	i nostri passaporti.	
IMPIEGATO	**La camera numero trentacinque.**	Room number 35. Here is the key.
	(KYAH-veh)	
	Ecco la chiave.	
	(MEE-lleh)	
MARK	**Grazie mille!**	Thanks a million! (*literally*, a thousand thanks)
IMPIEGATO	**Prego.**	You're welcome.

Now, without looking back, try to complete the missing dialogue parts. Check your answers only *after* attempting to fill in the missing parts from memory.

Scusi, signore, ci può dare una c<u>amera</u> per una s<u>ettimana</u>?

Non ho una p<u>renotazione</u>.

Impossibile, signore.

Perché?

P<u>erché</u> è molto pieno.

Senta, io e la mia famiglia abbiamo b<u>isogno</u>
urgente di una camera. Siamo americani.

29

Va b_ene____. C'è una p_iccola____ camera al terzo p_iano____.

Q_uanta____ costa?

Cinquantamila l_ire____.

Can you make sentences found in the dialogue out of the following scrambled words?

chiave / Ecco / la

_Ecco la chiave_____

signora / la / Questa / moglie / mia / è / Mary Smith

_Questa é mia moglie la signora Mary Smith_____

chiama / si / Come

_Come si chiama_____

Study and repeat aloud these words referring to a hotel room. Then write the Italian word and draw a line to the appropriate item in the picture.

lo specchio
mirror

(LAHM-pah-dah)
la lampada
lamp

(LAH-vah-boh)
il lavabo
sink (for washing)

(ah-shoo-gah-MAH-noh)
l'asciugamano
towel

(kah-sseh-TTOH-neh)
il cassettone
chest of drawers

(DOH-chah)
la doccia
shower

la vasca
bathtub

(koo-SHEE-noh)
il cuscino
pillow

(BAH-nyoh)
il bagno
toilet

il letto
bed

il divano/il sofà
sofa

la porta
door

Pronomi e verbi
Pronouns and Verbs

You've already learned how to say "I" and "you" in Italian. Now it's time to move on to the forms for "he," "she," "we," and "they." Here are your new words:

(LOO-ee)

lui ——————————— he

lei ——————————— she (exactly the same as the polite "you")

noi ——————————— we

loro ——————————— they

Use this table to help you remember the Italian pronouns.

PRONOUNS				S U M M A R Y
io	I	**noi**	we	
tu	you (familiar)	**voi**	you (plural)	
lui	he	**loro**	they (masculine/feminine)	
lei	she/you (formal)			

Now, here are three common Italian verbs:

(pahr LAH reh)   *(kahn-TAH-reh)*   *(ah-rree-VAH-reh)*
parlare   **cantare**   **arrivare**
to speak   to sing   to arrive

Notice that they end in ⃞ **are** . So do many other verbs. Watch how they are conjugated.

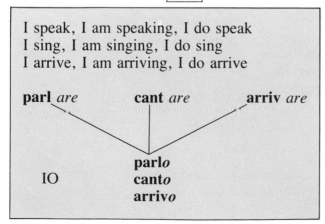

I speak, I am speaking, I do speak
I sing, I am singing, I do sing
I arrive, I am arriving, I do arrive

parl *are*   **cant** *are*   **arriv** *are*

IO   **parl***o*
           cant*o*
           arriv*o*

We speak, we are speaking, we do speak
We sing, we are singing, we do sing
We arrive, we are arriving, we do arrive

parl *are*   **cant** *are*   **arriv** *are*

NOI   **parl***iamo*
           cant*iamo*
           arriv*iamo*

You speak, you are speaking, you do speak
You sing, you are singing, you do sing
You arrive, you are arriving, you do arrive

parl *are*　　　　**cant** *are*　　　　**arriv** *are*

TU　　　　　　**parl***i*
　　　　　　　cant*i*
　　　　　　　arriv*i*

You speak, you are speaking, you do speak
You sing, you are singing, you do sing
You arrive, you are arriving, you do arrive

parl *are*　　　　**cant** *are*　　　　**arriv** *are*

VOI　　　　　**parl***ate*
　　　　　　　cant*ate*
　　　　　　　arriv*ate*

He/She speaks, he/she is speaking,
　　　　　　　　he/she does speak
He/She sings, he/she is singing,
　　　　　　　　he/she does sing
He/She arrives, he/she is arriving,
　　　　　　　　he/she does arrive
　　　　　　　also
You (polite) sing, you (polite) are singing,
　　　　you (polite) do sing

parl *are*　　　　**cant** *are*　　　　**arriv** *are*

LUI ⎫
LEI ⎭　　　　**parl***a*
　　　　　　　cant*a*
　　　　　　　arriv*a*

They speak, they are speaking, they do speak
They sing, they are singing, they do sing
They arrive, they are arriving, they do arrive

parl *are*　　　　**cant** *are*　　　　**arriv** *are*

　　　　　　　(PAHR-lah-noh)
　　　　　　　parl*ano*
　　　　　　　(KAHN-tah-noh)
LORO　　　　**cant***ano*
　　　　　　　(ah-RREE-vah-noh)
　　　　　　　arriv*ano*

Got it? Note that the pronouns are not necessary because the endings specify which person is involved. The pronouns are, in general, optional.

io parl*o*　or　**parl***o*　　　　**noi parl***iamo*　or　**parl***iamo*
tu parl*i*　or　**parl***i*　　　　　**voi parl***ate*　　or　**parl***ate*
lui ⎫　　　　　　　　　　　　**loro parl***ano*　or　**parl***ano*
lei ⎭ **parl***a* or **parl***a*

Notice as well that *parlano, cantano, arrivano* are *not* stressed on the ending *-ano*. Be careful! Note that the forms *parla/canta/arriva* and *parlano/cantano/arrivano* are used with corresponding non-pronoun subjects:

| Il ragazzo | parl*a* italiano. | Le zie | cant*ano* bene. | Maria | arriv*a* domani. |
The boy speaks Italian. | The aunts sing well. | Mary is arriving tomorrow.

| I ragazzi | parl*ano* italiano. | La zia | cant*a* bene. | Maria e Carla | arriv*ano* domani. |
The boys speak Italian. | The aunt sings well. | Mary and Carla are arriving tomorrow.

Here's a chart of | are | verb endings to help you remember.

VERB ENDINGS	S
"ARE" VERBS	U M M A R Y

io -o   noi -iamo

tu -i   voi -ate

lui }
lei } -a   loro -ano

Now test yourself. Add the correct endings to the verb *abitare,* which you have already encountered.

to live in a place

1. (io) abit _____   4. (lei) abit _____   7. (loro) abit _____

2. (tu) abit _____   5. (noi) abit _____   8. il ragazzo abit _____

3. (lui) abit _____   6. (voi) abit _____   9. i ragazzi abit _____

Molto bene!   See if you can put the correct endings on the following verbs, and if you understand the sentence.

La ragazza parl_____ italiano.   Tu parl_____ e io cant_____.

Gli zii arriv_____ domani.   Noi cant_____ e voi parl_____.

Note: To make any verb negative, just add | non | before it.

parlo —I speak | non | **parlo** —I do not speak

cantano —they sing | non | **cantano** —they do not sing

Slow down! If you are getting confused, just ease up your pace and review what you've learned so far. *Capisci?* (Do you understand?) See how much Italian you already know by doing the following "verb" crossword puzzle.

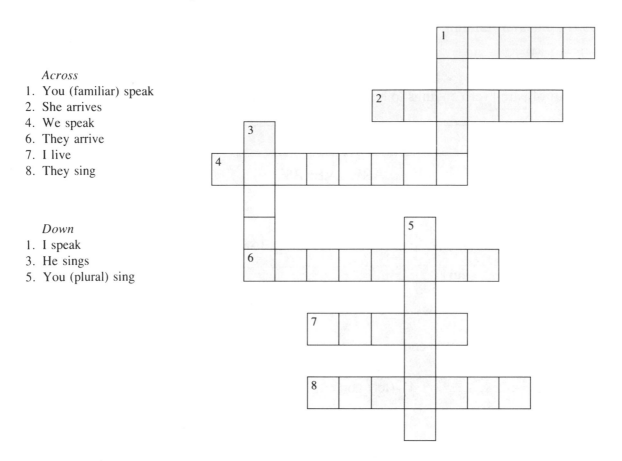

Across
1. You (familiar) speak
2. She arrives
4. We speak
6. They arrive
7. I live
8. They sing

Down
1. I speak
3. He sings
5. You (plural) sing

Now see if you remember what you have learned about forming questions by matching up the answers on the right to the questions on the left.

1. Che cosa è?
2. Chi non parla italiano?
3. Dove abita lei?
4. Come si chiama lei?
5. Quando arrivano le valige?
6. Quanto costa la camera?

a. Abito a Roma.
b. È una valigia.
c. Mi chiamo Giovanni Spina.
d. Il non parlo italiano.
e. Costa 50.000 lire.
f. Arrivano domani.

Test yourself on the many ways to say "the" by matching up the nouns on the right with the appropriate forms of "the" on the left.

1. l'   a. finestra
2. lo   b. porta
3. la   c. albergo
4. lo   d. camera
5. la   e. amica
6. la   f. amico
7. l'   g. specchio
8. il   h. zio
9. il   i. passaporto
10. l'   j. bagno

Now try to put the correct plural form (*le*, *gli*, or *i*) in front of these nouns (which are now plural).

__i__ finestre   __gli__ amici

__i__ porte   __gli__ specchi

__gli__ alberghi   __gli__ zii

__i__ camere   __le__ passaporti

__gli__ amiche   __le__ bagni

The following brief passage will allow you to test your comprehension of what you have learned so far. Read it several times, then try to choose the correct answer to each question.

Il signor Jones non ha una prenotazione all'albergo. Non

ci sono più camere. Allora, la signora Jones dice all'impiegato

che sono americani. L'impiegato dice che c'è una piccola
that
camera al terzo piano. La camera non ha il bagno e costa

cinquantamila lire.

Chi non ha la prenotazione?
☐ Il signor Jones non ha la prenotazione.
☐ L'impiegato non ha la prenotazione.

Che cosa dice la signora Jones?
☐ Dice "Buon giorno."
☐ Dice che sono americani.

Ha il bagno?
☐ Sì.
☐ No.

Ci sono camere?
☐ Sì.
☐ No.

Dov'è la piccola camera?
☐ Al terzo piano.
☐ A Chicago.

Quanto costa?
☐ 45.000 lire.
☐ 50.000 lire.

Matching 1-c, 2-g, 3-a, 4-h, 5-b, 6-d, 7-e, 8-i, 9-j, 10-f
Plurals le (finestre) le (porte) gli (alberghi) le (camere) gli (amici) gli (amiche) le (passaporti) i (specchi) gli (zii) i (bagni)
Comprehension Il signor Jones non ha la prenotazione. Dice che sono americani. No. No. Al terzo piano. 50.000 lire.

35

SEEING THE SIGHTS

(POON-tee) *(een-teh-REH-sseh)*
I punti d'interesse

3	*(JEE-roh)* *(PYEH-dee)* **In giro a piedi** Finding Your Way on Foot/Getting Around on Foot

"How do I get to . . . ?" "Where is the nearest subway?" "Is the museum straight ahead?" You'll be asking directions and getting answers wherever you travel. Acquaint yourself with the words and phrases that will make getting around easier. Don't forget to read each line out loud several times to practice your pronunciation, and act out each part to be certain you understand these new words.

(John and Anne set out on their first day to visit a museum.)

ANNE   *(kyeh-DYAH-moh)* *(VEE-jee-leh)*
John, chiediamo al vigile dove si
(moo-ZEH-oh)
trova il museo.

John, let's ask the policeman how to find the museum.

JOHN *(to the policeman)* **Scusi, signore, ci sa**

dire dove si trova il museo?

Excuse me, sir, can you tell us how to find the museum?

VIGILE   *(CHER-toh)* *(dee-REE-tee)*
Certo. Andate diritti fino a Via
(see-NEES-trah)
Verdi; poi a sinistra a Via Rossini; e

Certainly. Go straight to Verdi Street, then to the left at Rossini Street, and then to the right

(DEHS-trah)
poi a destra a Via Dante, dove c'è il
(seh-MAH-foh-roh)
semaforo. Il museo si trova a due
(ee-zoh-LAH-tee)
isolati dopo il semaforo.

at Dante Street, where the traffic lights are.

The museum can be found two blocks after the

traffic lights.

JOHN **Grazie mille.**

Thanks a million.

(cheh) (keh)
VIGILE **Non c'è di che.**

Don't mention it.

(after having followed the directions)
(KWEHS-toh)
ANNE **Questo non è il museo.**

This is not the museum.

(oo-FFEE-choh) (pohs-TAH-leh)
È l'ufficio   postale.

It's the post office.

(TAHR-dee)
JOHN **Pazienza. È tardi. Torniamo**

all'albergo.

Patience. It's late. Let's

go back to the hotel.

Now see if you can fill in the missing dialogue parts without looking back. Check your answers only after attempting to complete the missing parts from memory.

John, c_____ al vigile dove si trova il m_____.

Scusi, signore, ci sa d_____ dove si t_____ il museo?

C_____. Andate d_____ fino a Via Verdi; poi a s_____

a Via Rossini, e poi a d_____ a Via Dante, dove c'è il s_____.

Il museo si trova a due i_____ dopo il semaforo.

Grazie m_____.

Non c'è di c_____.

COME SI FA PER ANDARE A . . .?
How Do I Get to . . .?

La ragazza va | a | **Roma.**
goes

The girl goes *to* Rome.

Il signor Smith abita | in | **America.**

Mr. Smith lives *in* America.

La ragazza viene | da | **Roma.**
comes

The girl comes *from* Rome.

Odore | di | **piedi!**
smell
Smell *of* feet!

Il gatto è | su | **un tetto.**

The cat is *on* a roof.

Il museo è | lontano |
dal semaforo.

The museum is *far*
from the traffic lights.

Il gatto è | vicino a | **un fiore.**

The cat is *near* a flower.

La porta è | a destra | **e la**
finestra è | a sinistra |.

The door is *to the right* and
the window is *to the left*.

La pizza è | per | **lo zio.**

The pizza is *for* the uncle.

Gli spaghetti | con | **il formaggio.**

Spaghetti *with* cheese.

Maria arriva | dopo | **sua madre.**

Mary arrives *after* her mother.

L'uomo è | su | **un tetto.**

The man is *on* a roof.

Il gatto è | accanto a | **una gatta.**

The male cat is *next to* a female cat.

Can you match up the following?

1. con il formaggio   b.   a. after her mother
2. accanto a una gatta   c.   b. with cheese
3. dopo sua madre   a.   c. next to a female cat
4. a destra   e.   d. to the left
5. a sinistra   d.   e. to the right
6. a Roma   i.   f. the smell of feet
7. da Roma   h.   g. for the uncle
8. odore di piedi   f.   h. from Rome
9. per lo zio   g.   i. to Rome
10. vicino a un fiore   m.   j. in America
11. su un tetto   l.   k. far from the traffic lights
12. lontano dal semaforo   k.   l. on a roof
13. in America   j.   m. near a flower

I verbi ancora una volta
Verbs Once Again

In the previous unit you learned about "are" verbs. Now you will learn about "ere" verbs.

(SKREE-veh-reh) **SCRIVERE** to write	(veh-DEH-reh) **VEDERE** to see	(KREH-deh-reh) **CREDERE** to believe

I write,	I am writing,	I do write
I see,	I am seeing,	I do see
I believe,		I do believe

scriv *ere*   **ved** *ere*   **cred** *ere*

IO   **scriv***o*
        ved*o*
        cred*o*

We write,	we are writing,	we do write
We see,	we are seeing,	we do see
We believe,		we do believe

scriv *ere*   **ved** *ere*   **cred** *ere*

NOI   **scriv***iamo*
        ved*iamo*
        cred*iamo*

39

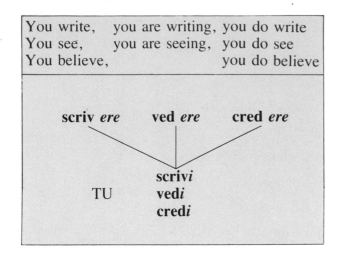

You write,   you are writing, you do write
You see,   you are seeing, you do see
You believe,   you do believe

scriv *ere*   **ved** *ere*   **cred** *ere*

TU   **scriv***i*
     ved*i*
     cred*i*

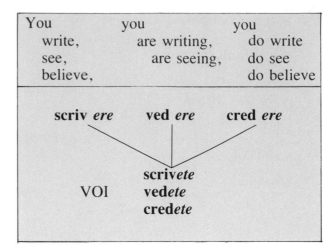

You   you   you
 write,   are writing, do write
 see,   are seeing,   do see
 believe,   do believe

scriv *ere*   **ved** *ere*   **cred** *ere*

VOI   **scriv***ete*
      ved*ete*
      cred*ete*

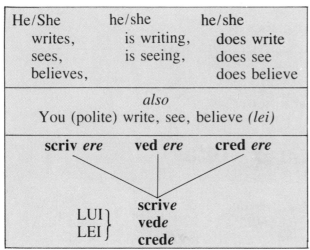

He/She   he/she   he/she
 writes,   is writing, does write
 sees,   is seeing,   does see
 believes,   does believe

also
You (polite) write, see, believe *(lei)*

scriv *ere*   **ved** *ere*   **cred** *ere*

LUI ⎱   **scriv***e*
LEI ⎰   **ved***e*
        cred*e*

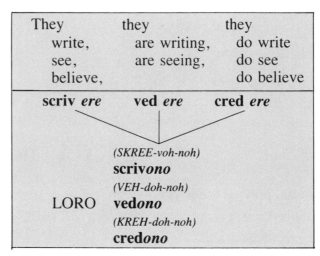

They   they   they
 write,   are writing, do write
 see,   are seeing,   do see
 believe,   do believe

scriv *ere*   **ved** *ere*   **cred** *ere*

          (SKREE-voh-noh)
          scriv*ono*
          (VEH-doh-noh)
LORO   **ved***ono*
          (KREH-doh-noh)
          cred*ono*

Once again, notice that the pronouns are optional and that *scrivono, vedono, credono* are not stressed on the ending *-ono*. To form the negative, just add *non* before the verb (as before). The following chart is a summary of "ere" verbs.

VERB ENDINGS		S
"ERE" VERBS		U
io cred ____ -o noi cred ____ -iamo		M M
tu cred ____ -i voi ____ -ete		A
lui ⎱ cred ____ -e loro ____ -ono		R
lei ⎰		Y

Now test your learning of these verbs in the following phrases, to get the control over an "ere" verb.

L'impiegato *scriv* _e____ .   Io non *cred* _o___ a Maria.   Tu non *ved* _i___ il semaforo.

Io *scriv* O a Maria.   I gatti non *scriv* ono.   I ragazzi non *ved* ono
                                                        il semaforo.

Noi *cred* iamo a Maria.   Voi *ved* ete il vigile.

Alcune parole utili
Some Useful Words

(CHEE-neh-mah)
il cinema
movie theater

(neh-GOH-tsee-oh)
il negozio
store

(mehr-KAH-toh)
il mercato
market

(BAHN-kah)
la banca
bank

(fahr-mah-CHEE-ah)
la farmacia
drugstore

(STRAII-dah)
la strada
street

(mahr-chah-PYEH-deh)
il marciapiede
sidewalk

(SPEH-zeh)
fare delle spese
to shop

If you unscramble the letters you will get words that you have just learned:

NBAAC   (la) _____   TACORME   (il) _____

RMFAAICA   (la) _____   RTADAS   (la) _____

CNIEAM   (il) _____   CAIRAMDPIEE   (il) _____

EGNOOIZ   (il) _____   PEESS   (fare delle) _____

ANSWERS

Vocabulary banca, farmacia, cinema, negozio, mercato, strada, marciapiede, spese

Verbs (scriv) e (cred) o (ved) i (scriv) o (ved) ono (scriv) ono (ved) ono (cred) iamo (ved) ete

41

Come si indicano le cose in italiano
How to Point Out Things in Italian

Words like "this" and "that" are important to know, particularly when you go shopping and want to buy that good-looking pair of gloves in the shop window. The Italian forms of these words vary, depending on whether the item is masculine or feminine, and whether you are pointing to one item or to many.

THIS AND THESE

WITH FEMININE NOUNS

Singular (this)
(KWEHS-tah)

| questa | ragazza |

| questa | madre |

Plural (these)
(KWEHS-teh)

| queste | ragazze |

| queste | madri |

WITH MASCULINE NOUNS

Singular
(KWEHS-toh)

| questo | ragazzo |

| questo | studente |

| questo | zio |

Plural
(KWEHS-tee)

| questi | ragazzi |

| questi | studenti |

| questi | zii |

In front of vowels, you may drop the vowel *in the singular* if you wish:

| questa amica | *or* | quest'amica |
| questo amico | *or* | quest'amico |

THAT AND THOSE

WITH FEMININE NOUNS

Singular (that)
Before Any Consonant

(KWEH-llah)
quella ragazza

Before Any Vowel
quell' amica

Plural (those)

(KWEH-lleh)
quelle ragazze

quelle amiche

WITH MASCULINE NOUNS

Singular
Before z or s Plus a Consonant

(KWEH-lloh)
quello zio

quello studente

Before Any Vowel
quell' amico

Before Any Other Consonant
(kwehl)
quel ragazzo

Plural

(KWEH-lyee)
quegli zii

quegli studenti

quegli amici

(KWEH-ee)
quei ragazzi

This table will help you remember these words.

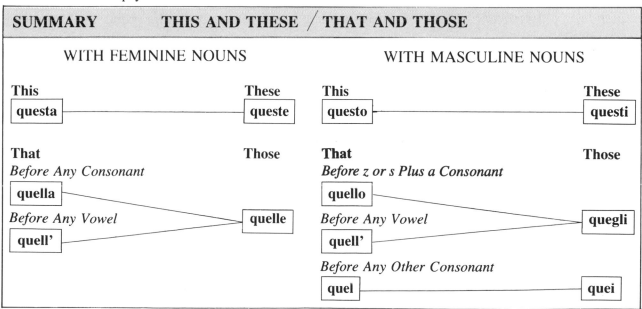

SUMMARY	THIS AND THESE / THAT AND THOSE		
WITH FEMININE NOUNS		**WITH MASCULINE NOUNS**	
This — questa	**These** — queste	**This** — questo	**These** — questi
That	**Those**	**That**	**Those**
Before Any Consonant — quella		*Before z or s Plus a Consonant* — quello	
Before Any Vowel — quell'	quelle	*Before Any Vowel* — quell'	quegli
		Before Any Other Consonant — quel	quei

43

Now practice what you have learned. Fill in the appropriate form of "this" or "that" for each of these singular nouns.

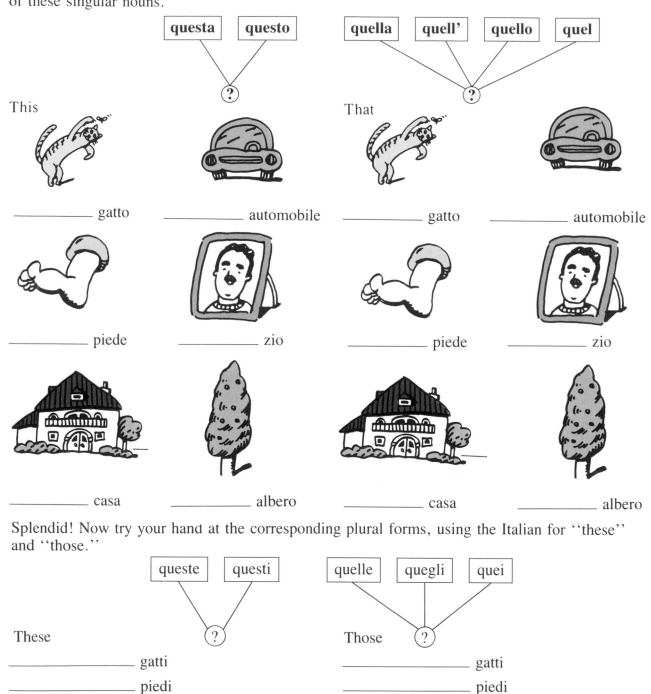

$\boxed{\textbf{questa}}$ $\boxed{\textbf{questo}}$?

$\boxed{\textbf{quella}}$ $\boxed{\textbf{quell'}}$ $\boxed{\textbf{quello}}$ $\boxed{\textbf{quel}}$?

This

_____ gatto

_____ automobile

That

_____ gatto

_____ automobile

_____ piede

_____ zio

_____ piede

_____ zio

_____ casa

_____ albero

_____ casa

_____ albero

Splendid! Now try your hand at the corresponding plural forms, using the Italian for "these" and "those."

$\boxed{\textbf{queste}}$ $\boxed{\textbf{questi}}$?

$\boxed{\textbf{quelle}}$ $\boxed{\textbf{quegli}}$ $\boxed{\textbf{quei}}$?

These

_____ gatti

_____ piedi

Those

_____ gatti

_____ piedi

_____ case   _____ case

_____ automobili   _____ automobili

_____ zii   _____ zii

alberi   alberi

Now you really have it. Can you change the following "this/these" forms to their corresponding "that/those" forms? Good luck!

questo marciapiede _____ marciapiede   questi alberghi _____ alberghi

questi marciapiedi _____ marciapiedi   quest'amica _____ amica

questa strada _____ strada   queste amiche _____ amiche

queste strade _____ strade   questo zio _____ zio

quest'albergo _____ albergo   questi zii _____ zii

For a quick refresher, complete the endings for the verb *vedere*, too.

1. Maria non ved_____ Carlo.

2. Noi ved_____ la zia di Maria.

3. I ragazzi ved_____ i fiori.

4. Io non ved_____ i fiori.

5. Tu ved_____ lo zio di Carlo.

45

Now fill in the blanks with one of the following: | a | da | di | vicino | accanto |

Maria va _____ Roma.

Il gatto è _____ al fiore.

Pino è il cugino _____ Gina.

Io abito _____ a Maria.

La ragazza arriva _____ Firenze.

Have fun with the following crossword puzzle.

Across
2. Post office
5. Movie theater
6. Store
7. Sidewalk
8. Street

Down
1. Bank
3. Pharmacy
4. Patience
7. Market

What's happening to Maria? Read the passage to review your words for directions.

Maria chiede al vigile dove si trova la banca. Il vigile dice di andare a destra e poi a sinistra.

Maria arriva al semaforo e non vede la banca, ma vede l'ufficio postale. Allora torna
but
all'albergo.

Now, select the appropriate answers.

Chi chiede al vigile dove
si trova la banca?

☐ L'ufficio postale.
☐ Il museo.
☐ Maria.

Che cosa dice il vigile?

☐ Dice di andare a destra e poi a sinistra.
☐ Dice di tornare all'albergo.
☐ Dice «Buon giorno».

Dove arriva Maria?

☐ Maria arriva all'aeroporto.
☐ Maria arriva a Roma.
☐ Maria arriva al semaforo.

Che cosa vede?

☐ Vede l'albergo.
☐ Vede l'ufficio postale.
☐ Vede il vigile.

Dove torna?

☐ Torna in America.
☐ Torna a Roma.
☐ Torna all'albergo.

Bus Map of Naples　　　　　　　　　*(Courtesy of Bonechi Publishers, Florence)*

The following dialogue contains some useful words and expressions that you might find helpful when you will need to use public means of transportation.

Remember to read each line out loud several times and to act out each part.

(prehn-DYAH-moh) (tah-SSEE)

MARY **Prendiamo il tassì per andare**　　　Shall we take the taxi to go to the movies?

al cinema?

MARK **Quanto lontano è?**　　　　　　　How far is it?

48

MARY	**Si trova in Via Verdi.**	It's on Verdi Street.
MARK	**No. Costa troppo.**	No. It costs too much.
MARY	**Allora prendiamo la** *(meh-troh-poh-lee-TAH-nah)* **metropolitana.**	Then let's take the subway.
MARK	**Penso che non ce ne sia una.**	I don't think there is one.
MARY	**Allora prendiamo l'autobus.**	Then let's take the bus.
MARK	**Va bene.**	Okay.

(A while later, they get on a bus.)

MARK	**Scusi, signore, questo autobus va fino a Via Verdi?**	Excuse me, sir, does this bus go to Verdi Street?
CONDUCENTE	*(shehn-DYAH-moh)* **Sì, ma lei dove va?**	Yes, but where are you going?
MARK	**Scendiamo al cinema. Quanto costa** *(bee-LLYEH-ttoh)* **un biglietto?**	We are getting off at the movie theater. How much does a ticket cost?
CONDUCENTE	**Mille lire, signore, e** *(dee vehr tee MEHN-toh)* **buon divertimento.***	1,000 lira *(see unit 25)*, sir, and enjoy yourself.
MARK	*(kohn-doo-TTOH-reh) (seem-PAH-tee-koh)* **Che conducente simpatico!** *(kohr-TEH-zee)* **Come sono cortesi gli italiani!**	What a nice driver! How courteous the Italians are!

Che cosa è?

_____ _____ _____ _____

*Obviously, Mark did not know that bus tickets are purchased before getting on a bus in Italy.

Altre parole che esprimono azioni

More Action Words

Now you will learn about "ire" verbs.

(dohr-MEE-reh)	*(pahr-TEE-reh)*	*(sehn-TEE-reh)*
dormire	**partire**	**sentire**
to sleep	to leave/depart	to hear

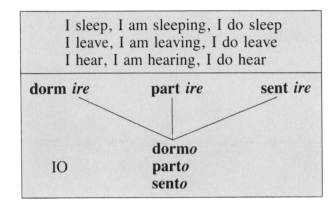

I sleep, I am sleeping, I do sleep
I leave, I am leaving, I do leave
I hear, I am hearing, I do hear

dorm *ire* **part** *ire* **sent** *ire*

IO
dorm*o*
part*o*
sent*o*

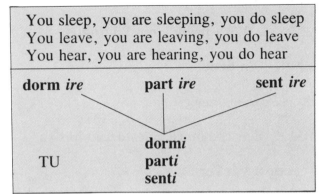

You sleep, you are sleeping, you do sleep
You leave, you are leaving, you do leave
You hear, you are hearing, you do hear

dorm *ire* **part** *ire* **sent** *ire*

TU
dorm*i*
part*i*
sent*i*

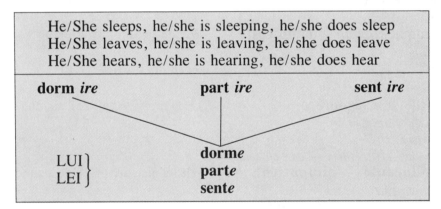

He/She sleeps, he/she is sleeping, he/she does sleep
He/She leaves, he/she is leaving, he/she does leave
He/She hears, he/she is hearing, he/she does hear

dorm *ire* **part** *ire* **sent** *ire*

LUI }
LEI }
dorm*e*
part*e*
sent*e*

We sleep, we are sleeping, we do sleep
We leave, we are leaving, we do leave
We hear, we are hearing, we do hear

dorm *ire* **part** *ire* **sent** *ire*

NOI
dorm*iamo*
part*iamo*
sent*iamo*

You sleep, you are sleeping, you do sleep
You leave, you are leaving, you do leave
You hear, you are hearing, you do hear

dorm *ire* **part** *ire* **sent** *ire*

VOI
dorm*ite*
part*ite*
sent*ite*

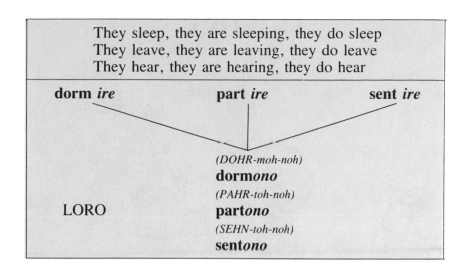

They sleep, they are sleeping, they do sleep
They leave, they are leaving, they do leave
They hear, they are hearing, they do hear

dorm *ire*   part *ire*   sent *ire*

(DOHR-moh-noh)
dorm*ono*

(PAHR-toh-noh)
LORO   **part*ono***

(SEHN-toh-noh)
sent*ono*

As in the case of "are" and "ere" verbs, notice that the pronouns are optional and that *dormono, partono, sentono* are not stressed on the ending *ono*. Remember that to form the negative you just put *non* before the verb. The following chart will help you remember the endings for "ire" verbs.

VERB ENDINGS

"IRE" VERBS

io _____	**-o**	noi _____	**-iamo**
tu _____	**-i**	voi _____	**-ite**
lui } lei } _____	**-e**	loro _____	**-ono**

S U M M A R Y

Practice the technique of forming "ire" verbs by adding the correct endings to the following:

(VOH-cheh)
L'autista sent_____ la voce del
voice
signor Smith.

Il signor Smith e sua moglie dorm_____
tutto il giorno.
all
Io part_____ domani.

Tu non part_____ domani.

Voi dorm_____ tutto il giorno.

Noi sent_____ la voce della signora
Smith.

SIGNORE . . .

(sah-LEE-reh)
salire
to get on

(ah-oo-TEES-tah)
l'autista/il conducente
driver

(kohm-PRAH-reh)
comprare
to buy

(SHEHN-deh-reh)
scendere
to get off

(fehr-MAH-tah)
la fermata
stop

(bee-LLYEH-ttoh)
il biglietto
ticket

(REHS-toh)
il resto
change

Here are some verbs that don't follow the rules. You've learned how to use common verbs that end in "are," "ere," and "ire." Unfortunately, using verbs isn't that simple! *Naturalmente!* There are exceptions to the rules, and we call them "irregular verbs." Here are some common irregular verbs—notice how they take on different forms, depending upon the subject. It is hard work, but you just have to learn these well, 'cause you will want to use them often.

IRREGULAR VERBS				
	ANDARE to go	VENIRE to come	FARE to do/make	DARE to give	DIRE to say/tell
IO (Je)	**vado**	*(VEHN-goh)* **vengo**	*(FAH-choh)* **faccio**	**do**	*(DEE-koh)* **dico**
TU (tu)	*(VAH-ee)* **vai**	*(VYEH-nee)* **vieni**	*(FAH-ee)* **fai**	*(DAH-ee)* **dai**	*(DEE-chee)* **dici**
LUI (il,elle) LEI	**va**	*(VYEH-neh)* **viene**	**fa**	**dà**	*(DEE-cheh)* **dice**
NOI (nous)	**andiamo**	**veniamo**	*(fah-CHAH-moh)* **facciamo**	**diamo**	*(dee-CHAH-moh)* **diciamo**
VOI (vous)	**andate**	**venite**	**fate**	**date**	**dite**
LORO (they)	**vanno**	*(VEHN-goh-noh)* **vengono**	**fanno**	**danno**	*(DEE-koh-noh)* **dicono**

Now fill in the blanks with the appropriate verb forms. How many can you complete without looking back?

Io *vado* a Roma e tu _vai_ a Firenze. Il ragazzo *va* al negozio e loro _vanno_ al cinema.
                                                                    store

Noi *andiamo* a Venezia e voi _andate_ a Pisa. Io *vengo* da Napoli e tu _vieni_ da Milano.

Il signore *viene* da Bologna e loro _vengono_ da Torino.

Voi *venite* da Palermo e noi _veniamo_ da Trieste.

(AHN-keh)
Tu *fai* delle spese e **anche** io _faccio_ delle spese.
     shop   also

Il ragazzo non *fa* delle spese, ma voi _fate_ delle spese **sempre.**
                                                              always

Noi *facciamo* delle spese e anche voi _fate_ delle spese.

Io *dico* «buon giorno» e tu _dici_ «**buona sera**».
                                    good evening/good afternoon

Have some fun finding the Italian translations for the following verbs in the word search puzzle. To reinforce your memory, write each one in the space provided.

x	x	v	a	n	n	o	x	x	x	x	x	x	x	v	x	x	x	x	d	x	x	x	x	x	x
x	x	x	x	x	x	x	x	x	x	x	x	x	e	x	x	x	a	x	x	x	x	x	f
x	d	x	x	x	v	i	e	n	e	x	x	x	n	x	x	x	a	x	x	x	x	x	a
x	x	i	x	x	x	x	x	x	x	x	x	x	g	x	x	n	x	x	x	x	x	c
x	x	x	c	x	x	x	x	x	x	x	x	x	o	x	x	n	x	x	x	x	x	c
x	x	x	x	o	x	x	x	x	x	x	x	x	x	x	o	x	x	x	x	x	i
x	x	f	a	n	n	o	x	x	x	x	x	x	x	x	x	x	x	x	x	x	o
x	x	x	x	x	o	x	d	i	c	o	x	x	x	d	i	a	m	o	x	x	x	x
v	a	d	o	x	x	x	x	x	x	x	x	x	x	x	x	x	x	x	x	x	x

1. they go _vanno_
2. she comes _viene_
3. I come _vengo_
4. I do _faccio_
5. they give _danno_
6. I say _dico_
7. they say _dicono_
8. we give _diamo_
9. they do _fanno_
10. I go _vado_

ANSWERS

Word search 1. vanno 2. viene 3. vengo 4. faccio 5. danno 6. dico 7. dicono 8. diamo 9. fanno 10. vado

Irregular verbs va (a Firenze.) vai (al cinema.) andate (a Pisa.) vieni (da Milano.)
vengono (da Torino.) faccio (delle spese.) fate (delle spese.) fate (delle spese sempre.)
dici («buona sera».)

53

Le preposizioni ancora una volta

Getting Back to Prepositions

Do you remember the Italian for those little words "of," "to," and "from"? (They are called *preposizioni*.) When *a, in, di, da,* and *su* occur right before "the," they "contract"; that is, they become one word with the various forms of "the."

di + il	su + il
È il libro del ragazzo.	Il gatto è sul tetto.
of the	on the
(It is the book *of the* boy.)	(The cat is *on the* roof.)

The contractions are summarized for you in the following chart.

PREPOSITIONS THAT CAN BE CONTRACTED							
+	LA	LE	L'	LO	GLI	IL	I
A	alla	alle	all'	allo	agli	al	ai
IN	nella	nelle	nell'	nello	negli	nel	nei
DI	della	delle	dell'	dello	degli	del	dei
DA	dalla	dalle	dall'	dallo	dagli	dal	dai
SU	sulla	sulle	sull'	sullo	sugli	sul	sui

Now try to use some of these in the following.

La ragazza arriva ___al'___ aeroporto domani.
at the

Il gatto è ___sull'___ albero.
on the

Quei libri **sono** ___delle___ amiche di Pino.
are   of the

Quelle penne sono ___dagli___ amici di Maria.
of the

Lo zio è ___nella___ banca.
in the

Quel signore è ___nella___ farmacia.
in the

Maria va ___al___ mercato.
to the

Giovanni fa delle spese ___nei___
in the

negozi di Roma.

Marco scende ___dell'___ autobus.
from the

Di

Some

The word "some" in Italian is expressed by using *di* plus *the* (see also the previous chart).

A   SOME

un libro

di + i

dei libri   (literally, [some] *of the* books)

una penna

di + le

delle penne

uno zio

di + gli

degli zii

un' amica

di + le

delle amiche

un amico

di + gli

degli amici

Now you try it.

una casa

un fiore

_____ case

_____ fiori

un'automobile

un biglietto

_____ automobili

_____ biglietti

uno studente

una metropolitana

_____ studenti

_____ metropolitane

Read the following brief passage. What you have learned will help you get where you are going. Then, select the appropriate answer to each question.

Il signor Rossi e sua moglie prendono l'autobus per due fermate. Poi prendono la
two   (KOH-zeh)

metropolitana. Loro scendono in Via Verdi. Arrivano al mercato e comprano molte cose.
things

Che cosa prendono il signor Rossi
e sua moglie per due fermate?

☐ Prendono la metropolitana.
☐ Prendono il tassì.
☐ Prendono l'autobus.

Poi che cosa prendono?

☐ Prendono la metropolitana.
☐ Prendono il tassì.
☐ Prendono l'autobus.

Dove scendono?

☐ Scendono in Via Rossini.
☐ Scendono in Via Verdi.
☐ Scendono in Via Dante.

Che cosa comprano?

☐ Comprano un libro.
☐ Comprano molte cose.
☐ Comprano una penna.

Now for review, fill in the missing verb endings.

1. Maria part_____ domani.

2. Loro dorm_____ tutto il giorno.

3. Io non dorm_____ al cinema!

4. Io part_____ domani e tu part

_____ questa **sera**.
evening

5. Tu dorm_____ sull'autobus.

6. Noi part_____ questa sera.

7. Voi non dorm_____ in quell'albergo.

Now let's see if you remember your prepositions.

Maria va _____ negozio.
to the

Io vengo _____ farmacia.
from the

Ecco la penna _____ amico di Maria.
of the

Maria **sale** _____ autobus.
gets on   the

Giovanni è _____ banca.
in the

CHE ORA È / CHE ORE SONO?

What Time Is It?

Tokio	Anchorage	New York	Parigi	Mosca
Sono le nove.	Sono le tre.	Sono le otto.	È l'una.	Sono le tre.

Expressing time is easy. Simply state the hour preceded by *le*. This is true for all hours except one o'clock, for which you use *l'*.

To add minutes, just use *e* ("and").

Sono le sei e dieci (6:10).   **Sono le sette e venti (7:20).**   **Sono le nove e trentanova (9:39).**

If the minute hand is close to the next hour, you can also tell time by quoting the next hour **meno** (minus) the number of minutes to go.

Sono le dieci e cinquanta. =   **Sono le undici e cinquantacinque. =**
Sono le undici meno dieci (10:50).   **Sono le dodici meno cinque (11:55).**

You can replace the quarter hours and the half-hours with the following expressions.

> **2:15 = le due e quindici = le due e** un quarto
>
> **3:30 = le tre e trenta = le tre e** mezzo / mezza
>
> **4:45 = le quattro e quarantacinque = le quattro e** tre quarti **=**
>
> **le cinque meno** un quarto

For A.M. you can use the expression | **di mattina** | ; for P.M. you can use | **di sera** | for the late afternoon and evening, and | **del pomeriggio** | for the early afternoon.

For official time, Italian uses the "24-hour clock."

> **Mario arriva al*le tredici e venti* = 13:20 = 1:20 P.M.**
> **Giovanni parte al*le diciotto e dieci* = 18:10 = 6:10 P.M.**
> **Il signor Smith arriva al*le venti e mezzo* = 20:30 = 8:30 P.M.**

COME SI CONTA IN ITALIANO
How to Count in Italian

I numeri cardinali
Cardinal Numbers

		(SEH-ee)		(OOHN-dee-chee)		(SEH-dee-chee)
1	uno	6 sei	11	undici	16	sedici
				(DOH-dee-chee)		(dee-chah-SSEH-tteh)
2	due	7 sette	12	dodici	17	diciassette
				(TREH-dee-chee)		(dee-CHOH-ttoh)
3	tre	8 otto	13	tredici	18	diciotto
(KWAH-ttroh)		9 nove		(kwah-TTOHR-dee-chee)		(dee-chah-NNOH-veh)
4	quattro	(DYEH chee)	14	quattordici	19	diciannove
(CHEEN-kweh)		10 dieci		(KWEEN-dee-chee)		(VEHN-tee)
5	cinque		15	quindici	20	venti

21 ventuno	24 ventiquattro	27 ventisette	30 trenta
22 ventidue	25 venticinque	28 ventotto	
23 ventitré	26 ventisei	29 ventinove	

	(cheen-KWAHN-tah)		
31 trentuno	50 cinquanta	62 sessantadue	81 ottantuno
32 trentadue	51 cinquantuno	. . .	82 ottantadue
. . .		70 settanta	. . .
(kwah-RAHN-tah)	52 cinquantadue		
40 quaranta	. . .	71 settantuno	90 novanta
41 quarantuno	60 sessanta	72 settantadue	91 novantuno
42 quarantadue	61 sessantuno	. . .	92 novantadue
. . .		80 ottanta	. . .

(CHEHN-toh) **100 cento**	**1,000 mille**	**1,002 milledue**	**3,000 tremila**
	1,001 milleuno	**2,000 duemila**	**10,000 diecimila**

Now try to write out in words the following:

Lui ha ―――――――― **soldi. Lei ha** ―――――――― **lire.**
has   95   cents   100

Marco ha ―――――――― **dollari. La penna costa** ―――――――― **soldi.**
88   67

(DOH-llah-ree)
Il biglietto costa ―――――――― **soldi. Maria ha** ―――――――― **dollari**
74   has   23   dollars

americani; Marco ha ―――――――― **dollari; Giovanni ha** ―――――――
32   29

dollari. Quanti dollari? ―――――――― **dollari.**
(23 + 32 + 29)   84

Che ora è? Now give the following times in words.

2:24 ―――――――――――――   4:12 ―――――――――――――

6:15 ―――――――――――――   8:20 ―――――――――――――

9:17 ―――――――――――――   11:01 ―――――――――――――

3:58 ―――――――――――――   5:30 ―――――――――――――

7:45 ―――――――――――――   1:10 ―――――――――――――

10:35 ―――――――――――――   12:47 ―――――――――――――

(meh-tsoh-JOHR-noh)	(meh-tsah-NOH-tteh)
mezzogiorno	**mezzanotte**
noon	midnight

The following humorous dialogue contains some useful words and expressions related to the telling of time.

Don't forget to read each line out loud several times and to act out each part.

(A stranger approaches Mark on the street.)

STRANIERO	**Scusi, signore, che ora è?**	Excuse me, sir, what time is it?
MARK	**È mezzanotte.**	It's midnight.
	(ahn-KOH-rah)	
STRANIERO	**Ma come, è ancora giorno?**	How can that be? It is still daytime?
MARK	**Scusi, allora è mezzogiorno.**	Excuse me, then it's noon.
	(SKEHR-tsah)	
STRANIERO	**Ma lei scherza?**	Are you joking?
	(oh-roh-LOH-joh)	
MARK	**No. Non ho l'orologio.**	No. I don't have a watch.
	(too-REES-tah)	
STRANIERO	**Lei è un turista?**	Are you a tourist?
MARK	**Sì.**	Yes.
	(VWOH-leh)	
STRANIERO	**Vuole comprare un orologio?**	Do you want to buy a watch? 500,000 lira.
	Cinquecentomila lire.	
MARK	**Troppo!**	That is too much!
STRANIERO	**Centomila lire.**	100,000 lira.
MARK	**No, grazie.**	No, thanks.
STRANIERO	**Ecco il suo orologio.**	Here is your watch. I am an honest
	(bohr-sah-YOH-loh)	
	Io sono un borsaiolo onesto!	pickpocket!

Now fill in the missing dialogue parts. Check your answers only after you have attempted to fill in the parts from memory.

Scusi signore, che o_____ è?

È m_____.

Ma come, è ancora g_____.

Scusi, allora è m_____.

Ma lei s_____?

No. Non ho l'o _____.

Lei è un t_____?

Sì.

Vuole c_____ un orologio?

Cinquecentomila lire.

Troppo!

Centomila l_____.

No, g_____.

Ecco il suo orologio. Io sono un

b_____ onesto!

I numeri ordinali 1–10
Ordinal Numbers 1–10

			(KWAHR-toh)		(SEH-ttee-moh)		(DEH-chee-moh)
First:	**primo**	Fourth:	**quarto**	Seventh:	**settimo**	Tenth:	**decimo**
(seh-KOHN-doh)		(KWEEN-toh)		(oh-TTAH-voh)			
Second:	**secondo**	Fifth:	**quinto**	Eighth:	**ottavo**		
(TEHR-tsoh)				(NOH-noh)			
Third:	**terzo**	Sixth:	**sesto**	Ninth:	**nono**		

Repeat aloud and write the floor designations in the appropriate blanks next to this control panel.

_____

_____

_____

_____

_____

_____

_____

_____

_____

Ricordati di . . .

Remember to . . .

(YEH-ree)
ieri Londra
yesterday

(OH-jjee) (pah-REE-jee)
oggi   Parigi
today

(doh-MAH-nee)
domani Roma
tomorrow

(AHN-keh)
anche Pisa
also/too

(DOH-poh)
dopo Madrid
after

By now, you should be able to make sense out of the following sentences.

(kwee)
Tu vieni **qui**.
here

Io vado **là (lì)**.
there

(MOHL-toh)
Mia moglie non ha **molto** denaro.
much   money

Mio marito ha **poco** denaro.
little

Adesso/ora andiamo a Bologna.
Now

Andiamo **almeno** fino a Palermo.
at least

Giovanni non sta **bene**. (John does not feel well.)
well

(MEH-lyee-oh)
Ora sta **meglio**. (Now he is better.)
better

(POH-ee)
Poi andiamo al cinema.
Then

Questo biglietto costa **troppo**.
too much

(voh-lehn-TYEH-ree)
Io vado a Milano **volentieri**.
gladly

Mia moglie **non** va **mai** al cinema.
never

Io **non** sento **niente/nulla**.
nothing

Io **non** vedo **nessuno**.
no one

See if you remember the meaning of these useful words by matching them with their English equivalents.

1. nessuno		a. yesterday	
2. bene		b. today	
3. meglio		c. tomorrow	
4. niente		d. again	
5. poi		e. also/too	
6. troppo		f. already	
7. mai		g. here	
8. volentieri		h. much	
9. ieri		i. little	
10. anche		j. now	
11. oggi		k. at least	
12. domani		l. well	
13. ancora		m. better	
14. già		n. then	
15. adesso/ora		o. too much	
16. almeno		p. gladly	
17. molto		q. never	
18. poco		r. nothing	
19. qui		s. no one	

Now put the appropriate words in the blanks below.

domani	oggi	anche	qui	molto	mai	niente	nessuno

?

Maria abita _____ a Roma.

Quando arriva Giovanni, _____ o _____?
                                              or

Domani arriva _____ la zia di Gina.

Lui non scrive _____ a suo zio.

Marisa non sa _____.
      knows

Io non vedo _____.

Luisa ha _____ denaro.
    has

Troppi verbi!

Too many verbs!

Previously, you learned about "ire" verbs. Now you will learn about a different kind of "ire" verb. These verbs take an "isc" in the *io, tu, lui / lei,* and *loro* forms. We'll show you how it is done.

(fee-NEE-reh)	(kah-PEE-reh)	(preh-feh-REE-reh)
finire	**capire**	**preferire**
to finish	to understand	to prefer

I finish, I am finishing, I do finish
I understand, I am understanding, I do understand
I prefer, I am preferring, I do prefer

fin *ire*   **cap** *ire*   **prefer** *ire*

IO   **fin***isco*
cap*isco*
prefer*isco*

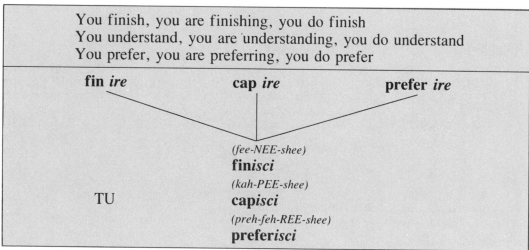

You finish, you are finishing, you do finish
You understand, you are understanding, you do understand
You prefer, you are preferring, you do prefer

fin *ire*   **cap** *ire*   **prefer** *ire*

TU
(fee-NEE-shee)
fin*isci*
(kah-PEE-shee)
cap*isci*
(preh-feh-REE-shee)
prefer*isci*

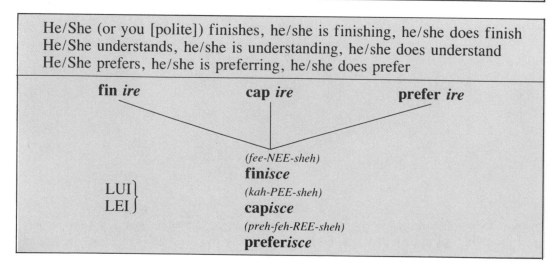

He/She (or you [polite]) finishes, he/she is finishing, he/she does finish
He/She understands, he/she is understanding, he/she does understand
He/She prefers, he/she is preferring, he/she does prefer

fin *ire*   **cap** *ire*   **prefer** *ire*

LUI }
LEI }
(fee-NEE-sheh)
fin*isce*
(kah-PEE-sheh)
cap*isce*
(preh-feh-REE-sheh)
prefer*isce*

We finish, we are finishing, we do finish
We understand, we are understanding, we do understand
We prefer, we are preferring, we do prefer

fin *ire*   **cap** *ire*   **prefer** *ire*

NOI   **fin***iamo*
             cap*iamo*
             prefer*iamo*

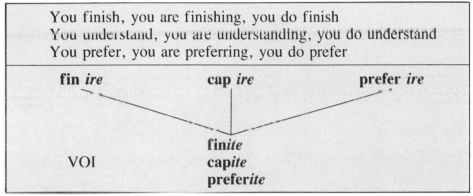

You finish, you are finishing, you do finish
You understand, you are understanding, you do understand
You prefer, you are preferring, you do prefer

fin *ire*   **cap** *ire*   **prefer** *ire*

VOI   **fin***ite*
             cap*ite*
             prefer*ite*

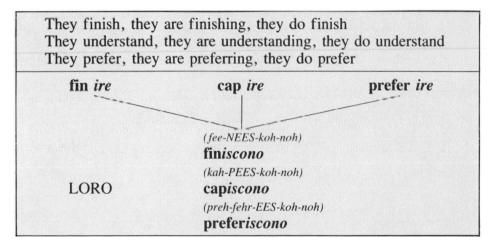

They finish, they are finishing, they do finish
They understand, they are understanding, they do understand
They prefer, they are preferring, they do prefer

fin *ire*   **cap** *ire*   **prefer** *ire*

             (fee-NEES-koh-noh)
             fin*iscono*
             (kah-PEES-koh-noh)
LORO   **cap***iscono*
             (preh-fehr-EES-koh-noh)
             prefer*iscono*

The table at the right will help you remember these "ire" verb endings.

SUMMARY	VERB ENDINGS
"IRE" VERBS WITH "ISC"	

io	_____	-isc	o	noi	_____	-iamo
tu	_____	-isc	i	voi	_____	-ite
lui } lei }	_____	-isc	e	loro	_____	-isc	ono

65

How can you recognize a special "ire" verb that takes these endings? You can't. *Mi dispiace!* (I'm sorry!) You cannot predict by yourself when to add the *isc*. You will have to learn the *isc* verbs through practice.

Let's review all the verb types! Test yourself by putting the right endings in the blanks. Look back at the charts if you have problems remembering.

io	noi

Io cant_____ molto bene.

Io non scriv_____ mai a mio zio.

Io non dorm_____ tutto il giorno.

Io cap_____ l'italiano.

Noi parl_____ l'italiano **come** gli italiani.
            like

Noi ved_____ Giovanni **stasera**.
            tonight

Noi fin_____ il libro domani.

Noi prefer_____ andare a Bologna.

tu	voi

Tu parl_____l'italiano molto bene.

Tu non ved_____ nessuno.

Tu part_____ domani per l'Italia.

Tu prefer_____ andare a Roma.

Voi cant_____ molto bene.

Voi scriv_____ molto bene.

Voi dorm_____ tutto il giorno.

Voi non cap_____ l'italiano.

lui/lei	loro

Lui arriv_____ domani.

Lei non cred_____ a Maria.

Il turista non sent_____
   la voce del vigile.

Giovanni non fin_____la pizza.

Loro arriv_____ dopo le sei.

Gli studenti scriv_____ **l'esame**.
            exam

Franco e Maria part_____ domani per
   l'Italia.

I signori Smith non cap_____ l'italiano.

ANSWERS

Verb review					
io	**tu**	**lui / lei**	**noi**	**voi**	**loro**
(cant) o	(parl) i	a (arriv)	iamo (parl)	ate (cant)	ano (arriv)
(scriv) o	(ved) i	e (cred)	iamo (ved)	ete (scriv)	ono (scriv)
(dorm) o	(part) i	e (sent)	iamo (fin)	ite (dorm)	ono (part)
(cap) isco	isci (prefer)	isce (fin)	iamo (prefer)	ite (cap)	iscono (cap)

66

Il mio e il tuo

Mine and Yours

What's mine and what's yours? Here's how to tell in Italian. Notice that the forms of these words change, depending on the noun.

WITH FEMININE NOUNS	WITH MASCULINE NOUNS	WITH FEMININE NOUNS	WITH MASCULINE NOUNS
MY		**OUR**	
(MEE-ah)	*(MEE-oh)*	*(NOHS-trah)*	*(NOHS-troh)*
la mia valigia	**il mio** biglietto	**la nostra** valigia	**il nostro** biglietto
(MEE-eh)	*(MYEH-ee)*	*(NOHS-treh)*	*(NOIIS-tree)*
le mie valige	**i miei** biglietti	**le nostre** valige	**i nostri** biglietti
YOUR (FAMILIAR)		**YOUR (PLURAL)**	
(TOO-ah)	*(TOO-oh)*	*(VOHS-trah)*	*(VOHS-troh)*
la tua valigia	**il tuo** biglietto	**la vostra** valigia	**il vostro** biglietto
(TOO-eh)	*(TWOH-ee)*	*(VOHS-treh)*	*(VOIIS-tree)*
le tue valige	**i tuoi** biglietti	**le vostre** valige	**i vostri** biglietti
HIS/HER *OR* YOUR (POLITE)		**THEIR**	
(SOO-ah)	*(SOO-oh)*	*(LOH-roh)*	
la sua valigia	**il suo** biglietto	**la loro** valigia	**il loro** biglietto
(SOO-eh)	*(SWOH-ee)*		
le sue valige	**i suoi** biglietti	**le loro** valige	**i loro** biglietti

Notice that "my," "your," and other possessive pronouns are preceded by the appropriate forms of "the." These are dropped only when the noun refers to a singular and unmodified family member (except for "their," which *always* retains the article "the"). For example:

mio zio	*but* **i** miei zii
tua sorella	*but* **la** tua sorella **piccola**
	small
nostro padre	*but* **il loro** padre

67

Notice, as well, that the forms *la sua, le sue, il suo,* and *i suoi* mean "his," "her," or "you" (polite).

Now test your knowledge by putting the appropriate possessive adjective in front of the following nouns.

_____ fiore	my	_____ zia	my (be careful!)
_____ fiori	my	_____ zie	my (be careful again!)
_____ casa	your (familiar)	_____ penna	his
_____ case	your (familiar)	_____ penne	his
_____ gatto	his	_____ orologio	her
_____ gatti	his	_____ orologi	her
_____ gatto	her (be careful!)	_____ biglietto	their
_____ gatti	her	_____ biglietti	their
_____ amico	our	_____ automobile	their
_____ amici	our	_____ automobili	their

If someone asks you, can you give the time in Italian? Read the passage and then answer the questions that follow.

Che ore sono? **chiede il padre a sua figlia.** **Sono le tre e mezzo,** **dice la figlia.**

A che ora parti per l'Italia? **chiede il padre.** **Alle cinque e venti,** *(rees-POHN-deh)* **risponde la figlia.**
answers

Ciao e buon viaggio. **Ciao papà.**
have a good trip · dad

Che cosa chiede il padre a sua figlia?
☐ Come stai?
☐ Che ore sono?
☐ Che fai?

Che ore sono?
☐ Sono le tre e un quarto.
☐ Sono le tre e venticinque.
☐ Sono le tre e mezzo.

A che ora parte la figlia?
☐ Alle cinque e venti.
☐ Alle cinque e un quarto.
☐ A mezzogiorno.

If you will be taking the train, the words and expressions in the following dialogue might prove to be useful to you.

Don't forget to read each line out loud several times and to act out each part.

MARY	*(EH-kkoh-chee) (stah-TSYOH-neh)* **Eccoci alla stazione** *(feh-rroh-vee-AH-ree-ah)* **ferroviaria.**	Here we are at the train station.
ANNE	*(RAH-pee-doh)* **Papà, prendiamo il rapido per** **andare a Firenze?**	Dad, are we taking the luxury (rapid) train to go to Florence?
MARK	**No. Costa troppo.**	No. It costs too much.
ANNE	**Allora prendiamo il** *(dee-reh-TTEE-ssee-moh)* **direttissimo?**	Then are we taking the fast train?
MARK	**Sì.** *(to a ticket clerk)* **Scusi, quanto** **costa un biglietto di andata e ritorno** **per quattro persone a Firenze?**	Yes. Excuse me, how much does a round-trip ticket to Florence for four persons cost?

69

IMPIEGATA	**Il direttissimo?**	The fast train?
MARK	**Sì.**	Yes.

IMPIEGATA *(skohm-pahr-tee-MEHN-toh)* **Scompartimento per** *(foo-mah-TOH-ree)* **fumatori o per non fumatori?**

Smoking or no smoking compartment?

MARK	**Non fumatori.**	No smoking.

IMPIEGATA **Duecentomila lire. Ecco i biglietti.**

200,000 lira. Here are the tickets.

MARK **Grazie. Quando parte il treno?**

Thank you. When does the train leave?

IMPIEGATA **Il treno parte alle quindici e trenta.**

The train leaves at 15:30 (3:30 P M).

Now try to complete the missing dialogue parts. Check your answers only after you have attempted to fill in the missing parts from memory.

Eccoci alla s_____ ferroviaria.

Papà, prendiamo il r_____ per andare a Firenze?

No. C_____ troppo.

Allora prendiamo il d_____?

Sì. Scusi quanto costa un biglietto di a_____

e r_____ per quattro persone a Firenze?

(oh-RAH-ree-oh)
L'orario
Train Schedule

Remember that train schedules use official time, based on a 24-hour clock:

> 1:00 p.m. = 13:00 hours = **le tredici**
> 2:00 p.m. = 14:00 hours = **le quattordici**
> 12:00 midnight = 24:00 hours = **le ventiquattro**

Note that the name of the city of departure *(Bologna)* is at the top of the schedule. Each city served by this line follows, with the departure time (from Bologna) for each train listed in the column on the left, followed by the arrival time on the right. Additional information regarding the type of each train is also given.

dp ab	ar an	Observations Bemerkungen	dp ab	ar an	Observations Bemerkungen

Firenze / Pisa

dp ab	ar an	Observations	dp ab	ar an	Observations
19 04	20 32	✗	16 24	19 02	✗ X Firenze
19 33	20 55		17 17	19 57	✗ X Firenze
21 13	22 39		18 53	22 10	R TEE ✗ X Firenze
22 01	23 20	✗	19 04	22 10	✗ X Firenze
22 23	23 30	Rapido	19 33	23 23	✗ X Firenze
23 23	0 50		21 13	23 48	

Milano / Roma

dp ab	ar an	Observations	dp ab	ar an	Observations
5 20	8 22		1 09	1) 6 30	⇌ —
6 12	9 00		1 34	7 15	⇌ —
6 44	9 12		5 35	10 40	
6 58	9 20		6 18	12 05	
7 20	9 50		8 05	12 55	✗
8 01	9 55	Rapido	8 17	13 15	✗
8 18	1)11 24		8 44	14 42	✗
10 36	13 00		9 09	13 45	✗
10 54	13 40	✗	10 04	14 05	R TEE ✗
11 00	13 50	✗	10 16	14 50	✗
12 00	13 55	R TEE ✗	10 23	1)15 50	✗
12 30	15 20	✗	13 05	17 10	R ✗
13 12	15 25	✗	13 12	18 50	✗
13 23	16 00	✗	13 47	17 45	P TEE ✗
14 05	16 40	✗	14 10	19 48	✗
15 02	17 10		14 55	19 13	Rapido ✗
15 42	17 30	R TEE ✗	15 10	1)19 46	✗
16 07	19 00		15 17	20 07	✗
17 15	19 05	R TEE ✗	16 24	17 40	✗
18 20	20 30	Rapido ✗	17 17	22 50	✗
18 49	1)21 25		18 13	1)23 07	✗
19 58	22 45		18 53	23 00	R TEE ✗
20 44	23 07		19 04	23 50	✗
21 44	23 35	R TEE ✗	19 24	1) 0 13	
21 50	23 40	R TEE ✗			1) Roma Tib.na
22 00	0 45				

1) Milano P.G.

Napoli / Torino

dp ab	ar an	Observations	dp ab	ar an	Observations
1 09	9 20	⇌ —	3 30	8 15	⇌ —
3 58	11 35		4 05	8 48	
8 44	17 22	✗	6 20	10 45	
10 23	19 48	✗	15 10	19 15	
13 47	1)20 10	R TEE ✗	18 37	22 50	
14 55	21 52	Rapido ✗	19 52	0 10	
15 10	2)22 08	✗			
18 00	2) 1 46	⇌ —			
19 24	3 01	⇌ —			
22 01	2) 5 10	⇌ —			
22 40	2) 5 36	⇌ —			

1) Napoli Merg.
2) Napoli C.F.

Venezia

dp ab	ar an	Observations
5 12	7 40	
5 58	8 15	
8 11	10 30	
11 13	12 48	✗
11 25	13 37	✗
12 25	13 31	✗
13 28	15 40	
14 49	16 37	R ✗
16 35	18 54	✗
17 22	19 14	✗
18 13	20 28	✗
21 01	23 08	
22 01	0 04	
22 25	0 38	

Palermo

dp ab	ar an	Observations
5 35	23 22	X Roma R ✗
13 05	8 25	R ✗ X Roma ⇌ —
15 10	10 58	⇌ —
18 15	13 20	⇌ —
22 01	17 35	⇌ —
22 40	17 57	⇌ —

Pisa / Verona

dp ab	ar an	Observations	dp ab	ar an	Observations
6 18	10 00	X Firenze	6 21	8 06	
8 05	10 36	✗ X Firenze	8 19	10 00	
9 09	12 30	✗ X Firenze	11 14	13 14	
9 56	12 30	Rapido X Firenze	△12 20	13 46	
10 16	13 10	X Firenze	12 55	14 33	
△10 30	13 10		16 10	17 50	
13 05	15 32	R ✗ X Firenze	△16 25	18 15	
13 47	16 22	R TEE ✗ X Firenze	17 46	19 10	
△14 55	17 14	Rapido ✗ X Firenze	18 59	20 49	
			22 10	23 42	

△ 29 V - 24 IX 83

(courtesy of Italian State Railways)

71

Il rapido is a luxury train that stops only at main railway stations. *Il direttissimo* is a fast train that stops at more railway stations. *Il diretto* is a "through" train that stops at many more railway stations.

Now fill in the following blanks, writing out the numbers in words, using the timetable.

From **Bologna** to **Venezia** is less than _____ ore.

From **Bologna** to **Milano** con il **rapido** is almost _____ ore.

From **Bologna** to **Torino** is more than _____ ore.

From **Bologna** to **Pisa** con il **rapido** is about _____ ore e _____ .

Voglio / Vorrei
I Want / I Would Like

(voh-LEH-reh)

"To want" is a very useful verb when requesting or asking for things. The Italian **volere** is irregular.

VOLERE

	(VOH-llyee-oh)				*(voh-LLYAH-moh)*	
io	**voglio**	I want		noi	**vogliamo**	we want
	(VWOH-ee)				*(voh-LEH-teh)*	
tu	**vuoi**	you [familiar] want	voi		**volete**	you [plural] want
lui } lei }	*(VWOH-leh)* **vuole**	he/she wants you (polite) want		loro	*(VOH-llyoh-noh)* **vogliono**	they want

If you want to be polite, then you should use the following form.

(voh-RREH-ee)
Vorrei ——————————————— I would like

Now try your hand at these. Fill in the blanks below with the appropriate forms of *volere*.

La figlia del signor Smith _____ un biglietto di andata e ritorno.
(wants)

Quelle persone _____ andare a piedi.
(want)

Io _____ andare con il direttissimo, ma tu _____ andare con il rapido.
(want) (want)

Noi _____ un biglietto per lo scompartimento per non fumatori.
(want)

Voi _____ due biglietti di andata e ritorno.
      want

Io _____ un orario per favore.
   would like

Io _____ anche un biglietto per Roma.
   would like

IN CARROZZA!
All Aboard!

(vyah-JJAH-reh)
viaggiare
to travel

il treno
train

(pah-sseh-JJEH-roh)
il passeggero
passenger

(seh-DEHR-see)
sedersi
to sit down

(ahl-TSAHR-see)
alzarsi
to get up

73

**la
sala d'aspetto**
waiting room

(kohn-doo-TTOH-reh)
il conduttore
conductor

(kah-mmee-NAH-reh)
camminare
to walk

(fah-KKEE-noh)
il facchino
porter

(oh-RAH-ree-oh)
l'orario
schedule

fare il biglietto
to buy a ticket

(pyah-ttah-FOHR-mah)
la piattaforma
platform

(kah-RREH-lloh)
il carrello per le valige
luggage cart

Now have fun with the following crossword puzzle.

Across

1. Train
3. Porter
7. Fast train

Down

2. Fast (express) train
4. To walk
5. Train schedule
6. To travel

I pronomi riflessivi

Reflexive Pronouns

A reflexive verb refers or "reflects" the action back to the subject. For example, "to wash" is a reflexive verb because you wash yourself, that is "reflect back" the action of the verb upon yourself. This is done by means of reflexive pronouns, like "myself" and "yourself." Here are the reflexive pronouns in Italian.

REFLEXIVE PRONOUNS		
mi —— myself		*(chee)* **ci** —— ourselves
ti —— yourself (familiar)		**vi** —— yourselves
si —— himself/herself/yourself (polite)/ itself/oneself		**si** —— themselves

Now let's conjugate a reflexive verb. To do thi just conjugate the verb as you would normally and simply put the reflexive pronouns *right before* the verb (even in the negative). For example:

io ———— **mi lavo** (I wash myself)
tu ———— **ti lavi** (you wash yourself)
lui ⎱
lei ⎰ ———— **si lava** (he/she washes himself/herself)
noi ——— **ci laviamo** (we wash ourselves)
voi ———— **vi lavate** (you wash yourselves)
loro——— **si lavano** (they wash themselves)

NEGATIVE

io _____ **non mi lavo**
tu _____ **non ti lavi**
lui/lei _____ **non si lava**
noi _____ **non ci laviamo**
voi _____ **non vi lavate**
loro _____ **non si lavano**

(lah-VAHR-see)

Notice that the reflexive form for "oneself" is attached to the infinitive form: **lavarsi**.

to wash oneself

Here are three useful reflexive verbs.

(ahl-TSAHR-see) **alzarsi** to get up	*(seh-DEHR-see)* **sedersi** to sit down	*(dee-vehr-TEER-see)* **divertirsi** to enjoy oneself

But the verb *sedersi*
is irregular, so this
is how you conjugate it.

SEDERSI			
io ——— mi siedo		noi ——— ci sediamo	
tu ——— ti siedi		voi ——— vi sedete	
lui ⎫		loro——— si siedono	
lei ⎭ ——— si siede			

Now try your hand at the following. Fill in the blanks with the correct reflexive pronoun and verb form.

Il signor Smith _____ nello scompartimento.
                        sits down

La signora Smith _____ alle sette e mezzo.
                        gets up

Io _____ alle sei e tu _____ alle sette.
        get up   get up

Noi _____ molto quando andiamo a Roma.
          enjoy ourselves

Voi non _____ mai quando andate in Italia.
            enjoy yourselves

I passeggeri _____ nello scompartimento.
            sit down

Io non _____ nello scompartimento per fumatori.
        sit down

Tu _____ nello scompartimento per non fumatori.
     sit down

The following passage is about train travel. Read it and then answer the questions that follow.

**Marco e Maria vanno alla stazione ferroviaria.
Fanno il biglietto di andata e ritorno per Venezia.
Viaggiano con il rapido fino a Bologna. E poi da
Bologna a Venezia vanno con il direttissimo.
Arrivano alle sedici.**

76

Dove vanno Marco e Maria?	☐ Vanno a Roma.
	☐ Vanno a Bologna.
	☐ Vanno a Venezia.
Che cosa fanno?	☐ Fanno le spese.
	☐ Fanno il biglietto.
	☐ Non fanno niente.
Come viaggiano fino a Bologna?	☐ Viaggiano con il diretto.
	☐ Viaggiano con il rapido.
	☐ Viaggiano con il direttissimo.
E da Bologna a Venezia?	☐ Con il diretto.
	☐ Con il rapido.
	☐ Con il direttissimo.
A che ora arrivano?	☐ Arrivano alle due.
	☐ Arrivano alle sedici.
	☐ Arrivano alle diciotto.

Now, as a brief summary of some of the important things you have learned, talk about yourself in Italian, by answering the following questions.

Come ti chiami? _____

Come si chiama tuo marito/tua moglie? _____

Dove abiti? _____

Come stai? _____

A che ora ti alzi la mattina? _____

A che ora vai a dormire la sera?_____

ANSWERS

Comprehension

Vanno a Venezia.   Fanno il biglietto.   Viaggiano con il rapido.   Con il direttissimo.   Arrivano alle sedici.

Fill-ins

Mi chiamo...   Mio marito/Mia moglie si chiama...   Abito a...(New York, Boston...)   Sto (bene, male...)   La mattina mi alzo alle (sei, sette...)   La sera vado a dormire alle (dieci, undici...)

Parlo un po' d'italiano. (I speak a little Italian). And so quick! By now you've learned quite a bit of Italian. Take a look at the rest of the world, too, and learn how to say the names of other countries—in Italian, of course.

COUNTRY	CITY	COUNTRY	CITY
(ah-oos-TRAH-lee-ah) l'Australia	Sydney	l'Italia	Roma
il Canada	Ottawa	*(jah-PPOH-neh)* il Giappone	Tokyo/Tokio
(peh-KEE-noh) la Cina China	Pechino Peking	il Messico	*(chee-TTAH)* la città del Messico
(FRAHN-chah) la Francia	Parigi	la Russia	Mosca
(jehr-MAH-nee-ah) la Germania	Berlino	*(SPAH-nyah)* la Spagna	Madrid
(een-geel-TEH-rrah) l'Inghilterra England	Londra	*(SVEE-tseh-rah)* la Svizzera	*(jee-NEH-vrah)* Ginevra
		(STAH-tee-oo-NEE-tee) gli Stati Uniti	Washington

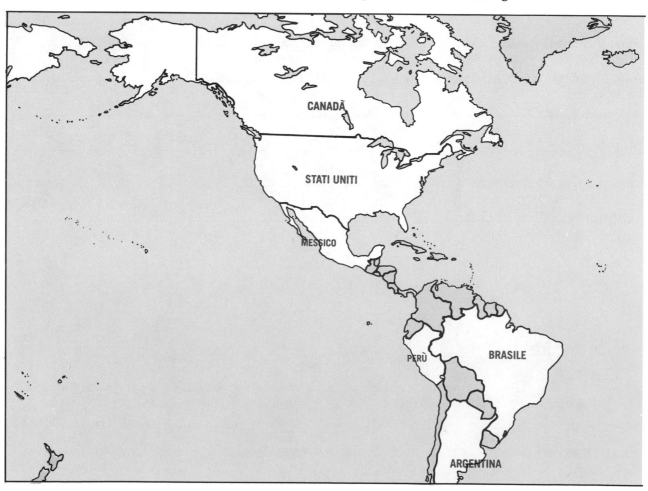

78

Parlo . . .
I Speak...

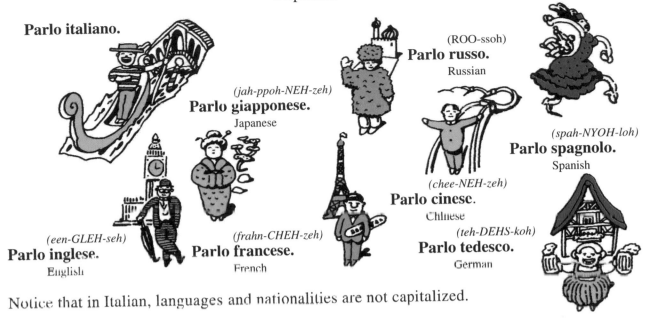

Parlo italiano.

(jah-ppoh-NEH-zeh)
Parlo giapponese.
Japanese

(ROO-ssoh)
Parlo russo.
Russian

(spah-NYOH-loh)
Parlo spagnolo.
Spanish

(chee-NEH-zeh)
Parlo cinese.
Chinese

(een-GLEH-seh)
Parlo inglese.
English

(frahn-CHEH-zeh)
Parlo francese.
French

(teh-DEHS-koh)
Parlo tedesco.
German

Notice that in Italian, languages and nationalities are not capitalized.

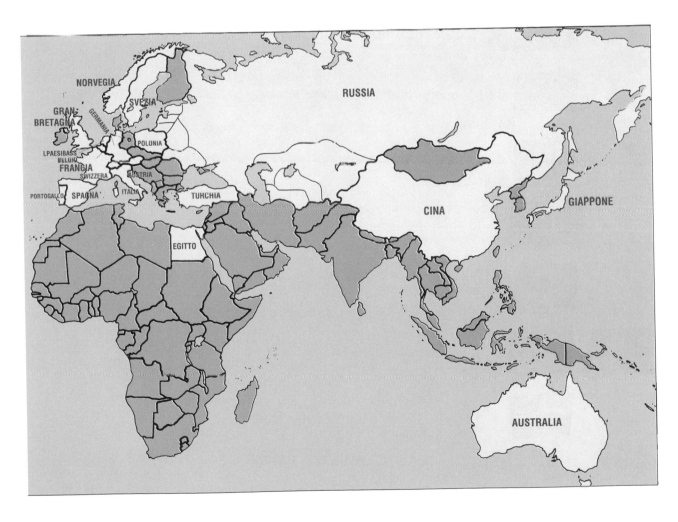

Sono
I Am

(EH-sseh-reh)
The verb *essere* is irregular.
to be

ESSERE			
io	**sono**	noi	**siamo**
tu	**sei**	voi	**siete**
lui lei	**è**	loro	**sono**

Now let's use this verb with nationalities.

1. Io sono americano e anche tu _____ americano.

(aoos-TREE-ah-koh)
2. Io sono austriaco e anche lui _____ austriaco.
Austrian

3. Io sono australiano e anche lei _____ australiana.
Australian

(BEHL-gah)   *(BEHL-jee)*
4. Io sono belga e anche noi _____ belgi.
Belgian

(een-GLEH-seh)
5. Io sono inglese e anche voi _____ inglesi.
English

(kah-nah-DEH-zeh)
6. Io sono canadese e anche loro _____ canadesi.
Canadian

(chee-NEH-zeh)
7. Io sono cinese e anche tu _____ cinese.
Chinese

(dah-NEH-zeh)
8. Io sono danese e anche quel signore _____ danese.
Danish

ANSWERS

Verbs 1. sei 2. è 3. è 4. siamo 5. siete 6. sono 7. sei 8. è

80

9. Io sono olandese e anche mia moglie _____ olandese.
(oh-lahn-DEH-zeh)
Dutch

10. Io sono francese e anche noi _____ francesi.
(ftahn-CHEH-zeh)
French

11. Io sono tedesco e anche voi _____ tedeschi.
(teh-DEHS-koh)   *(teh-DEHS-kee)*
German

12. Io sono italiano e anche i passeggeri _____ italiani.
(ee-tah-LYAH-noh)
Italian

13. Io sono giapponese e anche tu _____ giapponese.
(jah-ppoh-NEH-zeh)
Japanese

14. Io sono messicano e anche il mio amico _____ messicano.
(meh-ssee-KAH-noh)
Mexican

15. Io sono norvegese e anche noi _____ norvegesi.
(nohr-veh-JEH-zeh)
Norwegian

16. Io sono polacco e anche voi _____ polacchi.
(poh-LAH-kkoh)
Polish

17. Io sono russo e anche i miei amici _____ russi.
(ROO-ssoh)
Russian

18. Io sono spagnolo e anche tu _____ spagnolo.
(spah-NYOH-loh)
Spanish

19. Io sono svedese e anche la sua amica _____ svedese.
(sveh-DEH-zeh)
Swedish

20. Io sono svizzero e anche voi _____ svizzeri.
(SVEE-tseh-roh)
Swiss

21. Io sono turco e anche gli studenti _____ turchi.
(TOOR-koh)
Turkish

ANSWERS

9. è	11. siete	13. sei	15. siamo	17. sono	19. è	21. sono
10. siamo	12. sono	14. è	16. siete	18. sic	20. siete

Be careful with "is." Notice that is has an accent, whereas "and" does not. Also, you may recall from previous dialogues that "there is" is *c'è* with the plural form *(ci sono)* "there are." Remember that *ecco* is used to point out something. This table will help you remember these differences.

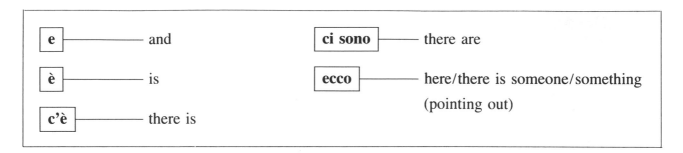

Notice that with *quale* (which) the final *e* is dropped in front of *è* ("is").

Qual è il tuo biglietto? (Which is your ticket?)

Qual è la tua chiave? (Which is your key?)

Try this now with the following questions.

_____ il tuo orologio? _____ la tua automobile? _____ il tuo passaporto?

Vado a . . .
I Am Going to . . .

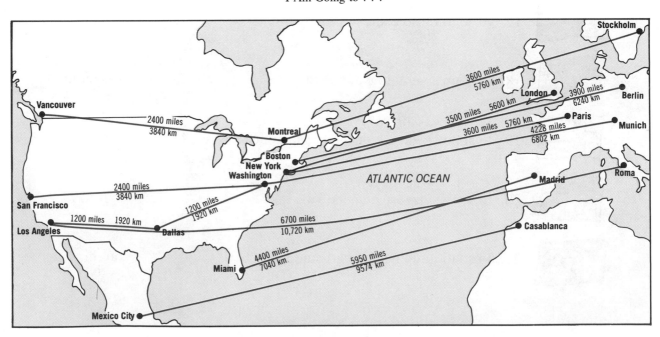

ANSWERS

Qual è   Qual è   Qual è

To say that something is "in" a **country**, use the corresponding preposition *in*. For example:

Dov'è Mosca? È *in* Russia. (Where is Moscow? It is in Russia.)

However, for the United States you have to use *negli Stati Uniti*. With any **city** *a* is used.

Dov'è la Statua della Libertà? È *a* New York.
      Statue   of   Liberty

You continue, using *in* or *a* in these sentences.

Dov'è la Torre Eiffel? È _____ Parigi.

Dov'è New York? È _____ Stati Uniti.

Dov'è Acapulco? È _____ Messico.

Dov'è Berlino? È _____ Germania.

Dov'è il Colosseo? È _____ Roma, _____ Italia.

Dov'è il Prado? È _____ Madrid, _____ Spagna.

Now try your skill with what you have just learned. Fill in the blanks as indicated.

_____ _____ Firenze. I fiorentini _____ molto simpatici.
  I am   in   Florentines   are

_____ Italia, si parla _____. Roma _____ _____
  In   one   Italian   is   the

capitale d'Italia, Parigi _____ _____ capitale della _____
                        is   the   France

_____ Madrid _____ _____ capitale della _____ .
  and   is   the   Spain

Capisco
I Understand

Look back to the section on "ire" verbs, if you have forgotten how to conjugate *capire*. Now try the following.

Io *capisco* l'italiano, ma tu non *capisci* l'italiano.
                      but

You continue.

1. Io _____ il tedesco, ma tu non _____ il tedesco.

2. Lui _____ lo spagnolo, ma loro non _____ lo spagnolo.

3. Maria _____ l'inglese, ma noi non _____ l'inglese.

4. I passeggeri _____ l'italiano, ma voi non _____ l'italiano.

Subway Map of Rome

Read the following dialogue, repeating each line out loud several times. Don't forget to act out each part.

(Knowing the frustration of not being understood, can you imagine how Anne felt when her wallet was stolen?)

ANNE	**Scusi, signore, lei parla inglese?**	Excuse me, sir, do you speak English?

VIGILE	**No. Solo italiano.**	No. Only Italian.

ANNE **Qualcuno ha rubato il mio**   Someone stole my wallet in the subway.
(pohr-tah-FOH-llyoh)
portafoglio nella metropolitana.
      (preh-OH-kkoo-pee)

VIGILE **Non si preoccupi, signorina!**   Don't worry, Miss! Fill out this form.

    Compili questo modulo.

ANNE **Parli più lentamente, per favore.**   Speak more slowly, please.

VIGILE **Va bene. Scriva il suo nome e il**   Okay. Write your name and your address, and
(een-dee-REE-tsoh)
suo indirizzo, e anche il numero di   also the phone number of your hotel.
(teh-LEH-foh-noh)
telefono del suo albergo.

ANNE **Non ho più soldi, carte di**   I have no more money, credit cards, or passport.
(KREH-dee-toh)   *(fah-ROH)*
credito, o passaporto. Cosa farò?   What am I going to do?

VIGILE **Per il passaporto, lei deve andare**   For the passport, you have to go to your
(ahm-bah-SHAH-tah)
alla sua ambasciata.   embassy.
      (pwoh) (ah-yoo-TAH-reh)

ANNE **Lei non mi può aiutare?**   Can't you help me?

      (preh-OH-koo-pee)
VIGILE **Non si preoccupi.**   Please don't worry. I am starting the search for
(koh-MEEN-choh) (chehr-KAH-reh)   *(SOO-bee-toh)*
Comincio a cercare il ladro subito.   the thief right now.

ANNE **Grazie mille.**   Thank you very much.

Now try to complete the missing dialogue parts without looking back. Check your answers after you have attempted this exercise from memory.

Scusi, signore, lei parla i _____?

No. Solo i _____.

Qualcuno ha rubato il mio p_____ nella metropolitana.

Non si preoccupi, signorina! Compili questo m_____.

Parli più l_____, per favore.

Va bene. Scriva il suo n_____ e il suo i_____, e anche il

numero di t_____ del suo albergo.

Non ho più s_____, carte di c_____, o passaporto. Cosa farò?

By rearranging the following words, you will get sentences found in the dialogue.

passaporto / Per / il / ambasciata / alla / deve / sua / lei / andare

_____

non / Lei / aiutare / può / mi

_____

The following brief passage reflects what you have learned about countries, languages, and nationalities. After you have read it, choose the appropriate completion to each sentence.

La signorina Smith è americana. Lei non parla italiano molto bene. Vuole andare in Svizzera, in Francia e in Germania, ma qualcuno ha rubato il suo portafoglio. Adesso parla a un vigile. Il vigile non parla inglese, ma capisce il francese. Allora, la signorina e il vigile parlano in francese.

La signorina Smith . . .
- ☐ parla italiano molto bene.
- ☐ non parla inglese.
- ☐ è americana.

Lei vuole andare . . .
- ☐ in Russia.
- ☐ in Francia.
- ☐ in Italia.

Qualcuno ha rubato . . .

- [ ] il suo portafoglio.
- [ ] il suo passaporto.
- [ ] i suoi soldi.

Adesso parla a . . .

- [ ] suo padre.
- [ ] sua madre.
- [ ] un vigile.

Il vigile capisce . . .

- [ ] il tedesco.
- [ ] il francese.
- [ ] lo spagnolo.

Now have fun with the following crossword puzzle.

Across
1. Spain
2. France
4. Germany
5. French

Down
1. Spanish
3. German

Northern Italy   *(Courtesy of Fisher Annotated Travel Guides ©—reprinted with permission)*

ALL'AGENZIA DI AUTOMOBILI DA NOLEGGIO
At the Car Rental Office

You may want to see the country close up. As you read the following dialogue, make sure that you repeat each line out loud several times. The words and expressions in it will prove useful if you want to rent a car.

(Mark has decided to rent a car and take his family for an excursion into the Italian countryside.)

MARK **Buon giorno. Vorrei noleggiare** *(noh-leh-JJAH-reh)*
una macchina. *(MAH-kkee-nah)*

Good day. I would like to rent a car.

IMPIEGATA **Per quanto tempo?**

For how long?

MARK **Per due settimane.**

For two weeks.

IMPIEGATA **Vediamo. Abbiamo una Lancia**
e una FIAT.

Let's see. We have a Lancia and a FIAT.

88

MARK	**Prendo la FIAT. Sono incluse**	I'll take the FIAT. Is the mileage included in the
	(MEE-llyah)	
	anche le miglia nel prezzo?	price?
	(behn-DZEE-nah)	
IMPIEGATA	**Sì, ma la benzina no. La sua**	Yes, but it does not include the gas. Your
	(GWEE-dah)	
	patente di guida e la sua carta di credito,	driver's license and credit card, please.
	per favore.	
	(foon-TSYOH-nah)	
MARK	**Mi fa vedere come funziona il**	Can you show me how the gearshift and the
	(MAHR-chah)	
	cambio di marcia e come	headlights work?
	funzionano i fari?	
IMPIEGATA	**Certo. Ecco la chiave e i**	Certainly. Here are the key and the papers.
	(doh-koo-MEHN-tee)(STEE ah)	
	documenti. Stia attento! Gli autisti	Be careful! Italian drivers are crazy!
	(PAH-tsee)	
	italiani sono pazzi!	
MARK	**Come tutti gli autisti oggi!**	Like all drivers today!

Now try to complete the missing dialogue parts without looking back. Check your answers after attempting the exercise from memory.

Buon giorno. V_____ n_____ una macchina.

Per q_____ t_____?

Per due s_____.

Vediamo. A_____ una Lancia e una FIAT.

Prendo la FIAT. Sono incluse anche le m_____ nel p_____?

Sì, ma la b_____ no. La sua p_____ di g_____

e la sua carta di credito, per favore.

Mi fa vedere come f_____ il cambio di m_____

e come funzionano i f_____?

Certo. Ecco la chiave e i d_____. S_____ a_____!

Gli a_____ italiani sono pazzi!

Alcune cose essenziali

Some Essentials

Here are some more words that you should know before you hit the road.

(ah-SSEE-koo-rah-tsyoh-neh)
l'assicurazione insurance

(ah-FFAH-reh)
un buon affare a good deal/bargain

(oo-tee-lee-TAH-ree-ah)
l'utilitaria compact car

una macchina grande a large car

(pool-MEE-noh)
il pulmino van

(eh-CHEH-ssoh)
la multa per eccesso

(veh-loh-chee-TAH)
di velocità speeding ticket

(pahr-KEH-jjoh)
il parcheggio parking

nord-sud-est-ovest north-south-east-west

(POON-tah)
l'ora di punta rush hour

(stah-TSYOH-neh) (sehr-VEE-tsyoh)
la stazione di servizio service station

(PYEH-noh)
fare il pieno to fill up

(TRAH-ffee-koh)
il traffico traffic

(jee-RAH-reh)
girare to turn

(rah-JOH-neh)
avere ragione to be right

(TOHR-toh)
avere torto to be wrong

Now choose one of the above words or expressions according to the meaning of each sentence. Don't forget to make necessary verb changes. *Buona fortuna!*

1. C'è molto t_____ durante l'ora di p_____.
   during

2. Maria ha r_____, la stazione di s_____ si trova a

   n_____, non a s_____, del semaforo.

3. Preferisco l'u_____, non la macchina g_____.

4. Alla stazione di servizio faccio sempre il p_____.

5. Hai t_____. Il p_____ costa poco. È un buon a_____.

6. Il vigile dà una m_____ per eccesso di v_____ al signor Smith.

7. Giovanni non g_____ a destra, lui g_____ a sinistra.

8. Va a est, non a o_____.

9. Qui non c'è il p_____.

LA SEGNALETICA / SEGNALI STRADALI

(seh-nyah-LEH-tee-kah)

Road Signs

If you're planning to drive while you're abroad, spend some time remembering the meanings of these signs.

Dangerous Intersection

Danger!

Stop

Speed Limit (in km/hr)

Minimum Speed

End of Limited Speed

No Entrance

Yield Right-of-way

Two-way Traffic

Dangerous Curve

Entrance to Expressway

Expressway Exit
(road narrows)

Customs

No Passing

End of No Passing Zone

One-way Street

Detour

Road Closed

Parking

No Parking

Roundabout

No Parking
(or waiting)

No Cyclists

Pedestrian Crossing

Railroad Crossing
(no gate)

Guarded Railroad Crossing

ALLA STAZIONE DI SERVIZIO
At the Service Station

Venice

(courtesy of Michelin Guide, Italy, *10th Edition—reprinted with permission)*

AUTISTA	**Il pieno, per favore.**	Fill it up, please.
IMPIEGATO	**Normale o super?**	Regular or super?
AUTISTA	**Normale. Le**	Regular. Would you mind checking the
	(dees-pyah-cher-EH-bbeh) (kohn-troh-LLAH-reh)	
	dispiacerebbe controllare	
	(OH-lee-oh) (AH-kwah)	
	l'olio, l'acqua e l'aria nelle gomme?	oil, water, and air in the tires?
IMPIEGATO	**Tutto è a posto.**	Everything is okay.
AUTISTA	**Voglio andare a Piazza San**	I want to go to San Marco Square. How does one
	Marco. Come ci si va?	get there?

93

IMPIEGATO (*points to map*) **Guardi. Lei si**	Look. You are here at
trova qui alla Stazione di Santa Lucia.	Santa Lucia Railroad
Prenda la strada che va intorno al	Station. Take the road that goes all around the
Canal Grande. Questa strada la porta	Grand Canal. This road will take you directly to
(*dee-reh-ttah-MEHN-teh*) **direttamente alla piazza.**	the square.
(*TRAH-ffee-koh*) AUTISTA **C'è molto traffico?**	Is there a lot of traffic?
IMPIEGATO **No. Non c'è affatto traffico,**	No. There is no traffic at all, because Venice
perché Venezia non ha strade, ha	does not have roads, it has only canals!
solo canali!	

Read over this dialogue several times and then test your memory by completing the missing dialogue parts. Check your answers only after you have attempted to complete the missing parts from memory.

AUTISTA _____ .

IMPIEGATO   **Normale o super?**

AUTISTA _____ . **Le dispiacerebbe controllare** _____ ?

IMPIEGATO   **Tutto è a posto.**

AUTISTA   **Voglio andare a Piazza San Marco.** _____ ?

IMPIEGATO   **Guardi. Lei si trova qui** _____

_____ . **Prenda la strada che va**

_____ . **Questa strada**

la porta _____ .

CLIENTE   **C'è** _____ ?

COMMESSO   **No. Non c'è** _____ **perché**

Venezia _____ !

94

L'AUTOMOBILE / LA MACCHINA
The Car

(voh-LAHN-teh)
il volante
steering wheel

(KLAHK-sohn)
il clacson
horn

(peh-DAH-leh)
il pedale del freno
brake pedal

(free-TSYOH-neh)
il pedale della frizione
clutch pedal

(tehr-jee-krees-TAH-llee)
i tergicristalli
windshield wipers

(KAHM-byoh)
la leva del cambio
gear shift

(kroos-KOH-ttoh)
il cruscotto
dashboard

(ah-cheh-leh-rah-TOH-reh)
l'acceleratore
accelerator

(bah-OO-leh)(pohr-tah-bah-GAH-llyee)
il baule / il portabagagli
trunk

(TAHR-gah)
la targa
plate

(pah-rah-OOR-tee)
il paraurti
bumper

(KOH-fah-noh)
il cofano
hood

(FAH-ree) (proh-yeh-TTOH-ree)
i fari / i proiettori
headlights

(bah-tteh-REE-ah)
la batteria
battery

(rah-dee-ah-TOH-reh)
il radiatore
radiator

(moh-TOH-reh)
il motore
motor

(pah-rah-BREH-tsah)
il parabrezza
windshield

(sehr-bah-TOH-yoh)
il serbatoio
gas tank

(kah-rroh-tseh-REE-ah)
la carrozzeria
body (of the car)

(pah-dee-LLYOH-neh)
il padiglione
roof

(pohr-TYEH-rah) (spohr-TEH-lloh)
la portiera / lo sportello
door

(POHM-pah)
la pompa
gas pump

(pah-rah-FAHN-goh)
il parafango
fender

(neh-oo-MAH-tee-chee)
i pneumatici /
tires *(GOH-mmeh)*
le gomme

Now fill in the names for the following auto parts.

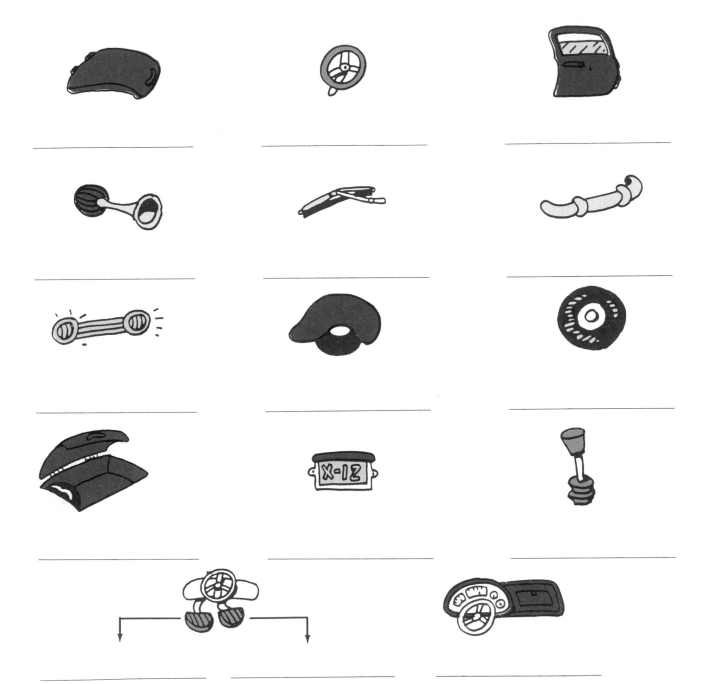

(ree-pah-RAH-reh) *(ah-jjoos-TAH-reh)*

Per riparare / aggiustare la macchina
Some Essentials for Repair

The following words and expressions will be useful to you if your car breaks down in Italy.

Mi può aiutare?   Can you help me?

La mia gomma è sgonfia.   My tire is flat.

La mia macchina non parte.	My car doesn't start.
I freni non funzionano.	The brakes don't work.
Ho bisogno di benzina.	I need gas.
(Mi faccia) il pieno, per favore.	Fill 'er up, please.

Come si fa per chiedere . . .

How to Ask for . . .

In order to get people to do things for you, you will have to know how to use verbs in a "command" or "imperative" way. Look at the following chart. This shows you how to form the imperative of regular verbs.

THE IMPERATIVE			
	PARL*ARE* CAMMIN*ARE*	SCRIV*ERE* RISPOND*ERE*	DORM*IRE* FIN*IRE*
Singular *Familiar* *Command:*	**Parla!** Speak! **Cammina!** Walk!	**Scrivi!** Write! **Rispondi!** Answer!	**Dormi!** Sleep! **Finisci!** Finish!
Singular *Polite* *Command:*	**Parli!** **Cammini!**	**Scriva!** **Risponda!**	**Dorma!** **Finisca!**
Plural *Command:*	**Parlate!** **Camminate!**	**Scrivete!** **Rispondete!**	**Dormite!** **Finite!**

The command "Let's speak, walk," and so on, is given by a form you already know.

Parliamo!	_____	Let's speak!
Scriviamo!	_____	Let's write!
Finiamo!	_____	Let's finish!
Dormiamo!	_____	Let's sleep!

Notice that, as in English, pronouns are not used with the imperative. Also notice that verbs like *finire,* which take the extra *isc* in the present indicative (remember?), also take it in the imperative singular command forms.

To make reflexive verbs imperative, add on the reflexive pronouns in the familiar and plural forms.

REFLEXIVE IMPERATIVES		
	ALZARSI	DIVERTIRSI
Singular Familiar Command:	(AHL-tsah-tee) **Alzati!**	(dee-VEHR-tee-tee) **Divertiti!**
Singular Polite Command:	*Si* **alzi!**	*Si* **diverta!**
Plural Command:	(ahl-TSAH-teh-vee) **Alzatevi!**	(dee-vehr-TEE-teh-vee) **Divertitevi!**
	and	
	(ahl-TSYAH-moh-chee) **Alziamoci!** Let's get up!	(dee-vehr-TYAH-moh-chee) **Divertiamoci!** Let's enjoy ourselves!

One more thing about imperatives: don't get discouraged! With a little practice, you will become familiar and quite proficient with these verb forms. To make any verb negative, you have learned to put *non* just before it. So too with imperative verbs. But there is one change you must make. For the singular familiar command in the negative, use the infinitive (*parlare, scrivere*).

NEGATIVE IMPERATIVES	
Singular Familiar Command:	**Non parlare!** Don't speak! **Non scrivere!** Don't write!
Other Command Forms:	**Non parli! Non scriva! Non parlate! Non scrivete!** (Just put *non* before the appropriate imperative form.)

Now try the following.

You are speaking to your friend. Tell him to do as you wish, filling in the blanks as indicated.

1. Giovanni, _____ italiano!
   speak (LEH-tteh-rah)

2. Giovanni, _____ la pizza!
   finish

3. Giovanni, _____ la **lettera!**
   write

4. Giovanni, non _____ lentamente!
   walk (be careful!)

5. Giovanni, _____ domani alle sei!
   get up

Now use polite forms, because you are speaking to a stranger.

Signora Smith, _____ italiano!
                    speak

Signora Smith, _____ la pizza!
                    finish

Signora Smith, _____ la lettera!
                    write

Signora Smith, non _____ lentamente!
                        walk

Signora Smith, _____ domani alle sei!
                    get up

Finally, try giving commands to a group of people.

Ragazzi, _____ italiano!
              speak

Ragazzi, _____ la pizza!
              finish

Ragazzi, _____ la lettera!
              write

Ragazzi, non _____ lentamente!
                  walk

Ragazzi, _____ domani alle sei!
              get up

The imperatives of the irregular verbs you have learned so far are as follows.

	ANDARE	VENIRE	FARE	DARE	DIRE	SEDERSI	ESSERE
Singular Familiar Command:	**Va'!**	*(VYEH-nee)* **Vieni!**	**Fa'!**	**Da'!**	**Di'!**	*(SYEH-dee-tee)* **Siediti!**	*(SEE-ee)* **Sii!**
Singular Polite Command:	**Vada!**	*(VEHN-gah)* **Venga!**	*(FAH-chah)* **Faccia!**	*(DEE-ah)* **Dia!**	**Dica!**	**Si sieda!**	*(SEE-ah)* **Sia!**
Plural Command:	**Andate!**	**Venite!**	**Fate!**	**Date!**	**Dite!**	*(seh-DEH-teh-vee)* **Sedetevi!**	*(SYAH-teh)* **Siate!**

For the negative of an irregular verb, use the infinitive (*Non andare! Non venire!* etc.).

Now choose the familiar or polite command forms of these verbs. *Stia attento!* (Be careful!)

1. Marco, _____ a casa!
              go   home

2. Anna, _____ qui!
                come

3. Signor Smith, _____ a casa!
                       go

4. Signora Smith, _____ questo!
                          do

5. Signorina Rossi, _____ qui!
                          come

6. Maria, _____ questo!
                  do

ANSWERS

Familiar or polite commands 1. va' (a casa!) 2. vieni (qui!) 3. vada (a casa!) 4. faccia (questo!) 5. venga (qui!) 6. fa' (questo!)

Plural commands parlate (italiano!) finite (la pizza!) scrivete (la lettera!) camminate (lentamente!) alzatevi (domani)

Singular commands parli (italiano!) finisca (la pizza!) scriva (la lettera!) cammini (lentamente!) si alzi (domani)

99

7. Giovanni, _____ la penna a Maria!
   give

8. Signor Verdi, _____ la penna alla signorina Smith!
   give

(veh-ree-TAH)

9. Signora Rossi, _____ la verità!   10. Gina, _____ la verità!
   say/tell   truth   say/tell

11. Pina, _____ qui!   12. Signorina Verdi, _____ qui!
    sit   sit

13. Signor Smith, _____ gentile!   14. Gino, _____ gentile!
    be   be

Using the imperative does not always mean you are giving orders. When someone asks for directions, your response will be "go to the right." That's a command, too, in a way. Giving directions in Italian is an essential communicative skill. Try your hand at giving

(ah-oo-toh-ree-MEH-ssah)

directions to the **autorimessa** in the diagram. Here are the verbs and expressions you will need.
garage

(jee-RAH-reh)
girare   **a destra**
to turn

andare diritto   **a sinistra**
straight ahead

Avere
To Have

Like "to be," *avere* is an essential verb for communicating in your new language. Notice that the "h" is not pronounced. It is always silent.

AVERE			
to have			
io _____ *(oh)* **ho**		noi _____ *(ah-BBYAH-moh)* **abbiamo**	
tu _____ *(AH-ee)* **hai**		voi _____ *(ah-VEH-teh)* **avete**	
lui ⎱ _____ *(ah)* **ha**	lei ⎰	loro _____ *(AH-nnoh)* **hanno**	
Singular Familiar Command: *(AH-bbee)* **Abbi!**	*Singular Polite Command:* *(AH-bbyah)* **Abbia!**	*Plural Command:* *(ah-BBYAH-teh)* **Abbiate!**	

ANSWERS

Directions

Gira / Giri a destra, poi a sinistra.
Va' / Vada diritto, gira / giri a destra.   Gira / Giri a sinistra, poi a destra, poi a sinistra.

7. da' (la penna)   8. dia (la penna alla)   9. dica (la verità!)   10. di' (la verità!)   11. siediti (qui!)
12. si sieda (qui!)   13. sia (gentile!)   14. sii (gentile!)

100

Capisci? Put the right form of *avere* in the spaces provided.

Quell'uomo _____ due valige.

Tu _____ sempre ragione.

Io non _____ la patente di guida.

Loro _____ torto.

Noi _____ una Lancia.

Gli autisti italiani _____
molta pazienza.

Voi _____ una FIAT.

Here are two more verbs that are useful, but first, review the verb *volere* in chapter 6.

(poh-TEH-reh) POTERE to be able to		(doh-VEH-reh) DOVERE to have to	
(POH-ssoh) io posso	(poh-SSYAH-moh) noi possiamo	(DEH-voh) devo	(doh-BBYAH-moh) dobbiamo
(PWOH-ee) tu puoi	(poh-TEH-teh) voi potete	(DEH-vee) devi	(doh-VEH-teh) dovete
lui⎱ (pwoh) lei⎰ può	(POH-ssoh-noh) loro possono	(DEH-veh) deve	(DEH-voh-noh) devono

Now use the right form of *potere* or *dovere* in the following sentences.

Io non _____ andare in Italia quest'**anno.**
      potere   *year*

I passeggeri _____ scendere a Bologna.
              dovere

Voi _____ comprare l'assicurazione per la macchina!
      dovere

I turisti _____ noleggiare quella macchina.
         potere

Io _____ portare la mia macchina alla stazione di servizio.
    dovere

Tu _____ portare la tua macchina a quella stazione di servizio.
      potere

                                   (lah-SHAH-toh)
Il signor Smith non _____ guidare in Italia perché ha lasciato la sua patente in
America.   *potere*   *he left*

Attenzione! (Watch out!) Driving in a foreign country means watching the road even when the scenery is breathtaking.

Che bella veduta! Yes, how beautiful! Read the passage that follows and determine what happened on this trip. Answer the questions that follow.

Un autista americano e un autista italiano hanno avuto un piccolo incidente. *(een-chee-DEHN-teh)* **L'autista**
had   Accident

italiano chiede come è successo. *(soo-CHEH-ssoh)* **Il danno non è grave, ma la macchina dell'italiano è**
it happened   *(DAH-nnoh)* damage *(GRAH-veh)* serious

(NWOH-vah) *(deh-CHEE-deh)* *(BREH-veh)* *(dees-koo-SYOH-neh)*
nuova. L'autista italiano decide di chiamare un vigile. Dopo una breve discussione, i due
new   decided   brief   discussion

(ah-jjoos-TAH-reh) *(oh-NYOO-noh)* *(PROH-pree-ah)*
autisti decidono di farsi aggiustare ognuno la propria macchina. Il vigile dice ai due
fix   each one own

autisti che bisogna stare attenti quando si guida.
be careful   one

102

Chi ha avuto un incidente?

☐ Due turisti americani.

☐ Un autista americano e un autista italiano.

☐ Un autista e un vigile.

Chi chiede come è successo?

☐ L'autista americano.

☐ Il vigile.

☐ L'autista italiano.

Com'è il danno?

☐ È grave.

☐ Non è grave.

☐ È molto grave.

Chi decide di chiamare il vigile?

☐ L'autista italiano.

☐ L'autista americano.

☐ Nessuno.

Che cosa decidono di fare, gli autisti?

☐ Decidono di andare insieme a Roma.

☐ Decidono di andare alla stazione di servizio

☐ Decidono di farsi aggiustare ognuno la propria macchina.

Che cosa dice il vigile?

☐ Dice che bisogna guidare solo le macchine nuove.

☐ Dice che bisogna stare attenti quando si guida.

☐ Dice che non bisogna fare un incidente.

Now see how many of the following words and expressions you remember or can figure out by matching them up with their English meanings.

1. incidente		a.	No Left Turn
2. danno		b.	One-Way
3. aggiustare		c.	No Parking
4. girare		d.	rush hour
5. guidare		e.	west
6. benzina		f.	east
7. clacson		g.	south
8. cruscotto		h.	(car) horn
9. pneumatici		i.	No Passing
10. volante		j.	gas
11. Divieto di sorpasso		k.	to drive
12. Divieto di svolta a sinistra		l.	to turn
13. Senso unico		m.	steering wheel
14. Divieto di sosta		n.	dashboard
15. ora di punta		o.	to fix
16. nord		p.	accident
17. sud		q.	tires
18. est		r.	damage
19. ovest		s.	north

As a quick review of those pesky imperative verbs, say the following in Italian.

Mark, get up! _____

Mrs. Smith, enjoy yourself! _____

John, don't go to the museum today! _____

Mr. Smith, don't go to the post office today! _____

Anne, John, speak Italian! _____

These words will be useful to you if you go camping to any of the many mountain spots throughout Italy. You will be able to buy equipment in most of the resort villages found in the Italian mountains.

(mah-teh-RAH-ssoh)(pneh-oo-MAH-tee-koh)
il materasso   pneumatico
air mattress

(KAH-pee)(vehs-tee-AH-ree-oh)
il capi di vestiario
articles of clothing

(pah-GAH-yeh)
le pagaie
paddles

(koh-PEHR-tah)
la coperta
blanket

(PEE-lah)(tahs-KAH-bee-leh)
la pila   tascabile
flashlight

(kah-NEHS-troh)
il canestro
basket

(roo-SHEH-lloh)
il ruscello
brook

(TEHN-dah)
la tenda
tent

(AHL-beh-roh)
l'albero
tree

(SOH-leh)
il sole
sun

(kah-NOH-ah)
la canoa
canoe

(stee-VAH-lee)
gli stivali
boots

(SEH-kkyoh)
il secchio
bucket

(ah-treh-tsah-TOO-reh)(ee-JEH-nee-keh)
attrezzature   igieniche
toilet articles

(SKAH-toh-lah)
la scatola
box

(fyah-MMEE-feh-ree)
i fiammiferi
matches

(STOO-fah)
la stufa
heater

(SAH-kkoh)(PEH-loh)
il sacco a pelo
sleeping bag

(TEHR-mohs)
il thermos
thermos

(skah-toh-LEH-tteh)
le scatolette
cans

(RAH-dee-oh)(pohr-TAH-tee-leh)
la radio   portatile
portable radio

(KAH-nnah) (PEHS-kah)
la canna da pesca
fishing pole

(kah-vah-TAH-ppee)
il cavatappi
corkscrew

(oo-TEHN-see-lee)(koo-CHEE-nah)
gli utensili da   cucina
cooking utensils

Practice your "outdoor" Italian. Find the camping words and expressions in the following puzzle and circle them. When you locate each one, write it down and pronounce it aloud. We've found the first one for you, as an example.

materasso pneumatico

_____   _____   _____

_____   _____   _____

_____   _____   _____

_____   _____   _____

_____   _____   _____

_____   _____   _____

```
q m a t e r a s s o p n e u m a t i c o a z w s p x e d c
r f v t g b y h n u i j m k q l a s o l e p o l a i j n u
h r b y g v t f c r l d x e s b z a p q x s w c g d e v f
r u b g t n h y m j a u k o p e q a e z w c s x a e d c r
m s k s c a t o l e t t e n j r i b r h u a v g i y c f t
x c d r z s e q a z a w s x e o d c t r f p m k e i n j u
z e a q t h e r m o s x c c a v a t a p p i d e v f r b g
t l n h y m j u k l c o p q a z w s x e d d c r f v t y h
z l a q x s w c d s a c c o a p e l o v f i r b g t n z a
p o l n y q a z w x b e d r f v i j n b r v p m q z x c v
y h n u t e n s i l i d a c u c i n a t g e b r f v f w s
q a z w s x e d c r l f v y h n z a q x w s e c c h i o d
x s c a n n a d a p e s c a w c d e v f s t u f a r a e w
z a q x s w c d e b f r g h y h u n k i j i l o n q m a c
i r a d i o p o r t a t i l e w c s d f g a h b o v m p o
m k o n j u b h y v g t c f r x a d w x f r q w a t i e a
a t t r e z z a t u r e i g i e n i c h e i p o u y f t r
z x e c v b n m a s d f g h q w e e r t y o u i z x e w t
q w n e r t y u i o p a s d f g s h j k l z x c v b r n m
p o d i u r w q a l k s j s c a t o l a d h f g m z i b y
z m a x n c b v l a p q o w i e r r u t y z q w e r t c p
p z o c s t i v a l i i v u b y o d q p w o b n v m c l z
```

ANSWERS

Word search	scatolette	capi di vestiario	sacco a pelo	
materasso pneumatico	thermos	cavatappi	pila tascabile	
coperta	utensili da cucina	albero	canoa	tenda
scatola	canestro	radio portatile	stivali	fiammiferi
	attrezzature igieniche	stufa	canna da pesca	pagaie	sole	secchio	ruscello

106

AL CAMPEGGIO
To the Campground

Now read the following two dialogues, which contain some useful words, expressions, and information on camping. Read them aloud, repeating each line several times, until you can pronounce them easily.

(Mark calls his friend Giovanni on the phone to ask for some camping information.)

GIOVANNI **Pronto. Chi parla?**

Hello. Who is it?

MARK **Ciao, Giovanni. Sono Mark. Mi**

Hi, Giovanni. It's Mark. Can you tell

sai dire se c'è un campeggio qui
(vee-CHEE-noh)
vicino?

me if there is a campground near

here?

GIOVANNI **Sì, volentieri. Prendi**
(ah-oo-toh-STRAH-duh) *(kee LOH-meh-tree)*
l'autostrada per venti chilometri, e
(CHEHR-kah) *(seh-NYAH-leh)* *(strah-DAH-leh)*
cerca un segnale stradale che
(EEN-dee-kah)
indica il campeggio.

Yes, gladly. Take the

highway for 20 kilometers,

and look for a road sign that indicates where the

campground is.

MARK **Lo conosci?**
(koh-NOH-shee)

Are you familiar with it?

GIOVANNI **Sì. Non ti preoccupare! È**
(preh-oh-kkoo-PAH-reh)
(FAH-chee-leh)
facile trovarlo. Tutti i campeggi
(pah-EH-zee)
italiani sono vicini a piccoli paesi.

Yes. Don't worry! It's easy to find. All Italian

campgrounds are near small towns.

MARK **Ci sono i bagni?**
(BAH-nyee)

Are there any bathrooms?

GIOVANNI **Penso di sì.**

I think so.

MARK **C'è acqua potabile?**
(poh-TAH-bee-leh)

Is there drinking water?

GIOVANNI **In Italia è preferibile bere**
(preh-feh-REE-bee-leh)
acqua imbottigliata o,
(eem-boh-ttee-LLYAH-tah)
naturalmente, vino!
(nah-toor-ahl-MEHN-teh) *(VEE-noh)*

In Italy it is preferable to drink

bottled water or, naturally, wine!

MARK **C'è l'elettricità?**
(eh-leh-ttree-chee-TAH)

Is there any electricity?

GIOVANNI **Non credo.**

I don't believe so.

MARK **Costa molto?**

Does it cost a lot?

GIOVANNI	**Costa molto poco.**	It costs very little.
	(fahn-TAHS-tee-koh)	
MARK	**Fantastico! Il campeggio italiano fa**	Fantastic! Italian camping is truly for me!
	(PROH-pree-oh)	
	proprio per me!	

AL NEGOZIO DI GENERI ALIMENTARI

(neh-GOH-tsee-oh)   *(JEH-neh-ree)*   *(ah-lee-mehn-TAH-ree)*

At the Grocery Store

(Mark Smith and his family enter a grocery store near the campground.)

	(deh-SEE-deh-rah)	
COMMESSA	**Buona sera. Desidera, signora?**	Good evening. Can I help you, madam?
	(PAH-kkoh)	
MARY	**Sì. Vorrei un pacco di spaghetti,**	Yes. I would like a package of spaghetti,
	(BOO-rroh) *(LEE-troh)*	
	cento grammi di burro, un litro di	100 grams (about ¼-pound) of butter, a liter
	(LAH-tteh) *(SAH-leh)* *(boh-TTEE-llyah)*	
	latte, un po' di sale, e una bottiglia	of milk, a bit of salt, and a bottle of wine.
	di vino.	
COMMESSA	**Trentamila lire.**	30,000 lira.
	(POH-lloh)	
MARK	**Vogliamo anche quel pollo e**	We also want that chicken and that box of
	quella scatola di fiammiferi, va bene?	matches, okay?

COMMESSA **Lei è un turista americano?**	Are you an American tourist?
MARK **Sì.**	Yes.
COMMESSA **Va bene.** *(She takes their money.)* **Dove va, al campeggio?**	Okay. Where are you going, to the campground?
MARK **Sì. Grazie e arrivederla.**	Yes. Thank you and good-bye.
COMMESSA **Arrivederla.**	Good-bye.

Now without looking back, match the following to form lines from the first dialogue.

Pronto. Chi . . .	italiani sono vicini a piccoli paesi.
Mi sai dire se . . .	acqua potabile?
Prendi . . .	preferibile bere acqua imbottigliata o, naturalmente, vino!
Non ti . . .	di sì.
Tutti i campeggi . . .	italiano fa proprio per me!
Ci sono . . .	preoccupare!
Penso . . .	parla?
C'è . . .	c'è un campeggio qui vicino?
In Italia è . . .	l'autostrada per venti chilometri.
Il campeggio . . .	i bagni?

Check your answers only after you have attempted to match up these items from memory. Now try to complete the missing parts from the second dialogue. Check your answers only after you have attempted to do this exercise from memory.

Buona s_____. D_____, signora?

Sì. Vorrei un p_____ di spaghetti, cento g_____

di b_____, un litro di l_____, un po' di s_____,

e una b_____ di v_____.

Trentamila l_____.

Vogliamo anche quel p_____ e quella s_____ di f_____,

va bene?

Lei è un t_____ a_____?

Sì.

Va bene. Dove va, al c_____?

Sì. Grazie e a_____.

Arrivederla.

In the first dialogue above you were introduced to the verb *bere*, "to drink." This is conjugated as follows.

BERE To Drink					
Io	*bevo*	il vino.	Noi	*beviamo*	il caffè. *(kah-FFEH)* coffee
Tu	*bevi*	il vino.	Voi	*bevete*	il caffè con latte.
Lei	*beve*	il latte.	Loro	*bevono* *(BEH-voh-noh)*	solo il vino.

Come si dice . . .?
How Do You Say . . .?

Here are some expressions that might come in handy on your camping excursion.

Ho bisogno di . . . *(bee-ZOH-nyoh)*	I need	**avere fame**	to be hungry
Lo so	I know it	**avere sonno**	to be sleepy
Non lo so	I do not know it	**avere sete**	to be thirsty
avere caldo	to be hot	**avere paura** *(pah-OO-rah)*	to be afraid
avere freddo	to be cold		

Now try to match each sentence with a picture.

1.

    a. Il ragazzo ha bisogno di pane.
       (PAH-neh)
       bread

       (DOH-nnah)
    b. La donna si vergogna.
       woman   is ashamed

2.

    c. La donna ha caldo.

    d. L'uomo ha sonno.

       (bahm-BEE-nee)
    e. I bambini hanno paura.
       children

3.

    f. L'uomo ha freddo.

4.

5.

6.

Camping is fun as long as the weather holds out. See how the Smith family fared on their trip. Test your readiness for camping by selecting the appropriate answers to the questions, based on the following passage.

La famiglia Smith è a un campeggio vicino a Roma.

(SPYAH-jjah)
Fa molto caldo e allora decidono di andare alla spiaggia.
                                                    beach

Ma l'acqua è fredda e allora solo Anne va nell'acqua.

(jeh-LAH-toh) (KAHM-pehr)
John prende un gelato dal camper, ma la madre non vuole.
ice cream   camper

(nahs-KOHN-deh)   (KAH-neh)
John nasconde il gelato e il cane lo mangia.
hides   dog   eats it

Dov'è il campeggio?
- ☐ È vicino a Roma.
- ☐ È vicino a Piazza San Marco.
- ☐ È vicino a Firenze.

Dove decidono di andare?
- ☐ A Roma.
- ☐ Nel camper.
- ☐ Alla spiaggia.

Com'è l'acqua?
- ☐ È calda.
- ☐ È fredda.
- ☐ È piena di vino.

Chi mangia il gelato?
- ☐ La madre.
- ☐ Il cane.
- ☐ John.

Che cosa prende, John?
- ☐ Prende una bottiglia di vino.
- ☐ Prende un gelato.
- ☐ Prende una scatola di fiammiferi.

Now have fun with the following crossword puzzle.

Across
3. Vorrei cento grammi di . . .
4. Loro . . . solo il vino.
5. Il sacco a . . .
6. Vorrei un litro di . . .

Down
1. L'uomo non ha caldo, ha . . .
2. L'uomo va a dormire perché ha . . .
3. Vorrei una . . . di vino.
5. La canna da . . .

10 | Il tempo / Le stagioni / *(stah-JOH-nee)*
I giorni della settimana / I mesi *(MEH-zee)*
Weather / Seasons / Days of the Week / Months

Italian months are very similar to English. Say them aloud a few times, until you are familiar with the Italian pronunciation.

(jeh-NNAH-yoh)	*(MAH-jjoh)*	*(seh-TTEHM-breh)*
gennaio	**maggio**	**settembre**
January	May	September
(feh-BBRAH-yoh)	*(JOO-nyoh)*	*(oh-TTOH-breh)*
febbraio	**giugno**	**ottobre**
February	June	October
(MAHR-tsoh)	*(LOO-llyoh)*	*(noh-VEHM-breh)*
marzo	**luglio**	**novembre**
March	July	November
(ah-PREE-leh)	*(ah-GOHS-toh)*	*(dee-CHEHM-breh)*
aprile	**agosto**	**dicembre**
April	August	December

113

Now do the same with these expressions relating to the seasons.

(een-VEHR-noh)
—È inverno
Winter

Fa molto freddo.
It's very cold.

(NEH-vee-kah)
Nevica.
It's snowing.

(JEH-lee-doh)
Fa un freddo gelido.
It's freezing.

(pree-mah-VEH-rah)
—È primavera
Spring

Fa fresco.
It is cool.

C'è il sole.
It is sunny.

(ehs-TAH-teh)
—È estate
Summer

Fa caldo.
It is hot.

(OO-mee-doh)
È umido.
It is humid.

(ah-FOH-zoh)
È afoso.
It is muggy.

(boo-rahs-KOH-soh)
Il tempo è burrascoso.
It's stormy.

(PYOH-veh)
Piove.
It's raining.

(TWOH-nah)
Tuona.
It's thundering.

(ah-oo-TOO-nnoh)
—È autunno
Fall

Fa fresco.
It's chilly.

(dee-ROH-ttoh)
Piove a dirotto.
It's raining cats and dogs.

(NEH-bbyah)
C'è la nebbia.
It's foggy.

CHE TEMPO FA?
How Is the Weather?

If you look carefully you will see that many expressions connected with the weather use the verb form *fa* . . .

Che tempo fa?	How is the weather?	**Fa caldo.**	It is hot.
Fa fresco.	It is cool/chilly.	**Fa molto freddo.**	It is very cold.
Fa freddo.	It is cold.	**Fa un freddo gelido.**	It is freezing.

Here are some other useful weather expressions.

C'è il sole.	It is sunny.	**Tuona.**	It is thundering.
È umido.	It is humid.	**Piove a dirotto.**	It is raining cats and dogs.
È afoso.	It is muggy.	**Nevica.**	It is snowing.
È burrascoso.	It is stormy.	**C'è la nebbia.**	It is foggy.
Piove.	It is raining.		

In general, if you want to say the weather is beautiful or bad, use the following expressions.

Fa bel tempo.	The weather is beautiful.	**Fa brutto tempo.**	The weather is bad/awful.

If you have learned the weather phrases well, you should be able to give the appropriate expression to describe each picture.

1. _____

2. _____

3. _____

4. _____

5. _____

6. _____

7. _____

8. _____

Look back at the calendar and read the months of the year out loud, again, and review the ordinal numbers in chapter 5. Then try the following. Be careful not to capitalize the months.

Il terzo mese _____

Il quinto mese _____

Il primo mese _____

Il quarto mese _____

Il secondo mese _____

Il sesto mese _____

Il decimo mese _____

Il settimo mese _____

Il nono mese _____

l'ottavo mese _____

Il mese dopo ottobre _____
after
(OOL-tee-moh)

l'ultimo mese _____
last

To say a date in Italian, just use the cardinal numbers in the following formula.

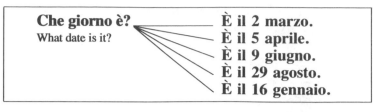

Che giorno è?
What date is it?
È il 2 marzo.
È il 5 aprile.
È il 9 giugno.
È il 29 agosto.
È il 16 gennaio.

The only exception is for the first day of each month, for which you use the ordinal number.

Che giorno è?
È il primo ottobre.
È il primo luglio.

Now you should be able to write out the following dates in Italian.

Che giorno è?

January 4	July 30
February 7	August 24
March 11	September 8
April 19	October 15
May 28	November 20
June 1 (Be careful!)	December 10

Here are the days of the week in Italian. Read them out loud several times; then see if you can figure out each of the logic puzzles that follow. Once again, notice that you do not capitalize the days of the week.

(loo-neh-DEE)
lunedì _____ Monday

(mahr-teh-DEE)
martedì _____ Tuesday

(mehr-koh-leh-DEE)
mercoledì _____ Wednesday

(joh-veh-DEE)
giovedì _____ Thursday

(veh-nehr-DEE)
venerdì _____ Friday

(SAH-bah-toh)
sabato _____ Saturday

(doh-MEH-nee-kah)
domenica _____ Sunday

116

1. il giorno **dopo** lunedì: _____
   after

2. il giorno dopo domenica: _____

3. il giorno **prima** di domenica: _____
   before

4. il giorno prima di venerdì: _____

5. il giorno dopo martedì: _____

6. il giorno dopo sabato: _____

7. il giorno prima di sabato: _____

(ah-jjeh-TTEE-vee)

Aggettivi
Adjectives

There are two main kinds of adjectives in Italian: one that ends in $\boxed{\text{-o}}$ and another that ends in $\boxed{\text{-e}}$. Adjectives usually follow the noun they modify and agree with its gender (masculine or feminine) and its number (singular or plural). Confused? Don't worry! Just look at the following examples and then try your hand at the activities that follow.

ADJECTIVES IN $\boxed{\text{-o}}$: ITALIANO

WITH MASCULINE NOUNS

Singular
il ragazzo italian $\boxed{\text{o}}$
the Italian boy

il padre italian $\boxed{\text{o}}$
the Italian father

Plural
i ragazzi italian $\boxed{\text{i}}$
the Italian boys

i padri italian $\boxed{\text{i}}$
the Italian fathers

WITH FEMININE NOUNS

la ragazza italian $\boxed{\text{a}}$
the Italian girl

la madre italian $\boxed{\text{a}}$
the Italian mother

le ragazze italian $\boxed{\text{e}}$
the Italian girls

le madri italian $\boxed{\text{e}}$
the Italian mothers

117

Get it? Adjectives that end in -e are even simpler. Simply use -e with any singular noun (masculine or feminine) and -i with any plural noun (masculine or feminine).

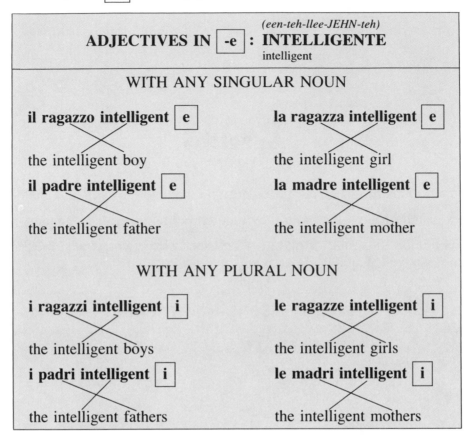

(een-teh-llee-JEHN-teh)
ADJECTIVES IN -e : INTELLIGENTE
intelligent

WITH ANY SINGULAR NOUN

il ragazzo intelligent e
the intelligent boy

la ragazza intelligent e
the intelligent girl

il padre intelligent e
the intelligent father

la madre intelligent e
the intelligent mother

WITH ANY PLURAL NOUN

i ragazzi intelligent i
the intelligent boys

le ragazze intelligent i
the intelligent girls

i padri intelligent i
the intelligent fathers

le madri intelligent i
the intelligent mothers

You can always refer to this chart if you forget later on.

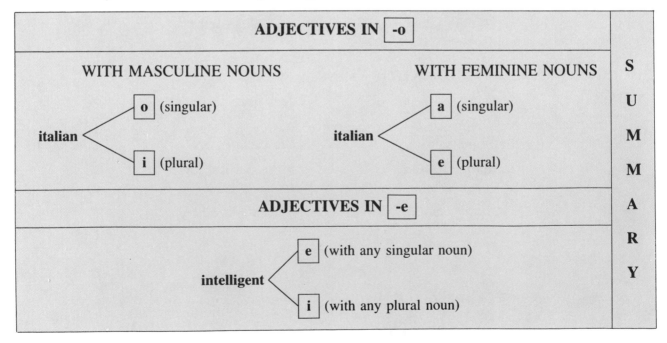

ADJECTIVES IN -o

WITH MASCULINE NOUNS

italian < **o** (singular) / **i** (plural)

WITH FEMININE NOUNS

italian < **a** (singular) / **e** (plural)

ADJECTIVES IN -e

intelligent < **e** (with any singular noun) / **i** (with any plural noun)

S U M M A R Y

118

Adjectives normally follow the noun in Italian. Some are also used in front of the noun.

il ragazzo simpatico   *or*   **il simpatico ragazzo**

the nice boy   the nice boy

A few adjectives, like the ordinal numbers you learned in chapter 5, are used only in front of the noun.

il primo ragazzo

the first boy

As in English, an adjective can be separated from the noun by certain verbs like "to be." However, the agreement patterns in the charts still apply, as you can see in these examples.

Il ragazzo è simpatico.
The boy is nice.

La ragazza è bella.
The girl is beautiful.

I ragazzi sono simpatici.
The boys are nice.

Le ragazze sono simpatiche.
The girls are nice.

Io sono alta e tu sei bassa.
I am tall and you are short.

(joh-VAH-neh)
Io sono giovane e
I am young and
(VEH-kkyoh)
tu sei vecchio.
you are old.

(CHEH-nah) *(BWOH-nah)*
La cena è buona.
The dinner is good.

La cena è pronta.
The dinner is ready.

La mia stanza è grande.
My room is big.

La mia stanza è piccola.
My room is small.

(KOH-moh-dah)
La mia stanza è comoda.
My room is comfortable.

La mia stanza
My room
(roo-moh-ROH-zah)
è rumorosa.
is noisy.

Here is a list of the adjectives just used. Match them to their English equivalents.

1. intelligente		a. short	
2. italiano		b. tall	
3. simpatico		c. beautiful	
4. bello		d. Italian	
5. alto		e. intelligent	
6. basso		f. nice	
7. giovane		g. comfortable	
8. vecchio		h. noisy	
9. buono		i. big	
10. pronto		j. small	
11. grande		k. good	
12. piccolo		l. ready	
13. comodo		m. young	
14. rumoroso		n. old	

It should be easy for you to put the correct ending on each of these adjectives.

Quelle ragazze sono intelligent_____ .   Questa pizza non è buon_____ .

Il passeggero italian_____ è simpatic_____ .   La cena è pront_____ .

Quella ragazza è bell_____ , alt_____   La mia stanza è piccol_____
  e giovan_____ .   ma comod_____ .

I miei due zii sono bass_____ e vecch_____ .

The following dialogue contains various words and expressions connected with the weather. Read it aloud several times and role-play each part.

(Anne has made an Italian friend, Gina. Anne has spent the night at Gina's house. It is now the morning after.)

ANNE   **Buon giorno, Gina. Sono le otto.**   Good morning, Gina. It's eight o'clock. It's

C'è un bel sole e fa bel tempo.   sunny and the weather is beautiful.

GINA *(ahn-KOH-rah)*
Ho ancora sonno.

(VOH-llyoh) *(ahn-KOH-rah)*
Voglio dormire ancora
un'altra ora.

I'm still sleepy.

I want to sleep another hour.

ANNE *(eem-poh-SEE-bee-leh) (preh-vee-ZYOH-nee)*
Impossibile! Le previsioni
(meh-teh-oh-roh-LOH-jee-keh)(EEN-dee-kah noh)
meteorologiche indicano che
(stah SEH-rah)
forse piove stasera. I due ragazzi con
(KOO-ee)
cui abbiamo un appuntamento ci
(ahs-PEH-ttah-noh) (doh-BBYAH-moh)(oo-SHEE-reh)
aspettano. Dobbiamo uscire
(mah-TTEE-nah)
questa mattina!

No way! (*literally,* Impossible!) The weather

forecast indicates that it may rain tonight. The

two boys with whom we have a date are waiting

for us. We have to go out this morning!

GINA **Solo un'altra mezz'ora?**

Only another half-hour?

ANNE **No. Adesso!**

No. Now!

(She starts exercising and making noise so that Gina is forced to get up from bed.)

ANNE **Finalmente! Com'è il mio ragazzo?**

Finally! How is my date?

GINA **È molto simpatico.**

He is very nice.

ANNE **Bene!**

Good!

GINA *(REE-kkoh)*
È anche molto ricco.

He is also very rich.

ANNE *(eem-POHR-tah)*
Non importa!

It doesn't matter!

GINA **Su! Andiamo!** *(to herself)*
Ma ho *ancora* sonno.

Come on! Let's go!
But I'm *still* sleepy.

121

Now try to complete the missing dialogue parts from memory. Check your answers after you have finished.

Buon giorno, Gina. S_____ le otto. C'è un bel s_____ e fa

b_____ t_____.

Ho ancora s_____. Voglio dormire ancora un'altra o_____.

Impossibile! Le p_____ m_____ indicano che forse

p_____ stasera. I due ragazzi con cui abbiamo un a_____ ci

aspettano. Dobbiamo uscire questa m_____!

Solo un'altra mezz'ora?

No. A_____! Finalmente. Com'è il mio ragazzo?

È molto s_____.

Bene!

È anche molto r_____.

Non i_____.

Here are words describing the various times of the day:

(mah-TTEE-nah)	(poh-meh-REE-jjoh)	(SEH-rah)	(NOH-tteh)
la mattina	**il pomeriggio**	**la sera**	**la notte**
morning	afternoon	evening	night

And here are two expressions using these words:

Buona sera.	Good evening./Good afternoon.
Buona notte. (can be used only when departing, not arriving)	Good night.

Now match these words with the pictures and write them in the blanks.

night

evening

afternoon

morning

IL LUNEDÌ
On Mondays

Il lunedì vado sempre a scuola. (On Mondays I always go to school.)

Il martedì mangio sempre la pizza.

Il mercoledì vado sempre al cinema.

Notice that to say "on Mondays, on Tuesdays, . . ." all you have to do
is use the masculine article **il**.
The only time you use the **la** form is for Sunday.

La domenica dormo tanto. (On Sundays I sleep a lot.)

123

See if you can read the following brief passage and then select the appropriate answer to each question.

Oggi è il quattro novembre.
today

(SOH-lee-toh)
Di solito il sabato faccio delle spese.
usually   I do my shopping.

Sono nato il quattordici febbraio   **e ho trentadue anni.**
I was born   I am thirty-two years old

(kah-lehn-DAH-ree-oh)   *(seh-nyeh-ROH)*
Oggi voglio comprare un calendario per il nuovo anno. Su questo calendario segnerò
                    calendar   I will mark down

(eem-pohr-TAHN-tee)   *(nah-TAH-leh)*   *(PAHS-kwah)*
tre date importanti: **Natale,**   **Pasqua,**
        important   Christmas   Easter

(kohm-pleh-AH-nnoh)
e il mio compleanno.
birthday

Che giorno è oggi?	☐ È il nove ottobre. ☐ È il quattro novembre. ☐ È il quindici febbraio.	Che cosa fai di solito il sabato?	☐ Non faccio niente. ☐ Faccio il pieno. ☐ Faccio delle spese.

Quando sei nato?   ☐ Sono nato il quattordici febbraio.
                          ☐ Sono nato a Natale.
                          ☐ Sono nato a Pasqua.

Quanti anni hai?	☐ Ho venti anni. ☐ Ho quarantadue anni. ☐ Ho trentadue anni.	Che cosa vuoi comprare oggi?	☐ Una macchina. ☐ Un calendario. ☐ Un libro.

Can you find these items in the picture? Say each one aloud as you locate it.

(pee-LOH-tah)
il comandante / il pilota
captain   pilot

(oh-roh-LOH-joh)
l'orologio
clock

(LEE-neh-ah)(ah-EH-re-ah)
la linea   aerea
airline company

(kohn-TROH-lloh)
la torre di controllo
control tower

(koh-pee-LOH-tah)
il co-pilota
copilot

(MOH-bee-leh)
la scala mobile
escalator

(bee-llyeh-tteh-REE-ah)
la biglietteria
ticket counter

(KAH-myohn)
il camion
truck

(ah-ssees-TEHN-teh)
l'assistente di volo
flight attendant

(trahs-pohr-tah-TOH-reh)
il nastro trasportatore
conveyor/moving belt

(doh-GAH-nah)
la dogana
customs/passport control

(doh-gah-NYEH-reh)
il doganiere
customs officer

(ah-EH-reh-oh)
L'AEREO
The Plane

When you reach Italy you will probably land at either the Rome or Milan airport. Domestic flights are available to major cities within Italy.

Read the following words and expression out loud several times. They might come in handy on an Italian airplane.

(eh-kwee-PAH-jjoh)
l'equipaggio
crew

(oo-SHEE-tah) (see-koo-REH-tsah)
l'uscita di sicurezza
emergency exit

| *(kah-BEE-nah)* | *(seh-DEE-leh)* | *(cheen-TOO-rah)* | *(see-koo-REH-tsah)* |

la pista   **la cabina**   **il sedile**   **la cintura di**   **sicurezza**
runway   cabin   seat   seat belt

(vah-SSOH-yoh)

il passeggero   **il vassoio**
passenger   tray

There are certain words and expressions in this dialogue that you might hear or need on a plane. Read each line out loud several times and act out each part.

(eem-BAHR-koh)

ASSISTENTE   **La carta d'imbarco, per**   Boarding pass, please.

           favore.

(EH-kkoh-lah)

MARK   **Eccola.**   Here it is.

(The Smiths take their seats on the plane.)

(deh-KOH-lloh)   *(KWAHL-kelt)*

PILOTA   **Il decollo é previsto tra qualche**   The takeoff is expected in a few minutes. All

(mee-NOO-toh)   *(preh-GAH-tee)*

           minato. I passeggeri sono pregati di   passengers are requested to fasten their

(ah-lah-CHAH-reh)
allacciare le cinture di sicurezza e di

non fumare.

(pehr-FEH-ttoh)
MARY   **Ah, che decollo perfetto! I piloti**

   italiani sono proprio bravi.

MARK *(to the attendant)* **Signorina,**

   quando si mangia?

ASSISTENTE **Tra qualche minuto, signore.**

MARK **Vorrei un cocktail, per favore.**
(SOO-bee-toh)
ASSISTENTE **Sì, subito.**

(An hour later the plane is about to land.)

(ah-tteh-RRAH-jjoh)
PILOTA **Signore e signori, l'atterraggio**
(preh-VEES-toh)
   è previsto tra qualche minuto.

MARK **Meno male! Mi fa male lo**
(STOH-mah-koh)
   stomaco.

(SOH-lee-toh) *(mahn-JAH-toh)*
MARY **Come al solito, hai mangiato**

   troppo!

seat belts and to refrain from smoking.

Ah, what a perfect takeoff! Italian pilots are

really great.

Miss, when do we eat?

In a few minutes, sir.

I would like a cocktail, please.

Yes, right away.

Ladies and gentlemen, we will

be landing in a few minutes.

Thank goodness! My stomach hurts.

As usual, you ate too much!

By matching the items in the left column to those in the right column, you will get dialogue lines.
Check your answers only after you have attempted to do this exercise from memory.

La carta . . .	è previsto tra qualche minuto.
Il decollo . . .	sono proprio bravi.
I passeggeri . . .	si mangia?
I piloti italiani . . .	hai mangiato troppo!
Signorina, quando . . .	l'atterraggio è previsto tra qualche minuto.
Signore e signori . . .	male lo stomaco.
Mi fa . . .	d'imbarco, per favore.
Come al solito . . .	sono pregati di allacciare le cinture di sicurezza e di non fumare.

This word-search puzzle may be a bit tough! However, all of the words except one are part of the vocabulary you just learned.

customs _____   customs officer _____

truck _____   clock _____

seat _____   cabin _____

crew _____   runway _____

tray _____   window _____

q	a	z	w	s	x	e	d	c	r	f	v	t	s	g	b	p	l	m	o	k	n	i
y	h	n	u	j	m	i	d	o	g	a	n	i	e	r	e	q	a	z	w	s	x	e
k	o	l	p	q	a	z	o	w	s	x	e	d	d	c	r	d	c	r	f	v	t	g
g	f	o	r	o	l	o	g	i	o	v	t	g	i	b	y	b	y	h	n	i	k	o
y	h	n	u	j	m	i	a	k	l	p	o	q	l	a	f	q	a	z	w	s	x	e
d	c	a	m	i	o	n	n	r	f	v	r	t	e	q	u	i	p	a	g	g	i	o
g	a	b	y	h	n	u	a	j	m	c	k	o	p	l	s	q	a	z	w	s	x	e
q	b	a	z	w	s	x	e	d	c	r	f	v	y	h	o	n	u	j	m	k	l	o
p	i	s	t	a	q	a	z	w	x	s	e	d	i	l	e	f	v	t	g	b	y	a
h	n	n	u	j	m	i	k	l	v	a	s	s	o	i	o	p	o	q	a	z	w	r
s	a	x	e	d	c	r	f	v	t	g	b	y	h	r	n	i	k	m	l	o	p	l
q	a	z	w	s	x	e	d	f	i	n	e	s	t	r	i	n	o	c	r	f	v	q
t	g	b	y	h	n	u	j	m	q	a	z	w	s	a	x	e	d	r	t	g	b	v

ANSWERS

Word search
dogana dogàniere camion orologio sedile cabina equipaggio pista vassoio finestrino

128

Un po' di grammatica

(grah-MMAH-tee-kah)

Some Grammar

As with English, knowing how to say "me, him, her," and so on, is essential in Italian. These words are called direct object pronouns. Study the following examples.

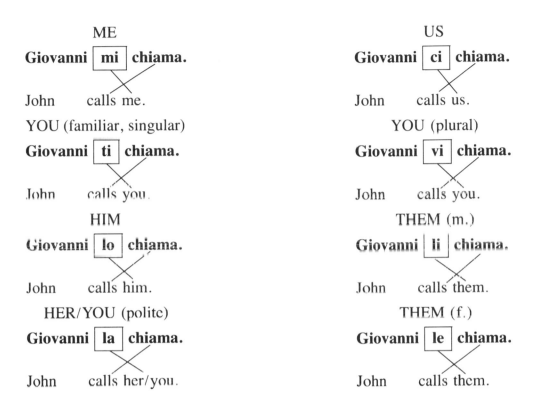

ME

Giovanni **mi** **chiama.**

John   calls me.

YOU (familiar, singular)

Giovanni **ti** **chiama.**

John   calls you.

HIM

Giovanni **lo** **chiama.**

John   calls him.

HER/YOU (polite)

Giovanni **la** **chiama.**

John   calls her/you.

US

Giovanni **ci** **chiama.**

John   calls us.

YOU (plural)

Giovanni **vi** **chiama.**

John   calls you.

THEM (m.)

Giovanni **li** **chiama.**

John   calls them.

THEM (f.)

Giovanni **le** **chiama.**

John   calls them.

Notice that these pronouns are put right before the verb, even in the negative:

Giovanni *non mi* chiama.

The forms **lo, la, li, le** also mean "it" and "them" according to gender.

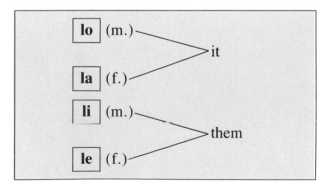

lo (m.)
la (f.)   it

li (m.)
le (f.)   them

129

Here are some examples.

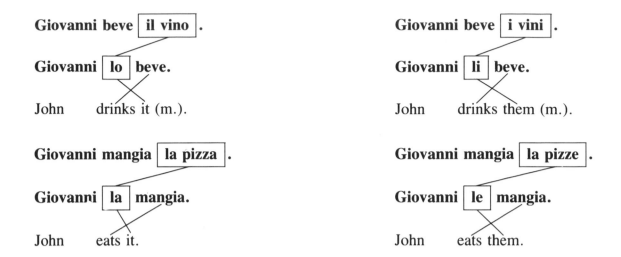

Giovanni beve	il vino	.		**Giovanni beve**	i vini	.
Giovanni	lo	**beve.**		**Giovanni**	li	**beve.**
John	drinks it (m.).			John	drinks them (m.).	

Giovanni mangia	la pizza	.		**Giovanni mangia**	la pizze	.
Giovanni	la	**mangia.**		**Giovanni**	le	**mangia.**
John	eats it.			John	eats them.	

Perhaps a chart will be useful to you if you forget later on.

DIRECT OBJECT PRONOUNS		S
mi _____ me		U
ti _____ you (familiar)		M
lo _____ him, it (m.)		M
la _____ her, you (polite), it (f.)		A
ci _____ us		R
vi _____ you (plural)		
li _____ them (m.)		Y
le _____ them (f.)		

See if you can select the right pronoun for each blank. **lo, la, li, le ??**

Il signor Smith chiama *la signorina*.   Il signor Smith _____ chiama.

Maria prende *il vino rosso*.   Maria _____ prende.

La ragazza compra *la penna*.   La ragazza _____ compra.

La ragazza compra *le penne*.   La ragazza _____ compra.

Giovanni chiama *la sua amica*.   Giovanni _____ chiama.

ANSWERS

Pronouns la (chiama.) lo (prende.) la (compra.) le (compra.) la (chiama.)

The answers to the following questions are scrambled. Try to rearrange the words so they make sense. If you have forgotten the meaning of some of the words, look for them in the glossary.

Chiede il passaporto, il doganiere? _____

passaporto / il / doganiere / il / chiede / Sì

Porta la carta d'imbarco, l'assistente di volo? _____

la / Sì / l'assistente / porta

Compra gli stivali, il ragazzo? _____

No / non / ragazzo / il / compra / li

Chi ha la carta d'imbarco? _____

signor / Smith / Il / ha / la

Chi ci chiama? _____

vi / chiama / Giovanni

IN CITTÀ
(chee-TTAH)

On the Town

Of course, you will want to do some sightseeing on your trip, and the following passage contains some useful information. Read it carefully and then select the appropriate answers to the questions.

La famiglia Smith è a Firenze. Prima vanno a vedere la Piazza del Duomo. Hanno una
(PREE-mah)
First

macchina fotografica e fanno molte fotografie. Poi vanno a vedere il Palazzo   Vecchio.
(foh-toh-GRAH-fee-kah)   (foh-toh-grah-FEE-eh)   (pah-LAH-tsoh)(VEH-kkyoh)
camera   photos

Comprano molte cartoline   e   ricordi. Vanno a vedere tanti monumenti e
(kahr-toh-LEE-neh)(ree-KOHR-dee)   (moh-noo-MEHN-tee)
postcards   souvenirs   monuments

edifici   famosi. Per andare in giro è necessario camminare molto.
(eh-dee-FEE-chee)(fah-MOH-see)   (neh-cheh-SSAH-ree-oh)
buildings   famous   around   necessary

Dov'è la famiglia Smith?
☐ È a Roma.
☐ È a Venezia.
☐ È a Firenze.

Dove vanno prima?
☐ Vanno a vedere la Piazza del Duomo.
☐ Vanno a vedere il Vaticano.
☐ Vanno a vedere un edificio famoso.

131

Con che fanno molte fotografie?

- [ ] Con un'aereo.
- [ ] Con un vassoio.
- [ ] Con una macchina fotografica.

Che cosa comprano?

- [ ] Comprano molti edifici.
- [ ] Comprano molte cartoline e ricordi.
- [ ] Comprano molti monumenti.

Che cosa vanno a vedere?

- [ ] Tanti monumenti e edifici famosi.
- [ ] La pista dell'aeroporto.
- [ ] La città di Firenze.

Per andare in giro, che cosa
è necessario fare?

- [ ] È necessario bere tanto vino.
- [ ] È necessario mangiare la pizza.
- [ ] È necessario camminare.

Firenze
Points of Interest

Florence

(courtesy of Pictograph)

ENTERTAINMENT
(dee-vehr-tee-MEHN-tee)
I Divertimenti

12	*(teh-AH-troh)* **Il teatro** / *(CHEE-nee-mah)* **Il cinema** / *(FEH-steh)* **Le feste**
	Theater / Movies / Holidays

AL TEATRO
At the Theater

Surely you will want to attend the opera during your stay in Italy. Read the Smith's dialogue aloud several times, until you can reconstruct it without looking back.

MARK **Dove andiamo stasera?**

Where are we going tonight?

MARY *(see-KOO-rah)* *(DRAH-mmah)* **Non sono sicura. C'è un dramma** *(een-teh-reh-SSAHN-teh)* **molto interessante di Pirandello al teatro.**

I'm not sure. There is a very interesting drama/play by Pirandello at the theater.

MARK *(PYAH-cheh)* **Il teatro non mi piace.**

I don't like the theater.

MARY *(OH-peh-rah)* **Allora andiamo all'opera. Stasera c'è *La Traviata* di Verdi. Che** *(MOO-zee-kah)* *(meh-loh-DEE-eh)* **musica! Che melodie!**

Then let's go to the opera. Tonight there's *La Traviata* by Verdi. What music! What melodies!

MARK   *(NOH-yah)*
Che noia!   What a bore!

MARY   **Mark, se non mi porti all'opera,**   Mark, if you do not take me to the opera, I won't

domani non vengo con te al cinema,   come with you tomorrow to the movies, so you

così non puoi vedere la tua   can't see your favorite actress, Sophia Loren.
(ah-TTREE-cheh)   *(preh-feh-REE-tah)*
attrice   **preferita, Sofia Loren.**
         (teh-SOH-roh)   *(koh-MEEN-choh)*
MARK   **Va bene, tesoro! Ma se comincio**   Okay dear! But if I start to snore don't get angry.
    (roo-SSAH-reh)   *(ah-rrah-BBYAH-reh)*
a russare non ti arrabbiare.
          (zbree-GYAH-moh-chee)
MARY   **Va bene. Sbrighiamoci! Sono già**   Okay. Let's hurry up! It's already 7:30 and the
                 (speh-TTAH-koh-loh)
le sette e mezzo e lo spettacolo comincia   show begins at 8:00.

alle otto.

MARK   **Sofia, mia bella Sofia, a domani!**   Sophia, my beautiful Sophia, see you tomorrow!

See how similar to English these words are.

il dramma
drama

la melodia
melody

il teatro
theater

Now try to complete Mary's part of the dialogue.

MARK   **Dove andiamo stasera?**

MARY   **Non** _____ . **C'è** _____

_____ .

MARK   **Il teatro non mi piace.**

MARY   **Allora** _____ .

134

Stasera _____. Che _____!

Che _____!

MARK **Che noia!**

MARY **Mark, se non mi** _____, **domani non** _____

_____, **così non puoi vedere** _____.

MARK **Va bene, tesoro! Ma se comincio a russare non ti arrabbiare.**

MARY **Va** _____. **Sbrighiamoci! Sono** _____.

e lo _____.

MARK **Sofia, mia bella Sofia, a domani!**

(ree-KOHR-dee)
Ti ricordi?
Do you remember?

Do you recall how to say "I would like"? This is a very useful expression that you will use frequently.

(johr-NAH-leh)
Vorrei un giornale.
newspaper

You continue.

_____
(MEH-tsoh)
essere nel mezzo.
in the middle

_____
il formaggio.

_____
(pah-rroo-KKYEH-reh)
andare dal parrucchiere.
to the hairdresser's

Mi dai i soldi?
Will You Give the Money to Me?

In the previous unit you learned about direct object pronouns. You will also need to know how to translate "to me, to him, to her," and the like. These are called indirect object pronouns. The following four are exactly the same as the direct object pronouns.

ME

Giovanni | **mi** | **chiama.**

John   calls me.

YOU (familiar, singular)

Giovanni | **ti** | **chiama.**

John   calls you.

US

Giovanni | **ci** | **chiama.**

John   calls us.

YOU (plural)

Giovanni | **vi** | **chiama.**

John   calls you.

TO ME

(ah-SSEH-nyoh)

Giovanni | **mi** | **dà l'assegno.**

John   gives the check to me.

TO YOU (familiar, singular)

Giovanni | **ti** | **dà l'assegno.**

John   gives the check to you.

TO US

Giovanni | **ci** | **dà l'assegno.**

John gives the check to us.

TO YOU (plural)

Giovanni | **vi** | **dà l'assegno.**

John gives the check to you.

This can be summarized in chart form.

			S
mi	——————	me, to me	U
ti	——————	you, to you (familiar, singular)	M M
ci	——————	us, to us	A
vi	——————	you, to you (plural)	R Y

Don't forget to keep these pronouns right before the verb, even in the negative.

Giovanni *non mi* chiama.
Giovanni *non mi* dà la penna.

The next examples show how to say "to him, to her, to you (polite, singular), to them."

HIM	TO HIM
Giovanni	**lo**	**chiama.**	**Giovanni**	**gli**	**dà l'assegno.**
John calls him.	John gives the check ⌐to him.⌐

HER/YOU (polite)	TO HER/TO YOU (polite)
Giovanni	**la**	**chiama.**	**Giovanni**	**le**	**dà l'assegno.**
John calls her/you.	John gives the check ⌐to her/you.⌐

THEM	TO THEM
Giovanni	**li**	**chiama.**	**Giovanni**	**gli**	**dà l'assegno.**
John calls them (m.).	John gives the check ⌐to them⌐ (m. and f.).

Giovanni | **le** | **chiama.**
John   calls them (f.).

Notice that there is only one form for "to them," although there is a more formal pronoun for "to them" that does not concern us here. *Gli* is the most commonly used one in spoken Italian. A summary of these pronouns might be helpful.

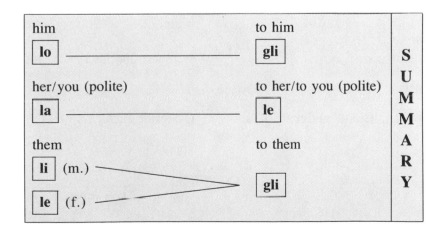

him	to him	S
lo ———————————	**gli**	U
her/you (polite)	to her/to you (polite)	M
la ———————————	**le**	M
them	to them	A
li (m.)		R
le (f.)	**gli**	Y

137

If you have studied these pronouns well, you should have no trouble inserting the proper one in each of the following blanks.

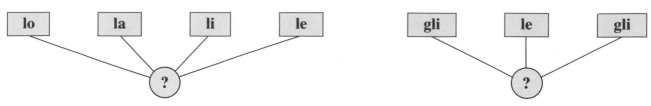

Il turista compra *l'orologio*. Il turista _____ compra.

Il turista compra *gli orologi*. Il turista _____ compra.

Il turista dà l'orologio *a suo figlio*. Il turista _____ dà l'orologio.

Il turista dà l'orologio *a sua figlia*. Il turista _____ dà l'orologio.

Il turista compra *la cartolina*. Il turista _____ compra.

Il turista compra *le cartoline*. Il turista _____ compra.

Il turista dà la cartolina *ai suoi amici*. Il turista _____ dà la cartolina.

Il turista dà la cartolina *alle sue amiche*. Il turista _____ dà la cartolina.

AL CINEMA
At the Movies

(Mark and Mary are at the movies the day after having gone to the opera. They are watching a rerun of the classic Ieri, oggi e domani.*)*

MARK *(feelm)*
Che bel film! E come è bella Sofia Loren!

What a beautiful film! And is Sophia Loren ever beautiful!

MARY *(SEHN-tsah)(soh-ttoh-TEE-toh-lee)*
Senza i sottotitoli non capisco niente.

Without subtitles I can't understand anything.

MARK **Non importa. Basta vedere Sofia.**

It doesn't matter. All that's important is to see Sophia.

MARY	*(VEE-ah)* **Andiamo via. Non mi piace sedermi** *(FEE-lah)* **nella prima fila.**		Let's go. I don't like to sit in the first row.
MARK	*(PYEH-noh)* **Ma il cinema è pieno di gente.**		But the movie theater is full of people.
MARY	*(EHS-koh)* **Io esco!**		I'm leaving (I'm going out)!
MARK	*(SEH-gweh)* **Va bene. Tuo marito ti segue.**		Okay. Your husband will follow (*literally:* is following you).

Read the dialogue several times and then try to complete the missing parts. Check your answers after you have attempted to do so from memory.

Che bel f_____! E come è b_____ Sofia Loren!

S_____ i s_____ non capisco niente.

Non i___ _____. B__ _____ vedere Sofia.

Andiamo via. Non mi p_____ sedermi nella prima f___ _____.

Ma il cinema è p_____ di gente. Io e_____!

Va bene. Tuo m_____ ti segue.

Here are two more verbs that you will use often.

(oo-SHEE-reh) **USCIRE** to go out			
io	*(EHS-koh)* _____ **esco**	noi	*(oo-SHAH-moh)* _____ **usciamo**
tu	*(EH-shee)* _____ **esci**	voi	*(oo-SHEE-teh)* _____ **uscite**
lui } lei }	*(EH-sheh)* _____ **esce**	loro	*(EHS-koh-noh)* _____ **escono**

Now fill in each blank with the correct form of *uscire*.

La signora Smith _____ alle sei.

Io non _____ mai.

Noi ___ _____ *(een-SYEH-meh)* **insieme** per andare
together
al cinema.

La moglie e il marito _____ insieme.

Tu _____ con Maria.

Voi non _____ mai insieme.

uscite (mai insieme.)

Verbs (to go out) esce (alle sei.) escono (insieme.) esco (mai.) esci (con Maria.) usciamo (insieme)

139

PIACERE			
to like			
io	*(PYAH-choh)* **piaccio**	noi	*(pyah-CHAH-moh)* **piacciamo**
tu	*(PYAH-chee)* **piaci**	voi	*(pyah-CHEH-teh)* **piacete**
lui lei	*(PYAH-cheh)* **piace**	loro	*(PYAH-choh-noh)* **piacciono**

This is a troublesome verb. In order to say "I like, you like," and so on, you must say "to be pleasing to."

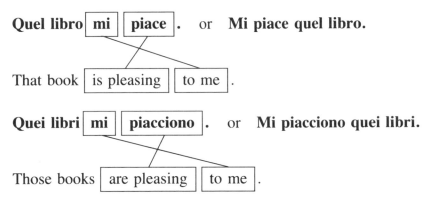

Quel libro | **mi** | **piace** . or **Mi piace quel libro.**

That book | is pleasing | to me .

Quei libri | **mi** | **piacciono** . or **Mi piacciono quei libri.**

Those books | are pleasing | to me .

Using the chart and the examples above, try to complete these sentences.

I like Mary. Mary is pleasing to me. **Mi _____ Maria.**

Mary likes me. I am pleasing to Mary. **Io _____ a Maria.**

We like the film. The film is pleasing to us. **Ci _____ il film.**

They like the films. The films are pleasing to them. **Gli _____ i film.**

I like the film. The film is pleasing to me. **Mi _____ il film.**

I don't like the films. The films are not pleasing to me. **Non mi _____ i film.**

LE FESTE
Holidays

Of course, you will want to join in the festivities, if you are in Italy during a holiday. Read this passage, and then answer the questions that follow.

La prima festa dell'anno è il capodanno.
(kah-poh-DAH-nnoh)
New Year's

il sei gennaio. Poi a primavera c'è la Pasqua.
(PAHS-kwah)
Easter

Poi c'è l'Epifania
(eh-pee-fah-NEE-ah)
Epiphany

Il quindici agosto c'è il Ferragosto. È una festa particolare in Italia.
(fehr-ah-GOHS-toh)
Assumption
(pahr-tee-koh-LAH-reh)
particular

Naturalmente il venticinque dicembre

c'è il Natale.
(nah-TAH-leh)

In italiano si dice «Buone feste!»

1. Qual è la prima festa dell'anno?
- [ ] Pasqua.
- [ ] Ferragosto.
- [ ] Capodanno.

2. Che festa c'è il sei gennaio?
- [ ] Ferragosto.
- [ ] Capodanno.
- [ ] Epifania.

3. Che festa c'è in primavera?
- [ ] Pasqua
- [ ] Natale.
- [ ] Ferragosto.

4. Che festa c'é il quindici agosto?
- [ ] Pasqua.
- [ ] Ferragosto.
- [ ] Natale.

5. Che festa c'è il venticinque dicembre?
- [ ] Pasqua.
- [ ] Capodanno.
- [ ] Natale.

6. Che vuol dire «Buone feste»?
- [ ] Hello.
- [ ] Good-bye.
- [ ] Happy holidays.

Let's finish this chapter with an easy one; fill in the blanks with the following words. This is Giovanni's weird dream. See what he dreamt about!

(bahn-DYEH-rah)

birra, albero, dorme, zia, bandiera, biglietti, fila
beer   flag

Giovanni e Maria comprano due _____ per andare al cinema.

Si siedono nella terza _____.

Giovanni compra e beve una _____.

(een-KOHN-trah)

Il film non è interessante. Al cinema, Maria **incontra** sua _____.
meets

Giovanni _____ durante tutto il film.

Quando Giovanni e Maria escono dal film vedono un _____ di Natale e

una _____ italiana.

ESCURSIONI A PIEDI E IL JOGGING
Hiking and Jogging

(Mark Smith is in great physical condition. He jogs every morning. This morning he is approached by a journalist who is writing an article on sports.)

GIORNALISTA **Buon giorno, signore. Sono** *(johr-nah-LEES-tah)* *(ahl-KOO-neh)* **un giornalista. Le posso fare alcune** *(doh-MAHN-deh)* **domande?**	Good morning, sir. I am a journalist. Can I ask you some questions?
MARK **Certo. Ma parli lentamente. Sono americano e non capisco tutto.**	Certainly. But speak slowly. I am an American and I don't understand everything.
GIORNALISTA *(SPEH-ssoh)* **Lei fa spesso il jogging?**	Do you jog often?
MARK *(OH-nyee)* **Sì. Ogni mattina.** **Incontro sempre un gruppo** **di turisti che fanno il jogging con me.** **Sembrano turisti spagnoli.**	Yes. Every morning. I always meet a group of tourists who jog along with me. They look like Spanish tourists.

143

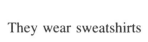

(spohr-TEE-veh)
Portano tute sportive   They wear sweatshirts

(SKAHR-peh) _(KOHR-sah)_
e scarpe da corsa.   and running shoes.

GIORNALISTA   **Le piacciono altri sport?**   Do you like any other sports?

(neh-AHN-keh) _(KAHL-choh)_
MARK   **No, neanche il calcio.**   No, not even soccer.

(They run into a group of hikers.)

GIORNALISTA   **Questi signori hanno un**   These people have a sleeping bag, a backpack,

(TSAH-ee-noh)
sacco a pelo, uno zaino,   cooking utensils and a canteen.

degli utensili da cucina e

(beh-ttoh-LEE-noh)
un bettolino.

MARK   **Lo so. Sono due giorni che sono**   I know. They have been here for two days.

qui. Credo che siano turisti francesi.   I think they are French tourists.

GIORNALISTA   **Come lo sa?**   How do you know?

(SEE-mee-leh)
MARK   **Parlano una lingua molto simile**   They speak a language very similar to Italian.

all'italiano.

(The journalist speaks to the hikers and then catches up to Mark.)

(ZBAH-llyah)
GIORNALISTA   **Lei si sbaglia, signore. Quei**   You're wrong, sir. They are Italians who

signori sono italiani ma parlano un   speak a dialect similar to French.
(dyah-LEH-ttoh)
dialetto italiano simile al francese.

MARK   **Ecco perché non li comprendo.**   That's why I don't understand them.

After reading the dialogue over several times, indicate if each of the following is true or false.

1. Il gruppo di turisti fa alcune domande a Mark. ☐ Vero
   True
   ☐ Falso
   False

2. Mark è americano e
   non capisce tutto.
   ☐ Vero
   ☐ Falso

3. Mark non fa mai il jogging.
   ☐ Vero
   ☐ Falso

4. Ogni mattina Mark incontra
   un gruppo di turisti che fanno·
   il jogging con lui.
   ☐ Vero
   ☐ Falso

5. I turisti portano tute sportive
   e scarpe da corsa.
   ☐ Vero
   ☐ Falso

6. A Mark piacciono molti sport.
   ☐ Vero
   ☐ Falso

7. I signori che incontrano hanno
   un sacco a pelo, uno zaino,
   degli utensili da cucina e
   un bettolino.
   ☐ Vero
   ☐ Falso

8. Quei signori parlano francese.
   ☐ Vero
   ☐ Falso

9. Mark vuole parlare ancora.
   ☐ Vero
   ☐ Falso

Are you ready for a hiking trip now? Let's see if you can identify this gear.

Che cosa è?   È una _____ .

Che cosa è?   È un _____ .

Che cosa è?   È uno _____ .

Che cosa sono?   Sono degli _____ .

Che cosa è?   È un _____ .

ANSWERS

Identification
2. Vero — tuta sportiva
4. Vero — sacco a pelo — zaino — utensili da cucina — bettolino

True/False
1. Falso
3. Falso
5. Vero
6. Falso
7. Vero
8. Falso
9. Falso

145

Ricordati . . .
Remember . . .

Nouns like *sport*, *film*, and *jogging* are all borrowed from English. The singular and plural forms are identical for these nouns.

lo sport ——→	**gli sport**
sport	sports
il film ——→	**i film**
film	films

In the first few units you learned about the pronouns "I, you, he, she," and so forth. The pronouns **lui, lei, noi, voi, loro** can also be used as object pronouns.

John calls him. **Giovanni** $\boxed{\text{lo}}$ **chiama.** *or* **Giovanni chiama** $\boxed{\text{lui}}$.

John calls her. **Giovanni** $\boxed{\text{la}}$ **chiama.** *or* **Giovanni chiama** $\boxed{\text{lei}}$.

Instead of **mi** the form **me** can be used; and instead of **ti** the form **te** can be used.

John calls me. **Giovanni** $\boxed{\text{mi}}$ **chiama.** *or* **Giovanni chiama** $\boxed{\text{me}}$.

John calls you. **Giovanni** $\boxed{\text{ti}}$ **chiama.** *or* **Giovanni chiama** $\boxed{\text{te}}$.

Notice that these pronouns come after the verb as in English.

Before the Verb	*After the Verb*
mi ———————	**me**
ti ———————	**te**
lo ———————	**lui**
la ———————	**lei**
ci ———————	**noi**
vi ———————	**voi**
li	
le	**loro**

The type used *after* verbs is also the *only* one used after prepositions.

Giovanni viene con $\boxed{\text{me}}$.   **Giovanni parla di** $\boxed{\text{te}}$.   **Giovanni arriva con** $\boxed{\text{loro}}$.

John is coming with me.   John is speaking of you.   John arrives with them.

146

See if you can replace each pronoun with an equivalent form. Don't get discouraged. These take a while to learn.

1. Il signor Smith *mi* chiama. Il signor Smith chiama _____ .

2. La signora Smith chiama *te*. La signora Smith _____ chiama.

3. Io *lo* chiamo. Io chiamo _____ .

4. Il giornalista chiama *lei*. Il giornalista _____ chiama.

5. Il passeggero *ci* chiama. Il passeggero chiama _____ .

6. Il passeggero chiama *voi*. Il passeggero _____ chiama.

7. L'autista *li* chiama. L'autista chiama _____ .

8. L'autista *le* chiama. L'autista chiama _____ .

(chee-KLEEZ-moh)   *(NWOH-toh)*

IL CICLISMO E IL NUOTO
Bicycling and Swimming

As you learn these words relating to cycling and swimming, you'll see some vocabulary patterns emerging that will help in recalling them.

(oh-KKYAH-lee) (proh-teh-TSYOH-neh)
gli occhiali di protezione
goggles

(chee-KLEES-tah)
Il ciclista
bicyclist

(SPEEN-jeh)   *(bee-chee-KLEH-ttah)*
spinge la sua bicicletta
pushes   bicycle

(sah-LEE-tah)
in salita.
uphill

(nwoh-tah-TOH-reh)
un nuotatore
swimmer

(RAH-nah)
il nuoto a rana
breaststroke

il nuoto a crawl
crawl

(DOHR-soh)
il nuoto sul dorso
backstroke

Add the appropriate word or expression that describes each picture.

_____

_____   _____

(sehn-TYEH-ree)   *(nah-too-RAH-lee)*

I SENTIERI NATURALI
Footpaths

This passage introduces some additional vocabulary. When you have mastered it, choose the correct answer to each of the questions that follow.

(SEH-nyee)

Nei sentieri naturali ci sono tanti alberi con segni.
markings

(een-dee-kah-TOH-ree)

Ci sono anche cartelli indicatori.
signposts

(PYAHN-teh)   *(FYOH-ree)*   *(een-SEH-ttee)*   *(ah-nee-MAH-lee)*

Ci sono anche piante,   fiori,   insetti   animali.
        plants   flowers   insects   animals

La natura italiana è molto bella.

Dove ci sono tanti alberi?
- ☐ Nell'acqua.
- ☐ Nei sentieri naturali.
- ☐ Nel vino.

Che cosa altro c'è?
What else
- ☐ Ci sono libri.
- ☐ Ci sono penne.
- ☐ Ci sono cartelli indicatori.

Ci sono piante, fiori, insetti e animali?
- ☐ Sì.
- ☐ No.

Com'è la natura italiana?
- ☐ È brutta.
- ☐ È bella.

ANSWERS

Comprehension   Nei sentieri naturali.   Ci sono cartelli indicatori.   Sì.   È bella.

Identification   il ciclista   il nuoto a rana   gli occhiali di protezione   il nuoto a crawl   il nuoto sul dorso

148

ORDERING FOOD

(ohr-dee-NYAH-moh)   *(mahn-JAH-reh)*
Ordiniamo da mangiare

14	*(PAHS tee)* *(CHEE-bee)* **I pasti /I cibi** Meals/Food

Che cosa dire quando ti *piace* qualcosa

What to Say When You *Like* Something

That troublesome verb *piacere* that you learned about in chapter 12 is used when talking about the things you may or may not like to eat.

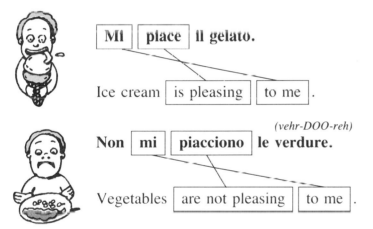

Mi | **piace** | **Il gelato.**

Ice cream | is pleasing | to me .

(vehr-DOO-reh)

Non | **mi** | **piacciono** | **le verdure.**

Vegetables | are not pleasing | to me .

Now choose either *piace* or *piacciono* to complete these sentences.

Mi _____ le verdure. Non mi _____ mangiare. Mi

_____ il gelato. Mi _____ il nuoto. Non mi

_____ andare in bicicletta. Mi _____ gli sport. Mi

_____ il calcio. Mi _____ il tennis e il ciclismo.

ANSWERS

Verbs piacciono (le) piace (mangiare.) piace (il) piace (il) piace (andare) piacciono (gli) piace (il)
piacciono (il)

149

The verb forms are the same, when used with other pronouns.

| Ti | piace | il gelato. |

Ice cream | is pleasing | to you

| Gli | piacciono | le verdure. |

Vegetables | are pleasing | to him .

| A Maria | piace | il gelato. |

Ice cream | is pleasing | to Mary

| Ai bambini | non piacciono | le verdure. |

Vegetables | are not pleasing | to the children .

Ti _____ il film.

Le _____ il tennis.

Vi _____ il gelato.

Gli _____ tutti gli sport.

Ci _____ le feste.

Gli _____ le verdure.

Now that you understand *piace* and *piacciono,* let's learn more about nouns.

Notice that nouns ending with an accented vowel do not change in the plural.

la città	**le città**
city	cities
il caffè	**i caffè**
coffee	coffees
il menù	**i menù**
menu	menus

Nouns ending in **-ista** can be either masculine or feminine.

il turista	**la turista**
male tourist	female tourist
il pianista	**la pianista**
male pianist	female pianist

Finally, notice this completely irregular noun.

	(WOH-mee-nee)
l'uomo	**gli uomini**
man	men

150

We want you to change these nouns from singular to plural. We've given you the correct article—you add the right noun form.

il gelato → i _____ , la caramella → le _____ ,

il padre → i _____ , la madre → le _____ ,

lo sport → gli _____ , il film → i _____ ,

il caffè → i _____ , la città → le _____ ,

il menù → i _____ , l'uomo → gli _____ .

(koh-lah-TSYOH-neh)
LA (PRIMA) COLAZIONE
Breakfast

(rees-toh-RAHN-teh)
un ristorante
(eh-koh-NOH-mee-koh)
economico

(The Smiths are having breakfast at a local inexpensive restaurant.)

(STRAH-noh)

MARK **Che strano! Di solito gli italiani**   How strange! Italians normally do not have

non fanno la prima colazione.   breakfast.

CAMERIERA **Buon giorno. Che cosa**   Good morning. Can I take your orders?

prendono?   *(literally,* what will you take)

(TAH-tsah) *(kah-ffeh-LLAH-tteh)*

MARY **Io vorrei una tazza di caffellate,**   I would like a cup of coffee
with milk,

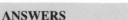

ANSWERS

Nouns gelati caramelle padri madri sport film caffè città menù uomini

(PAH-neh) (tohs-TAH-toh)
il pane tostato con burro   toasted bread with

(mahr-meh-LLAH-tah)
e marmellata,   butter and marmalade,

(bee-KKYEH-reh)
e un bicchiere di   and a glass

(SOO-kkoh) (ah-RAHN-chah)
succo d'arancia.   of orange juice.

MARK   **Mamma mia, che fame! Io prendo**   Good grief, what an appetite!

(pah-NEE-noh) (DOHL-cheh)
un panino dolce, un bicchiere di   I'll take a sweet roll,

(poh-moh-DOH-roh)
succo di pomodoro e un   a glass of tomato juice,

(kah-ppoo-CHEE-noh)
cappuccino.   and a cappuccino.

ANNE   **Io voglio solo una tazza di tè.**   I only want a cup of tea.

JOHN   **E io solo un espresso.**   And I only an espresso coffee.

CAMERIERA   **Grazie.**   Thank you.

(The Smiths finish their breakfast.)

(KOHN-toh)
MARK   **Cameriera, il conto, per favore.**   Waitress, the bill please!

CAMERIERA   **Ecco. Quarantamila lire in tutto.**   Here it is. 40,000 lira all together.

MARK *(to himself)*   **Più una mancia.**   Plus a tip.

MARY   **Va bene, signorina. Grazie.**   Okay, miss. Thank you.

After you have read the dialogue several times, try to match up the left column with the right one, to get lines from the dialogue. Check your answers.

Di solito gli italiani . . .   una tazza di caffellatte, il pane tostato con burro e marmellata e un bicchiere di succo d'arancia.

Che cosa . . .   una tazza di tè.

Io vorrei . . .   un espresso.

Io voglio solo . . .   non fanno la prima colazione.

E io solo . . .   prendono?

Io prendo . . .   il conto, per favore.

Cameriera, . . .   lire in tutto.

Quarantamila . . .   un panino dolce, un bicchiere di succo di pomodoro e un cappuccino.

(TAH-voh-lah)

LA TAVOLA
The Table

When the Smiths dine out, their place settings may look like this one. When you have read and pronounced the vocabulary, try to identify each object without referring to the Italian words.

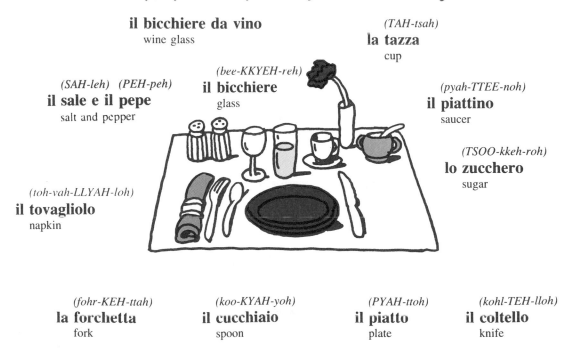

il bicchiere da vino
wine glass

(TAH-tsah)
la tazza
cup

(SAH-leh) (PEH-peh)
il sale e il pepe
salt and pepper

(bee-KKYEH-reh)
il bicchiere
glass

(pyah-TTEE-noh)
il piattino
saucer

(TSOO-kkeh-roh)
lo zucchero
sugar

(toh-vah-LLYAH-loh)
il tovagliolo
napkin

(fohr-KEH-ttah)
la forchetta
fork

(koo-KYAH-yoh)
il cucchiaio
spoon

(PYAH-ttoh)
il piatto
plate

(kohl-TEH-lloh)
il coltello
knife

How many words do you remember? Without looking at the picture, match up the two columns.

1. il coltello   a. wine glass

2. il sale   b. napkin

3. il cucchiaio   c. pepper

4. il bicchiere da vino   d. plate

5. il pepe   e. fork

6. il bicchiere   f. spoon

7. il piatto   g. sugar

8. il piattino   h. cup

9. la forchetta   i. saucer

10. la tazza   j. glass

11. il tovagliolo   k. knife

12. lo zucchero   l. salt

From the following list, choose the appropriate word for each blank.

tazza, bicchiere, forchetta, cucchiaio, cameriere, sale, pepe, zucchero, coltello

Questo panino è molto dolce. C'è molto _____.

Per mangiare la pizza, ho bisogno di una _____ e di un _____.

Ogni mattina io bevo una _____ di caffè.
(mee-NEHS-trah)

Per mangiare la minestra, ho bisogno di un _____.
    soup

Il _____ porta il conto.

Questo è un _____ di acqua.

Mi piace il cibo con tanto _____ e _____.

The answers are printed upside-down at the bottom.

ANSWERS

Matching 1-k, 2-l, 3-f, 4-a, 5-c, 6-j, 7-d, 8-i, 9-e, 10-h, 11-b, 12-g

Fill-ins zucchero forchetta / coltello cucchiaio tazza cameriere bicchiere sale / pepe

IL PASTO PRINCIPALE

(preen-chee-PAH-leh)

The Main Meal

What a feast! But to get a meal like this one, you'll have to learn how to order it.

(ahn-tee-PAHS-toh)
l'antipasto
appetizer

(proh-SHOO-ttoh)
il prosciutto
Italian ham

un piatto di minestra
bowl of soup

(meh-LOH-neh)
il melone
cantaloupe

(stoo-tsee-kah-DEHN-tee)
gli stuzzicadenti
toothpicks

un piatto di pasta
plate of pasta

(oh-LEE-veh)
le olive
olives

(een-sah-LAH-tah) (VEHR-deh)
l'insalata   verde
tossed salad

(ah-CHOO-geh)
le acciughe
anchovies

un piatto di verdure
plate of vegetables

il vino rosso / il vino bianco
red wine/   white wine

(PEH-sheh)
il pesce
fish

(FROO-ttah)
la frutta
fruit

(KAHR-neh)(MAHN-tsoh)
la carne di manzo
roast beef

By filling in the blanks and repeating each sentence several times, you will develop the ability to order the things you want.

Vorrei il _____ per antipasto.
ham and cantaloupe

Poi, vorrei un _____ .
bowl of soup

Mia moglie/Mio marito prende un _____ di spaghetti/ravioli/lasagne.
plate

Vorrei anche un piatto di _____ .
vegetables

Poi, vorrei un piatto di _____ .
fish

Mia moglie/Mio marito prende la _____ .
roast beef

Per finire, vorrei _____ e il _____ .
fruit   coffee

Per bere, vorrei una bottiglia di _____ .
red wine

ANSWERS

Ordering Food: prosciutto e (il) melone   piatto di minestra   piatto   verdure   pesce   carne di manzo   la frutta / caffè   vino rosso

155

LA CENA
(CHEH-nah)

The Evening Meal

To conclude the day's dining, read the following
passage and then respond to the questions.

In Italia ci sono due pasti principali:

il pranzo nel pomeriggio e la cena di sera.
   lunch

(VEHR-soh)

Di solito la cena è verso le otto, ma c'è chi
           around   he who

mangia anche alle nove o alle dieci. Gli italiani

(ah-bahs-TAHN-tsah)

mangiano abbastanza al pranzo e alla cena.
    quite well

(mee-neh-RAH-leh)   *(ah-ppeh-TEE-toh)*

Bevono di solito il vino e l'acqua minerale. «Buon appetito!» si dice prima di mangiare.
          mineral water   Good appetite   before

Quali sono i due pasti principali italiani?
- ☐ **Le cena e il pranzo.**
- ☐ Le lasagne e i ravioli.
- ☐ Gli spaghetti e il vino.

Quando si fa il pranzo?
- ☐ Alla mattina.
- ☐ Nel pomeriggio.
- ☐ A mezzanotte.

Quando si fa la cena?
- ☐ Alla mattina.
- ☐ Nel pomeriggio.
- ☐ Di sera.

Che cosa bevono di solito gli italiani?
- ☐ Niente.
- ☐ L'acqua.
- ☐ Il vino e l'acqua minerale.

Che cosa si dice prima di mangiare?
- ☐ Buon giorno.
- ☐ Buon appetito.
- ☐ Buona sera.

ANSWERS

Comprehension La cena e il pranzo. Nel pomeriggio. Di sera. Il vino e l'acqua minerale. Buon appetito.

156

Can you find *ten* words relating to food and eating in this word-search puzzle? After you have circled them, write them on the lines provided.

z	c	b	m	j	g	f	d	w	r	t	u	s	p	i
q	e	r	u	m	a	r	m	e	l	l	a	t	a	b
m	b	c	z	f	h	u	t	i	p	w	r	a	c	m
q	t	e	t	p	a	t	d	g	j	k	m	z	v	r
i	o	r	c	h	c	t	t	a	a	n	e	z	l	p
q	v	a	z	w	s	a	x	c	d	c	s	a	l	e
r	a	f	v	c	t	g	b	y	h	n	u	j	m	p
i	g	k	m	o	l	o	p	q	a	z	w	s	x	e
e	l	d	c	l	r	f	v	t	g	b	y	h	n	i
p	i	a	t	t	o	k	m	o	p	l	q	a	z	w
s	o	x	e	e	d	c	r	f	v	t	g	b	y	h
n	l	u	j	l	m	o	k	l	p	q	a	z	w	s
x	o	e	d	l	c	r	f	v	t	g	b	y	h	n
u	j	m	i	o	l	i	v	e	k	m	p	l	j	b

_____   _____   _____

_____   _____   _____

_____

157

You will remember that to order food or drink in
Italian, all you have to say is:

> **Vorrei** un piatto di spaghetti, per favore.
>
> **Vorrei** un piatto di ravioli, per favore.
>
> **Vorrei** una bottiglia di vino rosso, per favore.

To say "I am going to . . ." in Italian,
just use the verb in the normal way.

> Tomorrow I'm going to eat pizza. ⟶ Domani **mangio** la pizza.
>
> Tomorrow I'm going to drink wine. ⟶ Domani **bevo** il vino.

You will find some Italian food selections at the back of this book. Here are some items that
you might see on the menu when you dine out.

IL MENÙ

l'antipasto	appetizer	**la carne**	meat
		(deh-SSEHRT)	
la minestra	soup	**il dessert / il dolce**	dessert
(een-sah-LAH-tah)		*(beh-VAHN-deh)*	
l'insalata	salad	**le bevande**	drinks
le verdure	vegetables	**le acciughe**	anchovies
il pesce	fish	*(POH-lloh)*	
		il pollo	chicken
		(lah-TTOO-gah)	
		la lattuga	lettuce
		(ahs-PAH-rah-jee)	
		gli asparagi	asparagus
		(TROH-tah)	
		la trota	trout
		(vee-TEH-lloh)	
		la carne di vitello	veal
		(OO-vah)	
		l'uva	grapes
		il vino rosso	red wine

158

(The Smiths have decided to eat at an expensive restaurant.)

CAMERIERE **Buona sera. Vogliono**

vedere il menù?

Good evening. Would you (formal, plural) like to see the menu?

MARK **No, grazie. Non voglio**

vedere i prezzi.

No, thank you. I do not want to see the prices.

(ah-TEHN-tsyoh-neh)
MARY **Non faccia attenzione a mio**
(SKEHR-tsah)
marito. Lui scherza sempre.

Don't pay any attention to my husband. He always jokes around.

CAMERIERE **Abbiamo un antipasto**
(skwee-ZEE-toh) (WOH-vah)
squisito di uova con acciughe e
(SPEH-tsee-eh)
molte spezie.

We have a delicious appetizer of deviled eggs with anchovies and many spices.

(pee-KKAHN-teh)
ANNE **Troppo piccante!**

Too spicy!

MARK **Per il primo piatto,**

tutti prendiamo la minestra. Poi,
(pah-TAH-teh)
io prendo il pollo con le patate.

For the first dish, we will all have soup. Then, I'll have chicken with potatoes.

(koh-toh-LEH-ttah)
MARY **E io vorrei la cotoletta di**

vitello e l'insalata di lattuga con i
(poh-moh-DOH-ree)
pomodori.

And I would like a veal cutlet and the lettuce and tomato salad.

ANNE **Io prendo solo un po' di formaggio**
(DYEH-tah)
con il pane. Faccio la dieta.

I'll have only a bit of cheese with bread. I'm on a diet.

JOHN **Io vorrei la trota con le patate.**

I would like the trout with potatoes.

MARK **Una bottiglia di vino rosso, e alla**

fine l'espresso per tutti e un cognac per

me e mia moglie.

A bottle of red wine, and at the end espresso coffee for everyone and a cognac for me and my wife.

CAMERIERE **Prego.**

Thank you / Fine.

(The Smiths have finished the meal and are about to leave.)

(LAH-shah)

MARY   **Mark, lascia una mancia! Questo è**   Mark, leave a tip! This is an expensive restaurant.

(LOO-ssoh)

un ristorante di lusso.

(mahn-jeh-REH-moh)

MARK   **Va bene. Non mangeremo per una**   Okay. We won't eat for a week.

settimana!

When you have read the dialogue aloud until you are familiar with it, try to complete the missing parts without looking back. Then check your answers.

Buona sera. Vogliono vedere il m_____?

No, grazie. Non v_____ vedere i p_____.

Non faccia a_____ a mio marito. Lui s_____ sempre.

Abbiamo un antipasto s_____ di uova con a_____ e molte

s_____ .

Troppo p_____!

Per il primo p_____, tutti prendiamo la m_____. Poi, io prendo il

p_____ con le p_____.

E io v_____ la c_____ di v_____

e l'_____ di l_____ e p_____.

Io prendo solo un po' di f_____ con il p_____. Faccio la

d_____ .

Io vorrei la t_____con le patate.

Una b_____ di vino rosso, e alla f_____ l'espresso per tutti e un

cognac per m_____ e mia m_____.

Grazie.

Il signor Smith . . .

Mr. Smith . . .

You may have noticed that the final *-e* of *signore* is dropped before a name, such as Smith. This is true of all masculine titles ending in *-e*.

il signore	**il signor Smith** Mr. Smith
il professore	**il professor Rossi** Professor Rossi
il dottore	**il dottor Verdi** Dr. Verdi

The article used with titles is dropped when speaking directly to the person.

TALKING ABOUT SOMEONE	TALKING TO SOMEONE
Il signor Smith è americano. Mr. Smith is American.	**Buon giorno, signor Smith.** Good morning, Mr. Smith.
La signora Smith è intelligente. Mrs. Smith is intelligent.	**Buona sera, signora Smith.** Good evening, Mrs. Smith.

(sehn-TEER-see)

Sentirsi (bene, male)

To Feel (Well, Sick)

(BAH-nyoh)
bagno
restroom

donne uomini
ladies   gentlemen

It's easy to tell someone how you are feeling:

Mi sento bene.
Non mi sento bene. Mi sento male.

You continue. Answer the question and fill in the blanks.

Come ti senti? Mi _____ bene.

Come ti senti? Mi _____ male.

Here are some additional foods you might want to order. Say them aloud and then repeat them as you look at each picture.

Antipasti (Appetizers)	*Minestre* (Soups)

(free-TTAH-tah)
la frittata
omelet

(mee-nehs-TROH-neh)
il minestrone
minestrone

(pohl-peh-TTEE-neh)
le polpettine
meatballs

(TSOO-pah)
la zuppa
thick soup

Insalate (Salads)	*Verdure* (Vegetables)

l'insalata mista
mixed salad

gli asparagi
asparagus

l'insalata russa
Russian salad
potato salad

(spee-NAH-chee)
gli spinaci
spinach

Pesce (Fish)	*Carne* (Meats)

(kah-lah-MAH-ree)
i calamari
squid

(mah-YAH-leh)
la bistecca di maiale
pork steak

(gahm-beh-REH-ttee)
i gamberetti
prawns

(ah-NYEH-lloh)
la carne d' agnello
lamb

Dessert (Desserts)	*Bevande* (Drinks)

il gelato
ice cream

(ahl-KOH-lee-keh)
le bevande alcoliche
alcoholic beverages

i dolci
sweets

Now you should be able to zip right through the following brief passage and then select the appropriate answer to each question.

(trah-ttoh-REE-ah)

In Italia, si mangia al ristorante, alla trattoria, o al bar dove si mangiano i panini. I pasti
less formal restaurant   sandwiches

(kohn-SEES-toh-noh)

italiani consistono di un antipasto, un piatto di pasta o di minestra (zuppa, minestrone, e
consist

così via), e un piatto di carne o pesce, con patate, verdure, e così via. Poi c'è il dessert, la
so on

frutta e il caffè. Naturalmente si beve il vino o l'acqua minerale.

To wrap up our section on eating out, you fill in the menu; add the Italian words.

Dove si mangiano
i panini?

☐ A casa.
☐ In Francia.
☐ Al bar.

Nei pasti italiani,
non c'è . . .

☐ L'antipasto.
☐ La frutta.
☐ La Coca-Cola.

Che cosa si beve
in Italia ai pasti?

☐ La Coca-Cola.
☐ Il vino e
l'acqua minerale.
☐ Il tè.

MENU

(fish)

(soup)

(chicken)

(salad)

(sweet)

(vegetable)

(wine)

HOW'RE WE DOING?
Vediamo quanto hai imparato!
(Let's see how much you've learned!)

It's time for a breather! This is when you should go back over those sections where you are still having problems. You should also review any vocabulary you may have forgotten and reread the dialogues and comprehension passages. After you have done all that, have some fun with the following activities. If you have forgotten the meaning of any word or expression, you can look it up in the glossary. Are you ready?

First, try unscrambling the letters of the following words. To help you reconstruct the words, English meanings are provided. Each word begins with the letter *p*.

parrimaev _____ , porzez _____ ,
  spring   price

ploita _____ , puenmaocit _____ ,
  pilot   tire

pmoeriiogg _____ , patro _____ ,
  afternoon   door

patrofgolio _____ , poien _____ ,
  wallet   full

pttiao _____ , ppee _____ ,
  plate   pepper

ptniaa _____ , pscee _____ ,
  plant   fish

pstao _____ , paaatt _____ , pozaz _____ ,
  meal   potato   crazy

praaberazz _____ , paaarfnog _____ ,
  windshield   fender

praautri _____ , prahceggoi _____ ,
  bumper   parking

pssggraeeo _____ , ppaassotro _____ ,
  passenger   passport

pomissor _____ , pgeor _____ , pean _____ ,
  next   you're welcome   bread

pdrae _____ , pasee _____ , poacc _____ .
  father   country   package

164

After you have reviewed your verbs, try the following ''verb'' crossword puzzle.

Across

2. She understands
4. They live
6. They believe
8. I help
9. I see
12. You fasten (plural)
13. I am waiting
15. I drink
16. They finish
17. Walk! (singular, familiar)
20. I call
21. You wash yourself (singular, familiar)
22. You are (plural)
24. He answers
25. They sit

Down

1. We arrive
2. I sing
3. You know (singular, familiar)
4. He fixes
5. They are sleeping
7. I say
10. I am getting up
11. You go (singular, familiar)
13. We have
14. You drive (plural)
16. I make
18. She asks
19. You are leaving (singular, familiar)
23. I come
24. He steals

165

This one should be a snap! Read each sentence aloud, and these words will fall right into place.

accanto, acqua, adesso, destra, aereo, albergo, alto, altro, anche, antipasto, appuntamento, autorimessa

1. Maria si siede sempre _____ alla sua amica.

2. Vorrei bere un po' di _____ .

3. L'_____ di prosciutto è molto buono.

4. La mia macchina è nell'_____ .

5. Domani, il signor Smith ha un _____ con me.

6. Gira a _____ , non a sinistra!

7. _____ Gino parla italiano molto bene.

8. Lui non è _____ ; è basso.

9. La signora vuole un _____ panino.

10. Devi mangiare _____ , non dopo.

11. **Il pilota è già nell'** _____ .

12. Non ho una prenotazione per quell'_____ .

Here we go with plurals! Transpose each "singular" phrase to a "plural" phrase, as we have done with the first one.

il mio amico alto   __i__ mie __i__ amic __i__ alt __i__

la mia amica bella   l____ mi____ amich____ bell____

l'autobus comodo   gl____ autobus comod____

l'albero grande   gl____ alber____ grand____

un bambino bravo   de____ bambin____ brav____

166

una bandiera importante   dell_____ bandier_____ important_____

questa bicicletta nuova   quest_____ biciclett_____ nuov_____

questo caffè buono   quest_____ caffè buon_____

quel cane intelligente   que_____ can_____ intelligent_____

quella cartolina brutta   quell_____ cartolin_____ brutt_____

l'uomo famoso   gl_____ uomin_____ famos_____

la donna gentile   l_____ donn_____ gentil_____

lo zio giovane   gl_____ zi_____ giovan_____

il suo libro interessante   _____ suo_____ libr_____ interessant_____

Find the words that mean the following in the word-search puzzle and circle them. After you find each one, write it in the proper space.

gasoline	drink	ticket
bottle	room	key
dashboard	spoon	yesterday
milk	every	

a	d	h	k	m	b	p	t	x	c	r	u	s	c	o	t	t	o
t	b	e	n	z	i	n	a	c	u	w	z	a	a	c	f	i	g
l	e	o	r	u	g	x	b	u	f	j	n	r	m	v	z	h	n
c	v	g	k	o	l	s	w	c	h	i	a	v	e	a	d	g	i
g	a	h	l	p	i	t	x	c	q	r	u	p	r	a	f	j	l
z	n	v	m	w	e	r	u	h	o	a	f	j	a	l	z	v	b
m	d	g	d	y	t	l	h	i	e	r	i	d	v	n	e	q	m
l	a	t	t	e	t	a	m	a	s	u	c	n	w	q	h	f	s
a	p	s	o	b	o	t	t	i	g	l	i	a	v	n	w	x	b
y	o	q	x	c	m	e	f	o	r	w	m	q	e	r	i	n	p

Finally, choose the appropriate answer to each question.

Buon giorno, come sta?

☐ Bene grazie, e lei?
☐ Domani mattina.

Come si chiama, lei?

☐ Sono americano.
☐ **Mi chiamo Mark Smith.**

Dove abita, lei?

☐ **Vado in Italia.**
☐ Abito negli Stati Uniti.

A che ora parte il treno?

☐ Parte alle diciassette.
☐ Parte ieri.

Che ore sono?

☐ È il tre marzo.
☐ Sono le tre e venti.

Che giorno è oggi?

☐ È l'una.
☐ È il tre novembre.

Che tempo fa?

☐ Piove.
☐ Domani.

Che cosa prende?

☐ Un bicchiere di vino.
☐ Vado in Italia.

Perché mangia i ravioli?

☐ Perché mi piace.
☐ Perché mi piacciono.

Come si sente?

☐ Mi sento bene.
☐ **Mi sento.**

How did you do? Don't worry if you made mistakes. Learning a new language is a process of trial and error. It's time to go on!

ANSWERS

Comprehension Bene grazie, e lei? Mi chiamo Mark Smith. Abito negli Stati Uniti. Parte alle diciassette. Sono le tre e venti. È l tre novembre. Piove. Un bicchiere di vino. Perché mi piacciono. Mi sento bene.

168

STORES
(ehn-TRYAH-moh)   *(neh-GOH-tsee)*
Entriamo nei negozi

16	*(ah-bbee-lluy-MEHN-toh)* **Negozi di abbigliamento /** *(TAH-lyah)* *(koh-LOH-ree)* **Le taglie / I colori primari**

Ti provi i vestiti?
Trying on Clothes?

You can't leave Italy without doing some shopping. Let's hope that you fare better than some of these examples!

(TOH-llyehr-see)
togliersi
to take off

(vehs-TEER-see)
vestirsi
to get dressed

(kah-MEE-chah)
L'uomo si toglie la camicia.
shirt

(MEH-ttehr-see)
mettersi
to put on

(vehs-TEE-toh)
Mi metto il vestito.
dress / suit

La donna si veste molto
(eh-leh-gahn-teh-MEHN-teh)
elegantemente.
elegantly

Si metta questa camicia.
Put on this shirt.

Troppo grande!
Too big!

Si metta questo abito
Put on this suit.

Troppo grande!
Too big!

No, è perfetto. Le sta proprio bene.
No, it's perfect. It really suits you.

169

Stare is a verb that you will use while shopping:

STARE			
	to stay, to be		
io ——— sto		noi ——— stiamo	
(STAH-ee)			
tu ——— stai		voi ——— state	
		(STAH-nnoh)	
lui } ——— sta		loro ——— stanno	
lei }			

This verb also means "to suit someone" in the expression *stare bene a*:

Il vestito [**mi**] [**sta bene**] .

The dress [*suits*] [*me*] .

(*Literally*, the dress *stays well* on me.)

Le scarpe [**ti**] [**stanno bene**] .

The shoes [*suit*] [*you*] .

(*Literally*, the shoes *stay well* on you.)

L'ABBIGLIAMENTO MASCHILE
(mahs-KEE-leh)
Men's Clothes

(*Mark and his son are at a clothing store.*)

COMMESSO **I signori desiderano?**

Can I help you gentlemen?

MARK **Abbiamo bisogno di un nuovo**
(gwahr-dah-ROH-bah) *(PAH-yoh)*
guardaroba. Per mio figlio un paio
(kahl-TSEE-nee) *(pahn-tah-LOH-nee)*
di stivali, calzini,   pantaloni,
(GWAHN-tee) *(moo-TAHN-deh)*
guanti, e   mutande.

We need a new wardrobe. For my son a pair of boots, socks, trousers, gloves, and underwear.

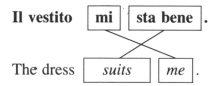

COMMESSO **Bene. E lei?**

Fine. And you?

MARK **Una camicia, una cravatta, una**
(krah-VAH-ttah)
(MAH-llyah) *(eem-pehr-meh-AH-bee-leh)*
maglia, un impermeabile,
(kah-PPEH-lloh)
e un cappello.

A shirt, a tie, a sweater, a raincoat, and a hat.

(*The two Smiths try on their clothes.*)

MARK **La camicia mi sta bene, ma il**

The shirt suits me, but not the rest.

	resto no. A mio figlio non sta bene	Nothing suits my son.

resto no. A mio figlio non sta bene

niente.

Nothing suits my son.

COMMESSO **Desiderano qualcos'altro?**
(mah-LLYEH-ttah)
Per suo figlio abbiamo una maglietta alla
(MOH-dah) *(cheen-TOO-rah)* *(beh-RREH-ttoh)*
moda, una cintura e un berretto.

Would you like something else?

For your son we have a fashionable

T-shirt, a belt, and a cap.

JOHN **No, grazie.**

No, thanks.

COMMESSO **Per lei abbiamo una giacca,**
(JAH-kkah)
(beh-LLEE-see-moh) *(kah-POH-ttoh)*
un bellissimo cappotto e un
(vehs-TEE-toh) *(GREE-doh)*
vestito all'ultimo grido.

For you we have a sports jacket, a very nice

coat, and

a suit in the latest style.

MARK **No, grazie.**

No, thanks.

COMMESSO **Neanche un fazzoletto**
(fah-tsoh-LEH-ttoh)
(ohm-BREH-lloh)
o un ombrello?

Not even a handkerchief

or an umbrella?

MARK **No.**

No.

COMMESSO **Ma non ha detto che aveva**

bisogno di un guardaroba nuovo?
(skehr-TSAH-voh)(voh-LEH-voh)

MARK **Scherzavo. Volevo solo**
(kah-PEE-vah)
vedere se lei capiva il mio italiano.
(pah-ROH-lah) *(FWOH-ree)*

But didn't you say that

you needed a new wardrobe?

I was only kidding. I wanted to see if you

understood my Italian.

COMMESSO **Capisce la parola fuori?**

Do you understand the word *out*?

MARK **Capisco. Andiamo, John.**

I understand. Let's go, John.

Ready to try your hand at completing the dialogue? Check your answers when you've finished.

I signori d_____?

Abbiamo b_____ di un n_____ guardaroba. Per mio figlio un

p_____ di stivali, c_____, p_____, g_____, e m_____.

Bene. E lei?

Una c_____, una c_____, una m_____, un i_____,

e un c_____.

La camicia mi s_____ bene, ma il r_____ no. A mio figlio non

s_____ bene niente.

Desiderano qualcos'altro? Per suo figlio abbiamo una m_____ di m_____,

una c_____ e un b_____.

No, grazie.

Per lei abbiamo una giacca, un bellissimo c_____ e un vestito all'ultimo g_____.

No, grazie.

Neanche un f_____ o un ombrello?

No.

Ma non ha detto che aveva b_____ di un guardaroba nuovo?

Il mio, il tuo . . .

Mine, Yours . . .

Remember those possessives? You can also use them to say "mine," "yours," and so on.

Il mio libro è nuovo.

My book is new.

Il mio è nuovo.

Mine is new.

I tuoi libri sono nuovi.

Your books are new.

I tuoi sono nuovi.

Yours are new.

La nostra penna è nuova.

Our pen is new.

La nostra è nuova.

Ours is new.

Le vostre penne sono nuove.

Your pens are new.

Le vostre sono nuove.

Yours are new.

Got it? All you do is get rid of the noun and keep the corresponding form of the possessive adjective.

Questo, quello
This, This One, That, That One

Now that you know about "mine" and "yours," you can apply the same rule to "this, this one" and "these."

Now it gets a little trickier. For "that, that one" and "those, those ones" you have to make some adjustments.

Do you think you've got it? Substitute the appropriate possessive pronoun for the noun in each of these sentences.

1. La mia penna è nuova.   _____ è nuova.

2. Il suo amico è francese.   _____ è francese.

3. I tuoi libri sono nuovi.   _____ sono nuovi.

4. I suoi calzini sono belli.   _____ sono belli.

5. Questi pantaloni sono belli.   _____ sono belli.

6. Queste mutande sono nuove.   _____ sono nuove.

7. Questa camicia è bianca   _____ è bianca.

8. Quella cravatta è bella.   _____ è bella.

9. Quelle maglie sono belle.   _____ sono belle.

10. Quell'impermeabile è nuovo.   _____ è nuovo.

11. Quel cappello è piccolo.   _____ è piccolo.

12. Quei vestiti sono alla moda. _____ sono alla moda.

Taglie
Sizes

While you are shopping, you may run into some unexpected problems with sizes, because the metric system is used throughout Italy. Here are some comparisons of sizes of men's clothing.

	TAGLIA AMERICANA	TAGLIA ITALIANA
Camicie	14	36
	15	38
	16	40
	17	42
Altre cose	34	44
Other things	36	46
	38	48
	40	50
	42	52
	44	54
	46	56

Now can you complete these sentences? The pictures will give you the necessary clues.

1. Quando fa freddo, mi metto il _____.

2. Quando fa fresco, mi metto la _____.

3. Quando nevica, mi metto gli _____.

4. Quando piove, mi metto l'_____.

5. Quando piove, porto l'_____.

6. Quando fa caldo, mi metto i _____ corti.

L'ABBIGLIAMENTO FEMMINILE
(feh-mmee-NEE-leh)
Women's Clothes

I colori primari
Basic Colors

You'll also have to be able to identify colors on your shopping trip. When you have learned these words, answer the questions that follow.

(reh-JJEE-seh-noh)(JAH-lloh)
un reggiseno giallo
yellow bra

(BOHR-sah)
una borsa rossa
red purse

(ah-TSOO-rroh)
un vestito azzurro
blue dress

un fazzoletto verde
green handkerchief

(moo-tahn-DEE-neh) (JAH-lloh)
le mutandine gialle
yellow panties

(soh-ttoh-VEHS-teh)
una sottoveste bianca
white slip

(kah-mee-CHEH-ttah)
una camicetta verde
green blouse

(GOH-nnah)
una gonna rossa
red skirt

Di che colore è?
What color is it?

Di che colore è la camicetta? _____

Di che colore è il reggiseno? _____

Di che colore sono le mutandine? _____

Di che colore è il vestito? _____

Di che colore il fazzoletto? _____

Taglie
Sizes

And here are some comparisons of women's sizes.

	TAGLIA AMERICANA	TAGLIA ITALIANA
Camicette	32	40
	34	42
	36	44
	38	46
	40	48
	42	50
	44	52
Altre cose	8	36
	10	38
	12	40
	14	42
	16	44
	18	46

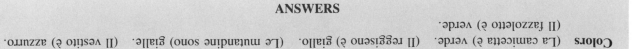

LE SCARPE PER UOMINI E DONNE
Shoes for Men and Women

Numeri di scarpa
Sizes

	UOMINI				
Numero americano	7	8	9	10	11
Numero italiano	39	41	43	44	45
	DONNE				
Numero americano	5	6	7	8	9
Numero italiano	35	36	38	38	40

Read the following passage about clothes and then check each statement as true or false.

Lina e Paola sono due amiche. Stasera si vestono per uscire a

una festa. Lina si mette una gonna azzurra e una camicetta rossa.
(STEH-sseh)
Anche Paola si veste con le stesse cose. Alla festa Lina e Paola si
same
(POHR-tah-noh)
incontrano e vedono che portano le stesse cose. Lina decide di
they are wearing
tornare a casa per mettersi un vestito nuovo.

1. Lina e Paola sono due amiche.
☐ Vero
☐ Falso

2. Stasera vanno al cinema.
☐ Vero
☐ Falso

3. Lina si mette una gonna azzurra e una camicetta grigia.
☐ Vero
☐ Falso

4. Paola si mette una gonna gialla e una camicetta verde.
☐ Vero
☐ Falso

5. Alla festa Lina decide di tornare a casa.
☐ Vero
☐ Falso

ANSWERS
True/False 1. Vero 2. Falso 3. Falso 4. Falso 5. Vero

17 I negozi di generi alimentari /
(oo-nee-TAH) *(PEH-zoh)*
Unità di peso e di misura
Food Stores / Weights and Measures

Shopping for food can be another pleasant experience, but not unless you know what the shops are! Study the vocabulary carefully.

(lah-tteh-REE-ah) **la latteria** dairy

(mah-cheh-LLAH-yoh) **il macellaio** butcher

(froo-ttee-VEHN-doh-loh) **il fruttivendolo** produce market

(pah-nee-FEE-choh) **il panificio** bread bakery

il latte milk   **la carne** meat   **la verdura** vegetables   **la frutta** fruit   **il pane** bread

(pehs-keh-REE-ah) **la pescheria** fish shop

(kohn-feh-tteh-REE-ah) **la confetteria** candy shop

(pahs-tee-cheh-REE-ah) **la pasticceria** pastry shop

(jeh-lah-teh-REE-ah) **la gelateria** ice cream shop

(eh-noh-TEH-kah) **l'enoteca** wine dealer

il pesce fish   **le caramelle** candy   **le paste** pastries   **le torte** cakes   **il gelato** ice cream   **il vino** wine

(doh-MAHN-dah)
Fare una domanda
To Pose a Question

Io faccio una domanda all'uomo.
I pose a question to the man.

Io *gli* faccio una domanda.
I pose a question *to him*.

Dal fruttivendolo
At the Produce Market

Expressions such as "at the market," "at the butcher's," "at the doctor's" or "to the market," "to the butcher's," "to the doctor's" are rendered in Italian by the preposition *da* and the appropriate noun.

Sono dal **fruttivendolo.**

I am at the market.

Vado dal **dottore.**

I am going to the doctor's.

Vado da **Giovanni.**

I am going to John's.

Troppe domande!
Too Many Questions!

(Mark Smith and his wife approach a policeman.)

MARK	**Scusi, signore, le vorrei fare una domanda.**	Excuse me, sir, I would like to ask you a question.
VIGILE	**Faccia pure!**	Go ahead!
MARK	**Ho bisogno di un po' di pane. Dov'è il panificio?**	I need some bread. Where is the bread bakery?
VIGILE	**Qui vicino in Via Verdi.**	Nearby on Verdi Street.
MARK	**Dove si compra la carne?**	Where does one buy meat?
VIGILE	**Dal macellaio, in via Rossini.**	At the butcher's, on Rossini Street.
MARK	**E il latte?**	And milk?
VIGILE	**Alla latteria, in via Dante.**	At the dairy, on Dante Street.
MARK	**Poi ho bisogno anche di verdura e frutta. Mi sa dire dov'è il fruttivendolo più vicino?**	Then I also need vegetables and fruit. Can you tell me where the nearest market is?
VIGILE	**In Via Nazionale.**	On National Street.

179

MARK	**Ho anche bisogno di un po' di pesce, un pacchetto di caramelle, una torta e due bottiglie di vino. Mi sa dire dove si trovano la pescheria, la confetteria, la pasticceria e l'enoteca?**	I also need a bit of fish, a package of candy, a cake and two bottles of wine. Can you tell me where to find a fish shop, a candy shop, a pastry shop and a wine shop?
VIGILE	**Basta, basta, signore! Lei fa troppe domande!**	Enough, enough, sir! You ask too many questions!
MARK	**Mamma mia! Che vigile impaziente!**	Heavens! (*literally*, my mom) What an impatient policeman!
MARY	*(rah-JOH-neh)* **No, Mark, il vigile ha ragione. Tu fai troppe domande.**	No, Mark, the policeman is right. You ask too many questions.

Read the dialogue aloud until you are familiar with the new vocabulary. Then check off each statement as either true or false.

1. Mark fa delle domande a una donna. ☐ Vero ☐ Falso

2. Mark non ha bisogno di pane. ☐ Vero ☐ Falso

3. La carne si compra dal macellaio. ☐ Vero ☐ Falso

4. Il latte si compra alla latteria. ☐ Vero ☐ Falso

5. La verdura si compra in una gelateria. ☐ Vero ☐ Falso

6. Il pesce si compra in una pescheria. ☐ Vero ☐ Falso

7. Il vino si compra in una confetteria. ☐ Vero ☐ Falso

8. Il vigile risponde a tutte le domande. ☐ Vero ☐ Falso

One of the following answers to each question is not correct.

Odd one out

Alla latteria si compra:
    il latte
    il burro
    il vino   _____

Dal macellaio si compra:
    la torta
    la carne
    il pollo   _____

ANSWERS

True/False 1. Falso **2.** Falso **3.** Vero **4.** Vero **5.** Falso **6.** Vero **7.** Falso **8.** Falso
Odd one out il vino la torta

180

Dal fruttivendolo si compra:
        la verdura
        il gelato
        la frutta   _____

Alla gelateria si compra:
        il pesce
        il gelato
        i dolci   _____

All'enoteca si compra:
        il pane
        il vino rosso
        il vino bianco   _____

Alla pasticceria si compra:
        la torta
        le paste
        la carne   _____

If you want to make a complaint, here are some suggestions.

Questo pane non è *fresco*!   This bread is not fresh!

Questo panino è *raffermo*!   This roll is stale!

(MAHR-choh)
Questo pomodoro è *marcio*!   This tomato is rotten!

Questo vino è *cattivo*!   This wine is bad tasting!

Si compra, si mangia . . .
One Buys, One Eats . . .

You might have noticed that expressions such as "one buys," and "one eats" are said in Italian by using *si* and the verb. However, be careful! The verb agrees with *what* one buys or eats.

Si compra il vino **all'enoteca.**
One buys wine at the wine shop.

Si comprano le caramelle **alla confetteria.**
One buys candy at the candy shop.

Si mangia la pizza **a Napoli.**
One eats pizza in Naples.

Si mangiano gli spaghetti **in tutta l'Italia.**
One eats spaghetti throughout Italy.

When you need to compare things, use *più* before the adjective to mean "more." To say "the most," simply use the appropriate definite article before *più*.

Mario è intelligente.   Mario is intelligent.
Gino è *più* intelligente.   Gino is more intelligent.
Pino è *il più* intelligente.   Pino is the most intelligent.

Maria è alta.   Mary is tall.
Gina è *più* alta.   Gina is taller.
Lina è *la più* alta.   Lina is the tallest.

181

UNITÀ DI PESO E DI MISURA

Weights and Measures

(peh-ZAH-reh)
pesare
to weigh

(PEH-zoh)
il peso
weight

As we said before, the metric system is used throughout Italy. Here is a chart that gives some metric terms.

(mee-LLEE-meh-troh) **millimetro (mm)**	millimeter	= .039 inch
(chehn-TEE-meh-troh) **centimetro (cm)**	centimeter	= .39 inch
(MEH-troh) **metro (m)**	meter	= 3.28 feet
(kee-LOH-meh-troh) **chilometro (km)**	kilometer	= .62 mile
(chehn-TEE-lee-troh) **centilitro (cl)**	centiliter	= .338 fluid ounce
(LEE-troh) **litro (l)**	liter	= .26 gallon
(mee-llee-GRAH-mmoh) **milligrammo (mg)**	milligram	= .015 grain
(chehn-tee-GRAH-mmoh) **centigrammo (cg)**	centigram	= .154 grain
(GRAH-mmoh) **grammo (g)**	gram	= 15.43 grains
(eh-ttoh-GRAH-mmoh) **ettogrammo (hg)**	hectogram	= 3.52 ounces
(kee-loh-GRAH-mmoh) **chilogrammo (kg)**	kilogram	= 2.2 pounds

(boh-TTEH-gah)
ALLA BOTTEGA DI GENERI ALIMENTARI

At the Grocery Store

These questions are so easy that we haven't given you the answers! If you can't figure out the new words from the pictures, check the glossary.

(sah-poh-NEH-ttah)
Vorrei una saponetta.

Quanto costa _____?

(bah-RAH-ttoh-loh)   *(soh-LOO-bee-leh)*
Vorrei un barattolo di caffè solubile.

Quanto costa _____?

Vorrei un rotolo di carta igienica.

Quanto costa _____?

(MEH-tsoh)   (chee-LYEH-jeh)
Vorrei mezzo chilo di ciliege.

Quanto costa _____?

Vorrei un litro di latte.

Quanto costa _____?

(doh DZEE-nah)
Vorrei mezza dozzina di limoni.

Quanto costa _____?

Vorrei un barattolo di verdura.

Quanto costa _____?

Vorrei un pacchetto di zucchero.

Quanto costa _____?

Vorrei una dozzina di uova.

Quanto costa _____

(SKAH-toh-lah) (bees-KOH-ttee)
Vorrei una scatola di   biscotti.

Quanto costa _____?

Notice that in Italian the article "the" must be used, especially at the beginning of a sentence, to express generalities.

Gli italiani mangiano gli spaghetti.
Italians eat spaghetti.

Lo zucchero costa molto.
Sugar costs a lot.

L'italiano è una bella lingua.
Italian is a beautiful language.

Il pane costa molto poco.
Bread costs very little.

This passage contains more information about shopping in Italy. Read it and then select the appropriate answer to each question.

In Italia la spesa si fa, in genere, ogni giorno.
      (JEH-neh-reh)
    food shopping   generally

(soo-pehr-mehr-KAH-tee)

Ma come negli Stati Uniti, oggi ci sono anche i supermercati, dove si può comprare il cibo
                    supermarkets

(soor-jeh-LAH-toh)   *(MEH-toh-doh)*   *(poh-poh-LAH-reh)*   *(mehr-KAH-toh)*

surgelato. Ma il metodo più popolare di fare la spesa è al mercato. Lì si compra sempre
frozen   method   popular   open-air market

"a buon mercato." Il cibo è fresco e buono.
    cheaply   food

Quando si fa, in genere, la spesa in Italia?
- ☐ Il sabato.
- ☐ Il venerdì.
- ☐ Ogni giorno.

Oggi ci sono anche . . .
- ☐ i supermercati.
- ☐ i negozi.
- ☐ le ciliege.

Che cosa si può comprare a un supermercato?
- ☐ Le scarpe.
- ☐ Il cibo surgelato.
- ☐ I cappotti.

Qual è il metodo più popolare di fare la spesa?
- ☐ Al supermercato.
- ☐ Alla bottega di generi alimentari.
- ☐ Al mercato.

Can you unscramble the letters to form the following words?

mrcteao _____
    open-air market

isbttooc _____
    biscuit/cookie

alotsca _____
    box

nzizaod _____
    dozen

cliiegai _____
    cherry

brttlaaoo _____
    jar/can

ettonapas _____
    soap bar

ANSWERS

Comprehension Ogni giorno. i supermercati. Il cibo curgelato. Al mercato.
Unscrambling mercato biscotto scatola dozzina ciliegia barattolo saponetta

184

Here are some items you might find in an Italian drugstore. Say them aloud as you find them in the showcase.

(dehn-tee-FREE-choh)
il dentifricio
toothpaste

(SPAH-tsoh-lah)
la spazzola
hairbrush

(spah-tsoh-LEE-noh)
lo spazzolino da denti
toothbrush

(speh-KKYEH-ttoh)
lo specchio / lo specchietto
mirror

una scatola di fazzoletti di carta
box of tissues

(PEH-ttee-neh)
il pettine
comb

(roh-SSEH-ttoh)
il rossetto
lipstick / rouge

(LAH-kkah)
la lacca per capelli
hairspray

(KREH-mah) (beh-LLEH-tsuh)
la crema (di bellezza)
facial cream

(SPEE-lleh) (see-koo-REH-tsah)
le spille di sicurezza
safety pins

(ZMAHL-toh) (OON-gyeh)
lo smalto per le unghie
nail polish

185

IN FARMACIA
At the Drugstore

(Mary Smith and Lina Rossi—an Italian friend—are at a drugstore.)

LINA	**Che cosa vuoi comprare, Mary?**	What do you want to buy, Mary?
MARY	**Non sono sicura.**	I'm not sure.
COMMESSO	**Desidera, signora?**	Can I help you, madam?
MARY	**Quanto costa la crema?**	How much does cold cream cost?
COMMESSO	**Ventimila lire.**	20.000 lira.
MARY	**E quel pettiné e quella spazzola?**	And that comb and that hairbrush?
COMMESSO	**Il pettine duemila e la spazzola cinquemila.**	The comb 2.000 and the hairbrush 5.000.
LINA	**Non c'è male, Mary.**	That's not bad, Mary.
MARY	**No, grazie.**	No, thanks.
COMMESSO	**Forse ha bisogno di uno spazzolino da denti e del dentifricio?**	Maybe you need a toothbrush and some toothpaste?
MARY	**No. Vorrei lo smalto per le unghie, il rossetto, il mascara, e la lacca per capelli.**	No. I would like nail polish, lipstick, mascara, and hairspray.
LINA	*(TROO-kkoh)* **Ah, ti vuoi mettere il trucco?**	Ah, you want to put on makeup?
MARY	**Sì, questa sera voglio uscire.**	Yes, tonight I want to go out.

After you have read the dialogue several times, check off each statement as either true or false.

1. Mary è sicura di quello che vuole comprare.
   - [ ] Vero
   - [ ] Falso

2. La crema costa ventimila lire.
   - [ ] Vero
   - [ ] Falso

3. Il pettine costa duemila lire.
   - [ ] Vero
   - [ ] Falso

4. La spazzola costa cinquemila lire.
   - [ ] Vero
   - [ ] Falso

5. Mary ha bisogno di uno spazzolino da denti.
   - [ ] Vero
   - [ ] Falso

6. Mary compra lo smalto per le unghie, il rossetto, il mascara, e la lacca per i capelli.
   - [ ] Vero
   - [ ] Falso

Some essential phrases:

Vorrei comprare . . .	*I would like* to buy . . .
Devo comprare . . .	*I have to* buy . . .
È necessario comprare . . .	*It is necessary* to buy . . .

Che, cui
That, Which, Who, Whom

The relative pronoun *che* translates as "that," "which," and "who" when used in sentences like the following.

Il libro che è rosso è interessante.

The book, which is red, is interesting.

La crema che voglio costa troppo.

The cream that I want costs too much.

Il ragazzo che mangia la pizza è mio fratello.

The boy who is eating pizza is my brother.

After a preposition, *cui* is used instead.

Ecco la borsa in cui metto il rossetto.

Here is the purse in which I put

the lipstick.

Questo è il ragazzo a cui parlo italiano.

This is the boy to whom I speak italian.

Now you choose either *che* or *cui*.

Maria compra la spazzola _____ costa
cinquemila lire.

Lina vuole il rossetto _____ costa molto.

L'uomo di _____ parlo è mio marito.

Maria dice _____ la sua amica
viene domani.

La donna per _____ compro la crema
è mia moglie.

Sapere, conoscere
To Know

These verbs may give you some trouble, so study them well.

	(sah-PEH-reh) SAPERE	*(koh-NOH-sheh-reh)* CONOSCERE		*(sah-PEH-reh)* SAPERE	*(koh-NOH-sheh-reh)* CONOSCERE
io	so	*(koh-NOHS-koh)* conosco	noi	*(sah-PPYAH-moh)* sappiamo	*(koh-noh-SHAH-moh)* conosciamo
tu	sai	*(koh-NOH-shee)* conosci	voi	*(sah-PEH-teh)* sapete	*(koh-noh-SHEH-teh)* conoscete
lui lei	sa	*(koh-NOH-sheh)* conosce	loro	*(SAH-nnoh)* sanno	*(koh-NOH-skoh-noh)* conoscono

What's the difference between these two verbs? Use *conoscere* when you want to say that you know or are acquainted with "someone"; use *sapere* when you want to say you know "something" or "how to do" something. Although there is some overlapping in use, this distinction is all you will need to know for your communicative purposes.

Now choose *sapere* or *conoscere* as the case may be.

Io non _____il signor Smith.

Gina _____parlare italiano molto bene.

Quell'uomo _____ lo zio di Carlo.

Noi _____ che lui arriva domani.

Tu _____ mia moglie?

188

I signori Smith non _____ parlare italiano molto bene.

Il signor Smith non mi _____ .

(Mark Smith and his son enter a drugstore.)

MARK   **Scusi, signore, lei ha**
    (see-gah-REH-tteh) *(ah-chen-DEE-noh)*
sigarette e un   accendino?

Excuse me, sir, do you have

cigarettes and a lighter?

COMNESSO   **No, lei deve andare da un**
    (tah-bah-KKAH-yoh)
tabaccaio.

No. You have to go to a tobacco shop.

MARK   **Allora mi dia uno spruzzatore**
    (deh-oh-doh-RAHN-teh)(rah-ZOH-yoh)
di deodorante e un rasoio con le
  (lah-MEH-tteh)   *(eh-LEH-ttree-koh)*
lamette. Il mio rasoio elettrico non

funziona in questo paese!

Then give me a can of deodorant and a razor

with blades. My electric razor

doesn't work in

this country!

COMMESSO   **Perché ha bisogno di un**
    (kohn-vehr-tee-TOH-reh)
convertitore.

Because you need

a converter.

             (kohm-plee-kah-TSYOH-nee)
MARK   **Quante complicazioni!**

So many complications!

COMMESSO   **Senta, signore. Ho la**
    (soh-loo-TSYOH-neh)   *(KREH-sheh-reh)*
soluzione. Si faccia crescere la barba

come me.

Listen, sir. I have the solution. Let your beard

grow like me.

(Mary and Anne now enter.)

MARY   **Ciao, Mark. Cosa fai?**

Hi, Mark. What are you doing?

MARK   **Compro delle cose.**

I am buying some things.

             (ahs-pee-REE-neh)
MARY   **Anch'io ho bisogno di aspirine,**
  (BEHN deh) *(tehr-MOH-meh-troh)*
bende e un termometro.

I too need aspirins, Band-Aids,

and a thermometer.

MARK   **Ti senti male?**

Do you feel sick?

MARY   **Mi fa male un po' la testa, e**   My head hurts a bit, and we need Band-Aids for

(TEHS-tah)

  abbiamo bisogno di bende per il nostro   our trip.

  viaggio.

COMMESSO   **Vuole anche delle spille di**   Do you want safety pins, a bit of talcum powder,

(TAHL-koh)

  sicurezza, un po' di talco e dei   and some diapers?

(pah-nnoh-LEE-nee)

  pannolini?

MARY   **Dei pannolini? Non ho bambini piccoli!**   Some diapers? I do not have small children!

When you are familiar with the dialogue, try to reconstruct it below.

Il / non / in / questo / mio / paese / funziona / rasoio

_____

convertitore / un / di / bisogno / Perché / ha

_____

me / come / crescere / barba / la / Si / faccia

_____

Anch'io / termometro / un / e / bende / bisogno / ho / di / aspirine

_____

spille / delle / sicurezza / di / anche / Vuole / talco / di / po' / un / e / pannolini / dei

_____

lamette / le / con / un / e / rasoio / mi / Allora / dia / spruzzatore / uno / deodorante / di

_____

19 | La lavanderia / La lavanderia a secco
(lah-vahn-deh-REE-ah)

Laundry / Dry Cleaner

Laundromats can be found throughout Italy in the major hotels. In general, the service in Italy for laundry and dry cleaning is quite good. However, you should always plan to bring along some wash-and-wear clothes, just in case! And remember, during the weekend of or near August 15, everything closes down in Italy.

(lah-vah-TREE-cheh)
la lavatrice
washer

(ah-shoo-gah-TREE-cheh)
l'asciugatrice
dryer

ALLA LAVANDERIA AUTOMATICA
(ah-oo-toh-MAH-tee-kah)

At the Laundromat

(Anne Smith is at the hotel laundromat where she runs into her Italian friend Lina.)

ANNE **Ciao, Lina. Mi puoi aiutare? È la**
(VOHL-tah)
mia prima volta a una lavanderia italiana.

Hi, Lina. Can you help me? It's my first time at an Italian laundromat.

LINA **Certo. Hai il sapone in polvere,**
(sah-POH-neh) (POHL-veh-reh)
(CHES-tah) (FEH-rroh) (STEE-roh)
una cesta, un ferro da stiro, e
(moh-LLEH-tteh)
delle mollette?

Certainly. Do you have   soap powder, a wash basket, an iron, and clothespins?

ANNE **Sì. Ho tutto. Vedo che c'è un'**

asciugatrice e un tavolo da stiro.

Meno male.

Yes, I have everything. I see that there is a dryer and an ironing board.

Thank goodness.

191

	(MEH-tteh-reh) (jeh-TTOH-neh)	
LINA	**Ora, devi mettere un gettone**	Now, you have to put a token in the washer and
	nella lavatrice e dopo nell'asciugatrice.	then in the dryer. Here. I have two tokens
	Ecco. Io ho due gettoni per te.	for you.
	(feh-SSOO-rah) (EH-kkoh-lah)	
ANNE	**Dov'è la fessura? Ah, eccola!**	Where is the slot? Ah, here it is!

(The machine does not start.)

	(NYEHN-teh)	
ANNE	**Perché sembra che niente**	Why does nothing seem
	(foon-TSYOH-nah)	
	funziona?	to work?
LINA	**Perché tu non sai fare.**	Because you don't know how to do things.

(Lina gives the machine a kick and the machine starts.)

	(MOH-doh)	
LINA	**Questo è il modo di fare le cose**	This is the way to do things the Italian way!
	all'italiana!	

(The machine begins to overflow with suds.)

	(soo-CHEH-deh)	
ANNE	**Mamma mia, che cosa succede?**	Oh dear! What's happening?
	(preh-oh-kkoo-PAH-reh)	
LINA	**Non ti preoccupare. C'è troppo**	Don't worry, there is too much soap. Look,
	(PAH-nnee)	
	sapone. Guarda, i tuoi panni non sono	your clothes are no longer dirty.
	(SPOHR-kee)	
	più sporchi!	

Read the dialogue several times out loud and then fill in the missing parts from memory. Afterwards, check your answers.

Ciao, Lina. Mi p_____ a_____? È la mia prima

v_____ a una l_____ italiana.

Certo. Hai il s_____ in p_____, una

c_____, un f_____ da stiro, e delle

m_____?

Sì. Ho tutto. Vedo che c'è un'a_____ e un t_____ da

stiro. Meno male.

Ora, devi m_____ un g_____ nella

l_____ e dopo nell'a_____. Ecco. Io ho due gettoni per te.

Dov'è la f_____? Ah, eccola!

Perché s_____ niente f_____?

Perché tu non s_____ fare.

Questo è il m_____ di fare le cose all'italiana!

Ci, ne

There, Some of

Notice that *ci* means "there" and that *ne* means "some of." Like the pronouns you learned earlier, these occur right before the verb.

Mark va *in Italia* domani.	**Mark *ci* va domani.**
Mark is going to Italy tomorrow.	Mark is going *there* tomorrow.

Io metto il rossetto *nella borsa*.	**Io *ci* metto il rossetto.**
I put the lipstick in the purse.	I put the lipstick *there*.

Voglio *del pane*.	***Ne* voglio.**
I want some bread.	I want *some* (of it).

Mangio *degli spaghetti*.	***Ne* mangio.**
I am eating some spaghetti.	I am eating *some* (of them).

Got it? Now it's your turn; you choose *ci* or *ne*.

Anne mette il gettone *nella fessura*. Anne _____ mette il gettone.

Lina ha *delle mollette*. Lina _____ ha.   Anne ha *cinque gettoni*. Anne _____ ha cinque.

Lina mette il sapone *nella lavatrice*. Lina _____ mette il sapone.

Anne mette un gettone *nell'asciugatrice*. Anne _____ mette un gettone.

Lina ha bisogno *di un ferro da stiro*. Lina _____ ha bisogno.

Anne non ha bisogno *di un tavolo da stiro*. Anne non _____ ha bisogno.

(sehr-VEE-tsee)

SERVIZI DI LAVANDERIA ALL'ALBERGO

Hotel Laundry Services

Here are some common expressions you may use when you use the laundry services of the hotel where you are staying.

Avete un servizio di lavanderia?	Do you have a laundry service?
(PAH-nnee) **Devo far lavare dei panni.**	I have some clothes to be washed.
(koo-CHEE-reh) *(boh-TTOH-neh)* **Mi può cucire questo bottone?**	Can you sew on this button?
(rah-mmehn-DAH-reh) **Mi può rammendare la manica?**	Can you mend the sleeve?
(stee-RAH-reh) **Mi può stirare questa camicia?**	Can you iron this shirt?
(AH-mee-doh) **C'è troppo amido nelle mie mutande!**	There's too much starch in my undershorts!
Dov'è la lavanderia a secco?	Where is the dry cleaner?
Mi può portare questo vestito alla lavanderia?	Can you take this suit to the cleaners?
(TOH-llyeh-reh) *(MAH-kkyah)* **Può togliere questa macchia?**	Can you take out this spot?

You might want to look over the words and expressions you have learned in this unit before you try to unscramble the following.

lvaandriea _____ lvaandriea a cceso _____
      laundry   dry cleaner

lvaartiec _____ ecirtaguiasc _____
      washer   dryer

ANSWERS

Unscrambling lavanderia lavanderia a secco lavatrice asciugatrice

ci (mette il) ci (mette un) ne (ha bisogno) ne (ha bisogno.)

194

spaone in plovree _____ sceta _____ tolgieer _____
          soap powder   wash basket   to take out

rrfeo da stoir _____ lltteeom _____ mcchaia _____
          iron   clothespins   spot

mtteere _____ ttgeone _____ fsseuar _____
          to put   token   slot

pnnai __ _____ ccuier _____ bttnooe _____
          clothes   to sew   button

rmmaenared _____ arestir _____ miado _____
          to mend   to iron   starch

(lah-mehn-TEH-leh)

Lamentele

Complaints

(ree-CHEH-veh)   *(kohn-TROH-llah)*

Il signor Smith riceve i suoi panni dalla lavenderia dell'albergo. Quando li controlla, decide
                                                         checks

(lah-mehn-TAHR-see) *(dee-reh-TTOH-reh)*   *(BOO-koh)*

di andare a lamentarsi dal direttore.   Nella sua camicia c'è un buco e ci hanno messo
   to complain   manager   hole   they put

troppo amido. Tra i panni trova un reggiseno e mutandine da donna. Trova anche un
              Among

calzino rosso e uno verde.

Wouldn't you know that Mark would have these kinds of laundry problems? Answer the true-and-false after you have read the passage.

1. Il signor Smith non ha lamentele.   ☐ Vero   4. **Nella sua camicia c'è**   ☐ Vero
                                      ☐ Falso   **un buco.**   ☐ Falso

2. Il signor Smith riceve i suoi panni   ☐ Vero   5. Trova panni da donna.   ☐ Vero
   dalla lavanderia a secco.   ☐ Falso   ☐ Falso

3. **Il signor Smith si lamenta dal**   ☐ Vero   6. Trova due calzini gialli.   ☐ Vero
   direttore.   ☐ Falso   ☐ Falso

ANSWERS

True/False 1. Falso 2. Falso 3. Vero 4. Vero 5. Vero 6. Falso

sapone in polvere cesta togliere ferro da stiro mollette mettere gettone fessura panni cucire bottone rammendare stirare amido

195

DAL PARRUCCHIERE
At the Beauty Shop / Hairdresser

*(Mary and Anne decide to go
to a beauty shop.)*

PARRUCCHIERE   **Desiderano?**

Can I help you?

(SHAHM-poh)

MARY   **Per mia figlia, uno shampoo, un**

For my daughter, a shampoo,

(trah-ttah-MEHN-toh) (FAH-chah)

trattamento alla faccia,

a facial massage,

(mah-nee-KOO-reh)   (PYEH-gah)

una manicure, e una messa in piega.

a manicure,

and a (hair) set.

Io vorrei solo una

(pehr-mah-NEHN-teh)

permanente.

I would like only a permanent.

(kah-PEH-llee)

Attenzione ai miei capelli!

Be careful with my hair!

Hanno un bel colore!

It is a beautiful color!

PARRUCCHIERE   **Va bene. Prima**

Okay. First you have

(lah-VAH-reh)

bisogna lavare   i capelli

to have your hair washed

(SOH-ttoh)

e poi deve andare sotto

and then you have to go

(KAHS-koh)

il casco.

under the hair dryer.

(after they have been under the hair dryer for a while:)

PARRUCCHIERE **Venga, signora! I capelli sono**   Come, madam! Your hair is dry.

   (ah-SHOO-ttee)   *(spah-tsoh-LAH-reh)*
asciutti. Prima le devo spazzolare   First I have to brush your hair

i capelli e poi le faccio la permanente.   and then I'll give you a

              (SPAH-tsoh-lah)
Un momento che prendo una spazzola   permanent. Hold on a moment; I'm going to get

    (bee-goh-DEE-nee)
e alcuni bigodini.   a brush and some curlers.

(as the beautician is about to finish:)

PARRUCCHIERE **Signora, si guardi nello**   Madam, you can look at yourself in the mirror.

          (vch rah MEHN-teh)
specchio! Lei è veramente bella!   You are truly beautiful!

MARY   **Mamma mia! I miei capelli**   Good heavens!

    (BYOHN-dee)
sono biondi!   My hair is blonde!

When you have the dialogue down cold, match up the phrases in the left column with those in the right column. Then, check your answers.

Per mia figlia . . .	solo una permanente.
Io vorrei . . .	lavare i capelli e poi andare sotto il casco.
Attenzione . . .	sono biondi!
Hanno un bel . . .	guardi nello specchio!
Prima bisogna . . .	spazzolare i capelli e poi le faccio la permanente.
I capelli . . .	prendo una spazzola e alcuni bigodini.
Prima le devo . . .	ai miei capelli!
Un momento che . . .	sono asciutti.
Signora, si . . .	colore!
I miei capelli . . .	uno shampoo, un trattamento alla faccia, una manicure, e una messa in piega.

Here are some more useful expressions for you.

   (shah-KKWAH-reh)
Mi può sciacquare i capelli?   Can you give me a rinse?

   (tah-LLYAH-reh)
Mi può tagliare i capelli?   Can you give me a haircut?

Non voglio la lacca, per favore.

(frahn-JEH-ttah)
Mi fa la frangetta?

No hair spray, please.

Can you give me some bangs?

One last word about those pesky object pronouns! What happens when the two types, direct and indirect (remember?), are used together? Watch!

Giovanni *mi* dà *il libro*.
John gives the book to me.

Maria *ti* dà *la penna*.
Mary gives the pen to you.

Lui *ci* dà *i libri*.
He gives the books to us.

Giovanni *me lo* dà.

John gives *it to me*.

Maria *te la* dà.

Mary gives *it to you*.

Lui *ce li* dà.

He gives *them to us*.

Confused? Don't worry. You probably won't need to know how to use the two types together. However, someone may use them when speaking to you. Just be aware that they both come before the verb and that minor changes are made: *mi* becomes *me*; *ti* becomes *te*; and so on.

DAL BARBIERE
At the Barber

Il signor Smith decide di andare

dal barbiere per farsi
to have

tagliare i capelli e la barba.
his hair cut

Al signor Smith non piace farsi la barba da solo.
to shave himself

(LOON-gah) (bah-ZEH-tteh) (BAH-ffee)
Ha la barba lunga, le basette, e i baffi.
long   sideburns   moustache

Decide di farsi tagliare tutto!
to have everything cut

Il barbiere è un uomo simpatico.

(MEHN-treh)   *(BRAH-noh)*
Comincia a tagliare i capelli del signor Smith, mentre canta un brano d'opera.
while   excerpt

(veh-LOH-cheh) (FOHR-bee-chee) (mah-kkee-NEH-ttah) (rah-ZOH-yoh)

È molto veloce con le forbici e la macchinetta. Con il rasoio, comincia a
quick   scissors   clippers   straight razor

(PEHN-sah)

fare la barba al signor Smith. Ma il barbiere pensa solo a cantare. Taglia la barba

del signor Smith e gli taglia anche tutti i

(KAHL-voh)

capelli! Adesso il signor Smith è calvo!
bald

Il barbiere dice al signor Smith: «Non si

(peh-ttee-NAHR-see)

preoccupi! Lei non deve più pettinarsi!»
You do not have to comb yourself anymore!

Are these passages getting easier for you? If not, go over this one again, and look up the words you don't recognize. Then select the correct answer to each question.

Dove decide di andare il signor Smith?
- [ ] Dal parrucchiere.
- [ ] Dal barbiere.
- [ ] Dal fruttivendolo.

Perché va a farsi tagliare la barba?
- [ ] Perché è calvo.
- [ ] Perché è simpatico.
- [ ] **Perché non gli piace farsi la barba da solo.**

Ha i baffi?
- [ ] Sì.
- [ ] No.

Che cosa fa il barbiere al signor Smith?
- [ ] **Gli taglia tutti i capelli.**
- [ ] Lo pettina.
- [ ] Gli fa la permanente.

ANSWERS

Comprehension Dal barbiere. Perché non gli piace farsi la barba da solo. Sì. Gli taglia tutti i capelli.

199

Review the words and expressions introduced in this unit, and then give this crossword puzzle a try.

Across
2. Curlers
4. To comb oneself
6. Hair dryer
8. Hair

Down
1. Blond
2. Sideburns
3. Moustache
4. Permanent
5. Razor
7. Bald
9. To wash

21 | (KYOHS-koh) (kahr-toh-leh-REE-ah)
Il chiosco / La cartoleria
Kiosk / Stationery Store

AL CHIOSCO
At the Kiosk

Naturally by this time, you know what to do with this dialogue.

(While walking through Rome, Anne and John Smith stop at a kiosk.)

JOHN   **Scusi, lei vende i giornali in**   (VEHN-deh) (johr-NAH-lee)

lingua inglese?

Excuse me, do you sell English language newspapers?

PROPRIETARIO DI CHIOSCO   **No signore. Lei**   (ree-VEES-teh)
è turista? Ho delle riviste americane.

No, sir. Are you a tourist? I have some American magazines.

JOHN   **No, grazie. Però vorrei comprare**   (peh-ROH)
(kahr-toh-LEE-neh) (frahn-koh-BOH-llee)
delle cartoline e dei francobolli.

No, thank you. However, I would like to buy some postcards and stamps.

PROPRIETARIO DI CHIOSCO   **Ecco, signore.**

Here you are, sir.

ANNE   **Io vorrei comprare delle riviste**

per la mia amica in America e delle

guide turistiche.

I would like to buy some magazines for my friend in America and some tourist guides.

PROPRIETARIO DI CHIOSCO   **Ecco, signorina.**

Here you are, miss.

ANNE   **Grazie. Quanto le devo?**

Thank you. How much do I owe you?

JOHN *(looking through wallet)* **Lascia** *(LAH-shah)* Forget it, Anne.
(PEHR-deh-reh)
perdere, Anne.

ANNE **Perché?**   Why?

JOHN **Perché non abbiamo soldi!**   Because we do not have any money!

Now you do the dialogue. Don't forget to check your answers.

JOHN **Scusi,** _____**?**

PROPRIETARIO DI CHIOSCO **No signore. Lei è turista? Ho delle riviste americane.**

JOHN **No,** _____**.**

PROPRIETARIO DI CHIOSCO **Ecco, signore.**

ANNE **Io** _____**.**

PROPRIETARIO DI CHIOSCO **Ecco, signorina.**

ANNE **Grazie.** _____**?**

JOHN **Lascia perdere, Anne.**

ANNE **Perché?**

JOHN **Perché** _____**!**

You may have noticed that *molto* has several meanings. Here are some of them.

Marco mangia *molti* spaghetti.   **Gina ha *molti* amici.**   **La ragazza è *molto* bella.**

Mark eats *a lot of* spaghetti.   Gina has *many* friends.   The girl is *very* beautiful.

It is usually an adjective and therefore agrees with the noun it modifies. However, when it means "very," it is *not* an adjective and it is not followed by a noun, so it does not agree with the following word.

La ragazza ha *molti* amici.

many

La ragazza è *molto* bella.

very

202

ALLA CARTOLERIA

At the Stationery Store

You may have to visit a stationery store so you can write home. If so, you'll need to know these words.

(BEE-roh)
la biro
ballpoint pen

(mah-TEE-tah)
la matita
pencil

(LEH-tteh-reh)
la carta da lettere
stationery

(BOOS-tah)
la busta
envelope

(bloh-KKEH-ttoh)
il blocchetto
writing pad

(tah-KKWEE-noh)(ah-PPOON-tee)
il taccuino per appunti
notebook

(ah-deh-ZEE-voh)
il nastro adesivo
transparent tape

(SPAH-goh)
lo spago
string

Have you learned them well enough to recognize them all scrambled up? Try to straighten them out.

agpso ^(lo) _____   orib ^(la) _____   mttaia ^(la) _____

ntsroa ovisade ^(il) _____   btsua ^(la) _____

ccaniuto per ppanuit ^(il) _____   bolhcctteo ^(il) _____

tcraa da ttleeer ^(la) _____

You're doing so well that you should have no trouble with this passage and the questions that follow.

(EHN-trah-noh)

Due signore entrano in una cartoleria. La prima signora compra un blocchetto di carta, una
enter   paper

biro, una busta, e dei francobolli perché vuole scrivere una lettera. L'altra signora compra

un taccuino per appunti, il nastro adesivo e lo spago. La prima signora è una turista

americana, e l'altra è una turista francese. Le due signore fanno conoscenza e poi vanno al bar a prendere un espresso.

1. Chi entra in una cartoleria?
☐ Due donne francesi.
☐ Due donne americane.
☐ Una francese e un'americana.

2. Chi compra la biro?
☐ La donna francese.
☐ La donna americana.
☐ Nessuno.

3. Chi compra lo spago?
☐ La donna francese.
☐ La donna americana.
☐ Nessuno.

4. Chi compra la matita?
☐ La donna francese.
☐ La donna americana.
☐ Nessuno.

5. Dove vanno le due signore?
☐ Al cinema.
☐ Al chiosco.
☐ Al bar.

You deserve an easy one, now! After reviewing the new words and expressions in this unit, you'll see some of them in the word-search puzzle. Write them out as you find them.

_____   _____   _____
          kiosk   newspaper   magazine

_____   _____   _____
          stamp   ballpoint pen   pencil

a	a	a	a	a	a	c	h	i	o	s	c	o	b	b	b	b	b	b	b
b	b	b	b	b	b	b	b	b	b	b	b	b	b	b	r	d	d	d	d
i	c	v	g	i	o	r	n	a	l	e	c	c	c	y	i	y	y	y	y
r	p	p	p	p	p	p	p	p	p	p	p	p	p	p	v	j	j	j	j
o	t	u	v	b	n	m	m	m	m	m	m	m	m	m	i	m	m	m	m
r	r	r	r	r	r	r	r	r	r	r	r	r	r	s	a	e	r	t
b	b	b	m	a	t	i	t	a	a	a	a	a	a	t	a	a	a
f	r	a	n	c	o	b	o	l	l	o	x	x	x	a	u	u	u

22 | (joh-yeh-LLYEH-reh) (oh-roh-loh-JAH-yoh)
Il gioielliere / L'orologiaio
Jeweler / Watchmaker

IL GIOIELLIERE
The Jeweler

(brah-chah-LEH-ttoh)
il braccialetto
bracelet

(koh-LLAH-nah)
la collana
necklace

(SPEE-llah)
la spilla
brooch

(kah-TEH-nah)
la catena
chain

(ah-NEH-lloh)
l' anello
ring

(oh-reh-KKEE-noh)
l' orecchino
earrings

l'orecchino
(pehn-DEHN-teh)
pendente
pendant earrings

(As Mark and his wife are shopping at a jewelry store near the Ponte Vecchio in Florence, a tall, handsome man comes into the store.)

GIOIELLIERE **Desidera, signore?**	Can I help you, sir?
UOMO **Sì. Vorrei comprare qualcosa per mia moglie. Un braccialetto o un anello d'oro.**	Yes, I would like to buy something for my wife. A bracelet or a gold ring.

GIOIELLIERE **Ecco un braccialetto** *(ahr-JEHN-toh)* **d'argento e un anello d'oro.**	Here is a silver bracelet and a gold ring.
UOMO **Li prendo tutti e due.**	I'll take them both.
GIOIELLIERE **Vuole vedere qualcos'altro?**	Do you want to see something else?
UOMO **Sì. Una spilla degli orecchini.**	Yes. A brooch and earrings.
GIOIELLIERE **Pendenti?**	Pendants?
UOMO **Sì. E poi vorrei anche una collana** **e una catena.**	Yes. And then I would also like a necklace and a chain.
GIOIELLIERE **D'oro?**	Gold?
UOMO **Naturalmente.** *(takes out a gun)* **E adesso mi dia tutti i soldi che ha!**	Naturally. And now give me all the money you've got!

When you're sure you have mastered this dialogue, go ahead and reconstruct it—but be sure to check it when you're finished.

Desidera, signore?

Sì. Vorrei comprare q＿＿＿＿＿＿ per mia moglie. Un b＿＿＿＿＿＿ o un

anello d'＿＿＿＿＿＿ .

Ecco un braccialetto d'＿＿＿＿＿＿ e un a＿＿＿＿＿＿ d'oro.

Li p＿＿＿＿＿＿ tutti e due.

Vuole vedere qualcos'altro?

Sì. Una s＿＿＿＿＿＿ e degli o＿＿＿＿＿＿ .

P＿＿＿＿＿＿?

Sì. E poi vorrei anche una c＿＿＿＿＿＿ e una c＿＿＿＿＿＿ .

D'oro?

Naturalmente. E adesso mi dia tutti i s＿＿＿＿＿＿ che ha!

(zmeh-RAHL-doh)
lo smeraldo

(PYEH-treh) (preh-TSYOH-seh)
PIETRE PREZIOSE
Precious Stones

(roo-BEE-noh)
il rubino

(PLAH-tee-noh)
il platino

(toh-PAH-tsee-oh)
il topazio

(DZAH-ffee-roh)
lo zaffiro

(PEHR-luh)
la perla

l' argento
silver

The English and Italian are so similar that you should be able to identify these jewels.

Can you match each stone with its color?

1. lo smeraldo   a. bianco
2. il rubino   b. azzurro
3. il topazio   c. verde
4. lo zaffiro   d. rosso
5. la perla   e. giallo

(dyah-MAHN-teh)
il diamante

l' oro
gold

Gli Avverbi
Forming Adverbs

To form adverbs from adjectives, simply do the following. If the adjective ends in *-e*, just add *-mente*.

The only adjustment to be made occurs when the adjective ends in *-le* or *-re* preceded by a vowel. In this case, you drop the *-e*.

elegante	**elegante*mente***
elegant	elegant*ly*
intelligente	**intelligente*mente***
intelligent	intelligent*ly*

(proh-BAH-bee-leh)	
probab*ile*	**probabil*mente***
probable	probab*ly*
popol*are*	**popolar*mente***
popular	popular*ly*

If the adjective ends in *-o*, change the *-o* to *-a* and add *-mente*.

sicuro	**(sicura)**	**sicura*mente***	**lento**	**(lenta)**	**lenta*mente***
sure		sure*ly*	slow		slow*ly*

ANSWERS

Matching 1-c, 2-d, 3-e, 4-b, 5-a

L'OROLOGIAIO
The Watchmaker

(ZVEH-llyah)
la sveglia
alarm clock

(POHL-soh)
l' orologio da polso
wrist watch

l' orologiaio
watchmaker

(oh-roh-loh-jeh-REE-ah)
l' orologeria
watchmaker's shop

If you have to get your watch fixed, here are some useful expressions.

(ah-jjoos-TAH-reh)
Mi può aggiustare il mio orologio?   Can you fix my watch?

(ah-VAHN-tee)
Il mio orologio va avanti.   My watch is fast.

(een-DYEH-troh)
Il mio orologio va indietro.   My watch is slow.

Il mio orologio non va.   My watch has stopped.

(kah-ree-KAH-reh)
Devo caricare il mio orologio.   I have to wind my watch.

Here we go with another passage; test yourself by completing the statements.

Il mio orologio non va bene. Un giorno va avanti e un altro va indietro. Oggi non va e non lo posso caricare. Allora lo porto dall'orologiaio e l'orologiaio lo aggiusta. Il giorno dopo l'orologio va ancora avanti! Forse devo comprare un orologio nuovo.

L'uomo dice che il suo orologio non _____ .

Un giorno l'orologio va _____ e un altro va _____ ,

Oggi non va e l'uomo non lo può _____ .

Allora l'uomo porta l'orologio dall' _____

  e l'orologiaio lo _____ .

Ma il giorno dopo l'orologio va _____ !

L'uomo dice che deve comprare un orologio _____ .

Now, for a brief summary of several important things. How do you say the following things in Italian?

May I help you? _____

I would like to buy something. _____

My watch is fast. _____

Your watch is slow. _____

I have to buy a new watch. _____

23 Il negozio di articoli da regalo / *(ahr-TEE-koh-lee)* *(reh-GAH-loh)* Il negozio di musica / *(MOO-zee-kah)* Il negozio di fotografie *(foh-toh-grah-FEE-eh)*

Gift Shop / Music Store / Photography Shop

AL NEGOZIO DI ARTICOLI DA REGALO

At the Gift Shop

You certainly won't want to go home without some Italian presents! Here is what to look for.

(sehr-VEE-tsee-oh)
il servizio da tè
tea service

(PEH-lleh)
la pelle
leather

(reh-GAH-loh)
il regalo
present

(BOHR-sah)
la borsa
purse

(ah-NEH-lloh)
l'anello
ring

(bohr-SEH-ttah)
la borsetta
small purse

(KYAH-veh)
la chiave
key

(proh-FOO-moh)
il profumo
perfume

(pohr-tah-FOH-llyoh)
il portafoglio
wallet

(SHAHR-pah)
la sciarpa
scarf

(CHOHN-doh-loh)
il ciondolo
charm

(ree-cheh-VOO-tah)
la ricevuta
receipt

(KWAH-droh)
il quadro
painting

210

Are you ready for the dialogue? Follow it up with the true-false questions.

(Mary Smith and her son John go into a gift shop.)

COMMESSA **Desiderano?** — Can I help you?

MARY **Sì. Vorrei portare dei regali ai miei amici in America. Mi può aiutare?** — Yes. I would like to bring my friends in America some gifts. Can you help me?

COMMESSA **Volentieri. Forse un po' di profumo, una borsetta, o una sciarpa?** — Gladly. Maybe some perfume, a small purse, or a scarf?

MARY **No. Voglio qualcosa per uomo.** — No. I want something for men.

JOHN **Sì. Abbiamo molti zii in America.** — Yes. We have many uncles in America.

COMMESSA **Allora un portafoglio o un quadro?** — Then a wallet or a painting?

JOHN **No. Costano troppo.** — No. They cost too much.

COMMESSA **Lei può portare un regalo gratis ai suoi zii.** — You can bring a free gift to your uncles.

JOHN **Ah, sì? Che?** — Yes? What?

COMMESSA **I miei saluti!** — My greetings!

1. Mary vuole comprare dei regali per i suoi amici. ☐ Vero ☐ Falso

2. Mary compra il profumo. ☐ Vero ☐ Falso

3. Mary vuole una sciarpa. ☐ Vero ☐ Falso

4. Mary vuole qualcosa per uomo. ☐ Vero ☐ Falso

5. Il portafoglio e il quadro costano poco. ☐ Vero ☐ Falso

6. Il commesso dà un regalo gratis a John. ☐ Vero ☐ Falso

ANSWERS

True/False 1. Vero 2. Falso 3. Falso 4. Vero 5. Falso 6. Falso

211

AL NEGOZIO
DI MUSICA
At the Music Store

We haven't given you all the translations for this new vocabulary, but you should be able to figure them out.

(RAH-dee-oh)
la radio

(reh-jees-trah-TOH-reh)
il registratore
tape recorder

(teh-leh-vee-ZOH-reh)
il televisore

(moo-zee-kah-SSEH-ttah)
la musicassetta

(náhs-troh) (mah-nyéh-tee-koh)
il nastro   magnetico
tape

il compact disc

Did you get them all? Then go ahead with the following paragraph.

(KLAH-ssee-kah)
Il signor Smith ama la musica classica.
loves
Cerca un negozio di musica in tutta la città.

Finalmente ne trova uno. Ascolta i dischi
Finally
per tre ore! Suo figlio, invece, ama solo la

musica «folk». Anche il figlio entra nel negozio.

212

(kee-TAH-rrah)
Lui compra una chitarra e si mette a cantare.

(eem-bah-rah-TSAH-toh)   starts to
Imbarazzato, il signor Smith torna all'albergo.
Embarrassed

Now you can probably rearrange these sentences without even looking back.

classica / ama / Smith / Il / la / signor / musica

_____

tutta / in / città / la / Cerca / negozio / musica / di / un

_____

trova / Finalmente / uno / ne

_____

figlio / Suo / ama / solo / invece / folk / musica / la

_____

chitarra / Lui / una / compra / cantare / a / mette / e / si

_____

IL NEGOZIO DI FOTOGRAFIE
At the Photography Shop

Once again we have left out some translations—but you will recognize the words from the pictures.

(FOH-toh)
la foto

(een-grahn-dee-MEHN-toh)
l'ingrandimento

il negozio di fotografie

(dee-ah-poh-zee-TEE-veh)
le diapositive
slides

la pila
battery

(foh-toh-GRAH-fee-kah)
la macchina fotografica

(peh-LLEE-koh-lah)
la pellicola
film

(Mark is picking up the photos he had brought in to be developed.)

MARK	**Sono pronte le mie foto?**	Are my prints ready?
	(EH-kkoh-leh)	
COMMESSO	**Sì, eccole.**	Yes, here they are.
MARK	**Mamma mia, come sono brutto!**	Heavens, how ugly I am!
COMMESSO	**No, signore. Lei ha torto.**	No, sir. You are wrong.
MARK	**Lei è molto gentile. Senta, la mia macchina fotografica non funziona. La può aggiustare?**	You're very kind. Listen, my camera doesn't work. Can you fix it?

COMMESSO	**Certo.**	Certainly.
MARK	**Ecco un'altra pellicola. Questa volta voglio le diapositive.**	Here is another roll of film. This time I want slides.
COMMESSO	**Va bene, signore. Grazie e arrivederla.**	Okay, sir. Thank you and good-bye.
MARK	**Arrivederla.**	Good-bye.

Be sure you thoroughly understand the dialogue before going on to the completion exercise below (and check your answers!).

Sono pronte le mie f_____?

Sì, eccole.

Mamma mia, come sono b_____!

No, signore. Lei ha t_____.

Lei è molto g_____. S_____, la mia m_____

f____ _____ _____ non funziona. La può a_____?

Certo.

Ecco un'altra p_____. Questa volta voglio le d____ _____.

Va bene, signore. Grazie e arrivederla.

A_____.

Before you leave this chapter, go over the new vocabulary again; then practice it by unscrambling these words.

qdruao _____   grlcao _____
                painting   gift
dioar _____   chidisragi _____
              radio   record player
rgiestraerot _____   tlveeirose _____
                  tape recorder   television set
msuicassatte _____   dscoi _____
                      cassette   record
plleicoal _____
                film

ANSWERS

Unscrambling quadro regalo radio giradischi registratore televisore musicassetta disco pellicola

215

This dialogue contains words and expressions that you might find helpful if you break your glasses in Italy.

DALL'OPTOMETRISTA
At the Optometrist

OPTOMETRISTA	**Buon giorno, signore.**	Good morning, sir.
	(oh-KKYAH-lee)(ROH-ttee)	
MARK	**Ho gli occhiali rotti.**	My glasses are broken.
OPTOMETRISTA	**Mi faccia**	Let me see. Only one lens
	vedere. È rotta solo una	is broken.
	(LEHN-teh) (mohn-tah-TOO-rah)	
	lente. La montatura	The frame is intact.
	(een-TAH-ttah)	
	è intatta.	
MARK	**Il prezzo?**	The price?

216

OPTOMETRISTA **Cinquantamila lire.**		50.000 lira.
MARK **Cinquantamila lire!**		50.000 lira!
Per solo una lente?		For just one lens?
OPTOMETRISTA **Purtroppo!**		Unfortunately!/That's the way it is!
MARK **Li posso ritirare martedì?**		Can I get them Tuesday?
OPTOMETRISTA **No, ma venga giovedì.**		No, but come back Thursday.
MARK **Va bene. Grazie e arrivederla.**		OK. Thank you and good-bye.

Now here are some lines from the dialogue. Matching them won't be difficult.

Ho gli . . .	una lente?
È rotta solo . . .	venga gìovedì.
La montatura . . .	occhiali rotti.
Per solo . . .	ritirare martedì?
Li posso . . .	una lente.
No, ma . . .	è intatta.

DAL CALZOLAIO
At the Shoemaker

(kahl-tsoh-LAH-yoh)
il calzolaio
shoemaker

(STREEN-geh)
le stringhe
shoelaces

(SAHN-dah-loh)
il sandalo
sandal

le scarpe
shoes

See how quickly you can read this paragraph. Then go over it until it all comes easily, and answer the questions that follow.

(SAHN-dah-lee)

La signora Smith porta le sue scarpe e i suoi sandali dal calzolaio. I sandali hanno bisogno
shoes

(TAH-kkoh)   *(STREEN-geh)*

di un tacco nuovo e le scarpe hanno bisogno di stringhe. Va dal calzolaio in Via Veneto. È un
heel   shoelaces

uomo molto simpatico. La signora Smith gli chiede se può aggiustare le sue scarpe e i suoi

(sah-RAH-nnoh)

sandali. Il calzolaio dice che saranno pronti tra due giorni. Quando la signora Smith va a
they will be

(KYOO-zoh)   *(FEH-ree-eh)*

prendere le scarpe e i sandali vede un cartello sulla porta: "Chiuso per le ferie."
sign   Closed for the holidays.

Dove va la signora Smith?

☐ Dall'optometrista.
☐ Dal gioielliere.
☐ Dal calzolaio.

Di che cosa hanno bisogno i sandali?

☐ Di un colore nuovo.
☐ Di un tacco nuovo.
☐ Di niente.

Di che cosa hanno bisogno le scarpe?

☐ Di stringhe.
☐ Di un tacco nuovo.
☐ Di niente.

Dov'è il calzolaio?

☐ In Via Nazionale.
☐ In Via Veneto.
☐ A casa.

Quando saranno pronti i sandali e le scarpe?

☐ Domani.
☐ Tra una settimana.
☐ Tra due giorni.

Che cosa vede sulla porta la signora Smith?

☐ Vede un cartello.
☐ Vede una foto.
☐ Vede una lettera.

25	*(BAHN-keh)* ## Le banche Banks (Banking)

BIGLIETTI DENARO
Denominations

Notice that Italian denominations are high in comparison to American ones. In fact, a 1,000 lira note is worth less than *one* American dollar. There are also coins for 100, 200, and 500 lira. However, if your expected change is less than 100 lira you might get a token or even a piece of candy! These are probably worth more than the actual change you would otherwise get. You can get good exchange rates at most banks and hotels. And many stores give a good exchange rate as well.

(Courtesy of Ernst Klett Verlag, Stuttgart)

LE BANCHE, IL CAMBIO, E GLI
(KAHM-byoh)

ASSEGNI TURISTICI
(ah-SSEH-nyee)

Banks, Money Exchange, and Traveler's Checks

Gente e cose
People and Things

(deh-NAH-roh)
il denaro
money

l'assegno turistico
traveler's check

(kohn-TAHN-tee)
i contanti
cash

(PREHS-tee-toh)
il prestito
loan

la banca
bank

(eem-pyeh-GAH-toh)
l'impiegato di banca
bank employee

(dee -reh-TTOH-reh)
il direttore
manager

(kah-SSYEH-rah)
la cassiera (f)
(kah-SSYEH-reh)
il cassiere (m)
teller

(spohr-TEH-lloh)
lo sportello
teller's window

il conto
account

il biglietto di banca
bank note

(lee-BREH-ttoh)
il libretto di assegni
checkbook

(MOH-doo-loh) *(vehr-sah-MEHN-toh)*
il modulo di versamento
deposit slip

il modulo di
(preh-leh-vah-MEHN-toh)
prelevamento
withdrawal slip

Come si fa . . .

How to . . .

(kahm-BYAH-reh)
il cambio / cambiare
to exchange

(vah-LOO-tah)
la valuta
exchange rate

(pah-GAH-reh)
pagare
to pay

(vehr-SAH-reh)
versare /

(deh-poh-zee-TAH-reh)
depositare
to deposit

(preh-leh-VAH-reh)
prelevare
to withdraw

riscuotere un assegno
to cash a check

aprire un conto
to open an account

(feer-MAH-reh)
firmare
to sign

After all of that vocabulary, see how much of it you can remember. Match each word or expression to each picture by checking off the appropriate box.

☐ il denaro
☐ lo sportello

☐ il libretto di assegni
☐ i contanti

☐ il direttore
☐ il biglietto

☐ il cassiere
☐ il direttore

☐ il modulo di versamento
☐ il modulo di prelevamento

☐ i contanti
☐ l'assegno turistico

221

Did you get them all? Let's try some more:

1. Io vorrei _____ mille dollari americani.
   exchange

2. Io vorrei _____ cinquecentomila lire (500,000 lira).
   withdraw

3. Io vorrei _____ un assegno.
   cash

4. Io vorrei _____ 500,000 lire.
   deposit

(Mark Smith enters a bank; there are several people ahead of him.)

CASSIERE	**Desidera?**	May I help you?
UOMO	**Vorrei riscuotere un assegno.** *(kohm-PEE-lee)*	I want to cash a check.
CASSIERE	**Per favore compili questo modulo di prelevamento, lo firmi, e ritorni.**	Please fill out this withdrawal slip, sign it, and come back.
UN GIOVANE	*(PREHS-tee-toh)* **Vorrei un prestito.**	I would like to apply for a loan.

CASSIERE	**Per favore, attenda là il**	Please wait over there for the manager. He takes
	(OH-koo-pah)	
	direttore. Lui si occupa	care of loans.
	dei prestiti.	
DONNA	**È possibile aprire un conto e fare**	May I open an account and make a deposit?
	un versamento?	
CASSIERE	**Deve andare da un altro**	You must see another bank employee for that,
	impiegato, al prossimo sportello.	at the next teller's window.

(Finally Mark approaches the teller.)

MARK	**Buon giorno, signore. Ho bisogno**	Good day, sir. I need to exchange this $1,000
	di cambiare questo assegno turistico	American traveler's check for Italian lira.
	di mille dollari americani in lire	
	italiane.	
CASSIERE	**Molto bene. Vuole i soldi in**	Very well. Do you want the money in large or
	biglietti di taglio grosso o piccolo?	small bills?
MARK	**Grosso, per favore.**	Large, please.
CASSIERE	**Ecco, signore. Per favore firmi**	Here you are, sir. Please sign this receipt.
	(ree-cheh-VOO-tah)	
	questa ricevuta.	
MARK	**Grazie e arrivederla.**	Thank you and good-bye.

After you have become familiar with the dialogue, try to complete the following sentences from it.

Vorrei riscuotere un _____.

Vorrei un _____.

È possibile aprire _____ _____ e fare un _____?

Ho bisogno di _____ questo assegno _____ di _____

_____ americani in _____ _____. Per favore firmi questa _____.

If you got all that, then this paragraph and the questions that follow will be a breeze!

Il signor Smith entra in una banca con sua moglie. Chiede al cassiere di cambiare cento dollari americani. Il cassiere gli chiede di compliare un modulo e di firmarlo (sign it)**. Il signor Smith non lo vuole firmare e allora decide di non cambiare più i cento dollari.**

Chi entra in una banca?

☐ Il signor Smith e suo figlio.
☐ Il signor Smith e sua moglie.
☐ Il cassiere.

Che cosa chiede al cassiere?

☐ Gli chiede come sta.
☐ Gli chiede di versare un assegno.
☐ Gli chiede di cambiare dollari americani.

Quanti dollari vuole cambiare?

☐ Cento.
☐ Duecento.
☐ Trecento.

Che cosa gli chiede il cassiere?

☐ Di bere il caffè.
☐ Di prelevare i soldi.
☐ **Di firmare il modulo.**

Che cosa decide di fare il signor Smith?

☐ Di cambiare i soldi.
☐ Di non cambiare i soldi.
☐ Di chiamare il direttore.

This crossword puzzle is a final check on how much you have learned about money and banking.

Across
3. Exchange
4. Money
5. Checkbook
7. Teller (f.)
8. Account
9. Deposit

Down
1. Slip
2. Teller's window
3. Cash
4. Manager
6. Bank note

There are some new words in this dialogue. If you need help, check the vocabulary on the next page.

LINA **Che cosa fai?**
(JOH-koh) (pohs-TEE-noh)

PINO **Gioco a postino.**

What are you doing?

I'm playing postman.

LINA **E le lettere dove sono?**
(kah-SSEH-tteh)

PINO **Nelle cassette delle lettere delle**

case dei nostri vicini.
(PREH-zoh)

And where are the letters?

In our neighbors' mailboxes.

LINA **E dove hai preso le lettere?**
(bah-OO-leh)

PINO **Dal baule nella tua camera dove**
(TYEH-nee)
tieni quel pacchetto di lettere con un
(ah-TTOHR-noh)
bel nastro rosa attorno.

And where did you get the letters?

From the trunk in your room where

you keep that package of letters with

a beautiful pink ribbon around them.

LINA **Mamma mia! Sono le mie lettere**
(ah-MOH-reh)
d'amore!

Heavens! They are my love letters!

Are you sure you've got it? Then go ahead and fix up these sentences.

a / Gioco / postino

_____

E / dove / lettere / sono / le

_____

delle / cassette / lettere / Nelle / case / delle / dei / vicine / nostri

---

dove / E / hai preso / lettere / le

---

tieni / dove / Dal / camera / baule / tua / nella / pacchetto / quel / di / bel / lettere / un / con / attorno / nastro / rosa

---

d'amore / Sono / lettere / mie / le

---

la cassetta delle lettere
mailbox

il postino / il portalettere
mailman

(teh-leh-GRAH-mmah)
il telegramma
telegram

la posta / le lettere / le cartoline
mail   letters   cards

lo sportello
office window

il pacco / il pacchetto
package

You learned the last dialogue so quickly that we have another for you!

(John wants to mail a package to the U.S. Anne goes with him to the post office.)

JOHN   **È molto lontano l'ufficio postale?**   Is the post office very far?

ANNE   **No, è vicino all'albergo,**   No, it's near the hotel,

   ma c'è sempre tanta gente.   but there's always a lot of people.

   Gli italiani non sempre fanno   Italians don't always line up in
      (KOH-dah) (ohr-dee-NAH-tah)
   la coda   ordinata,   an orderly way, so let's hurry.
      (zbree-GYAH-moh-chee)
   allora sbrighiamoci!

(They reach the post office and find that it isn't busy.)

JOHN   **Meno male che non c'è nessuno.**   Thank heavens that no one is here.

ANNE   **John, ecco lo sportello per i pacchi.**   John, here is the parcel post window.
                       (mahn-DAH-reh)
JOHN   **Ecco signore. Voglio mandare**   Here you are, sir. I want to send this package to

   questo pacco negli Stati Uniti.   the U.S.

IMPIEGATA   *(weighs the package)*
    (ah-ffrahn-kah-TOO-rah)
   L'affrancatura per questo pacco è di   The postage for this package is 10,000 lira. Go to

   diecimila lire. Vada all'altro sportello   the other window for stamps.

   per i francobolli.

(John buys stamps and Anne goes to the postcard window.)

ANNE	**Quattro cartoline, per favore.**	Four postcards, please.
IMPIEGATA	**Ecco signorina.**	Here you are, miss.
ANNE	**Quanto è l'affrancatura per via**	What's the postage for airmail and for
	(ah-EH-reh-ah) *(rah-kkoh-mahn-DAH-tah)*	
	aerea e per posta raccomandata?	registered mail?
IMPIEGATA	**In tutto, ottomila lire.**	In all, 8,000 lira.

When you have read the dialogue several times, check off each statement as either true or false.

1. L'ufficio postale è molto lontano.
   ☐ Vero
   ☐ Falso

2. Gli italiani fanno sempre la coda ordinata.
   ☐ Vero
   ☐ Falso

3. Oggi non c'è tanta gente.
   ☐ Vero
   ☐ Falso

4. L'affrancatura per il pacco di John è di diecimila lire.
   ☐ Vero
   ☐ Falso

5. Anne compra tre cartoline.
   ☐ Vero
   ☐ Falso

6. L'affrancatura per Anne è di diecimila lire.
   ☐ Vero
   ☐ Falso

Ricordati ...
Remember ...

Here are a few useful expressions. Can you understand them?

(speh-DEE-reh)
mandare/spedire una lettera

depositare la valigia

229

spedire un telegramma

l'impiegata

You may have noticed that the adjective *buono* is used both before and after the noun. When it is used before the noun, you must make a few adjustments.

The form *buon* is used before a singular masculine noun beginning with any vowel or consonant, except *z* or *s* plus a consonant.

Buon giorno.
Buon appetito.

And in front of a feminine singular noun beginning with any vowel, the appropriate form is *buon'*.

Buon'amica.

Let's take a breather and do an easy one! Fill in the blanks as suggested by the pictures.

Maria scrive una _____ .

Giovanni spedisce dei _____ in Italia.

La signora ha bisogno di un _____ .

Gina mette le lettere nella _____ .

I verbi ancora una volta!

Verbs Again!

Notice that verbs ending in *-care* and *-gare* require an *h* when the verb ending starts with an *i*.

That's not so hard to remember, is it? Now let's wind up the post office chapter by adding the missing letters to the following words.

il post——no, la—— assetta delle l ——tter——, la post——, il t——l——gramma,

lo sportel——o, l'——ffrancatur——

Now, how do you say the following in Italian? This is a difficult exercise. So, even if you do not get the answers perfectly, you will learn considerably by trying.

I'm looking for the mailbox. Are you looking for it too, John?

_____

Who is paying for the coffee? Are you paying for it, Mary?

_____

We're looking for Dante Street. Do you know where it is, sir?

_____

They never pay for coffee at the (coffee) bar.

_____

27 | Il servizio telefonico

(sehr-VEE-tsee-oh) *(teh-leh-FOH-nee-koh)*

Telephone Service

PRONTO . . . PRONTO

Hello . . . Hello

(John has become friendly with Paola,
a girl he met at the bank last week.
He is in a phone booth and Anne
is outside.)

PAOLA	**Pronto. Chi parla?**	Hello. Who is it?
JOHN	**Ciao, Paola. Sono John.**	Hi, Paola. It's John. (*literally*, I am John)
PAOLA	**Dove sei?**	Where are you?

(kah-BEE-nah) (teh-leh-FOH-nee-kah)

JOHN	**In una cabina telefonica vicino a casa tua. Vuoi uscire con me stasera?**	At a phone booth near your home. Do you want to come out with me tonight?
PAOLA	**Dove?**	Where?
JOHN	**Al cinema.**	To the movies.
PAOLA	**No. Non mi piace il cinema.**	No. I don't like the movies.

(bah-LLAH-reh)

JOHN	**Allora andiamo a ballare?**	Then shall we go out dancing?
PAOLA	**No. Non so ballare.**	No. I don't know how to dance.
JOHN	**Andiamo a un ristorante?**	Shall we go to a restaurant?
PAOLA	**No. Sono a dieta.**	No. I'm on a diet.

ANNE	*(who has been waiting to use the phone)* **Ti dico io dove devi andare, John! A un'altra cabina!**	I'll tell you where to go, John! To another booth!

Are you sure you have completely mastered the dialogue? Maybe you should read it once more, before answering the true-false exercise.

1. John è in una cabina telefonica. ☐ Vero ☐ Falso

2. John chiede a Paola di andare al bar. ☐ Vero ☐ Falso

3. A Paola piace il cinema. ☐ Vero ☐ Falso

4. Paola non sa ballare. ☐ Vero ☐ Falso

5. Paola decide di andare al ristorante. ☐ Vero ☐ Falso

6. Anne ha molta pazienza. ☐ Vero ☐ Falso

(teh leh-foh-NAH-tah)

TELEFONATA LOCALE O INTERURBANA?

(een-tehr-oor-BAH-nah)

Local or Long Distance?

The telephone system of another country always seems to have its mysteries. Here are some words and expressions that you might need.

il telefono — telephone

(teh-leh-foh-NAH-reh)
telefonare — to phone

formare il numero — to dial

la cabina telefonica — phone booth

(chehn-trah-lee-NEES-tah)
il/la centralinista — operator

la carta telefonica — phone card

Pronto — Hello

la guida telefonica — phone book

la telefonata interurbana — long distance call

When you have learned them thoroughly, write the appropriate word or expression in the blanks.

In Italia, si può usare la ——————————————————————————— .

Quando si risponde al telefono si dice «———————————————————————» .

I numeri di telefono si trovano nella ——————————————————————— .

Una telefonata "long distance": ———————————————————————— .

In una ——————————————————————— si trova il telefono pubblico.

Prima di parlare al telefono, bisogna ———————————————————— .

Lina forma il numero del macellaio. Un uomo risponde. Lina dice all'uomo che vuole

comprare un pollo. Gli dice che è molto urgente la situazione perché stasera arrivano i suoi

(preh-pah-RAH-reh)
zii dall'America. Vuole preparare una bella cena. L'uomo ascolta con pazienza. Poi dice:
to prepare
(zbah-LLYAH-toh)   (fyoh-RAH-yoh)
«Scusi, signora, ma lei ha sbagliato numero, Io sono un fioraio.»

You're doing great! Now prove to yourself how much you've learned by filling in the blanks:

L'uomo ascolta con —————————— .

Lina dice che è —————————— —————————— la situazione ——————————

—————————— —————————— i suoi zii dall'America.

L'uomo risponde. Io sono un —————————— .

28 | **I dentisti, i dottori, gli ospedali**
(dehn-TEES-tee) *(doh-TTOH-ree)* *(ohs-peh-DAH-lee)*
Dentists, Doctors, Hospitals

UNA RAPIDA OCCHIATA
(RAH-pee-dah) *(oh-KKYAH-tah)*
A Once-Over

We're getting close to the end! But you really *should* learn the parts of the body. Mario and Gino are testing each other. Let's join in!

MARIO **Chi comincia, tu o io?** Who'll start, you or I?

GINO **Comincia prima tu.** You start.

MARIO **Bene. Che sono questi?** Good. What are these?

GINO *(kah-PEH-llee)* **I capelli.** The hair(s).

MARIO **E che c'è nel mezzo agli** And what's between the eyes?

occhi?

GINO **Il naso.** The nose.

MARIO **Tra il naso e la bocca** Between the nose and the mouth,

molti uomini hanno... many men wear...

GINO *(BAH-ffee)* **i baffi.** a moustache.

MARIO *(oh-REH-kkee)* **Abbiamo due orecchi...** We have two ears...

235

GINO *(GWAHN-cheh)*
e due guance,
and two cheeks,

MARIO *(FAH-chah)*
ma solo una faccia
but only one face

GINO **e una testa.**
and only one head.

MARIO **Quando si ride, si vedono…**
When one laughs, one sees…

GINO *(DEHN-tee)*
i denti
the teeth

MARIO **e quando si va dal medico…**
and when you go to the doctor,

GINO *(LEEN-gwah)*
gli si fa vedere la lingua, aah.
you…show him your tongue, aah.

MARIO **Questo è…**
This is…

GINO *(MEHN-toh)*
il mento
the chin

MARIO **e quello è…**
and that is…

GINO *(KOH-lloh)*
il collo.
the neck.

MARIO **Ecco due…**
Here are two

GINO *(SPAH-lleh)*
spalle
shoulders

MARIO **e due…**
and two…

GINO *(GOH-mee-tee)*
gomiti…
elbows…

MARIO **due…**
two…

GINO **mani**
hands

MARIO **e dieci...**

GINO **dita.**

and ten...

fingers.

MARIO **Ora tocca a te.**

GINO **Questa è...**

(SKYEH-nah)
MARIO **la schiena,**

Now it's your turn.

This is

the back,

GINO **e qui davanti...**

(PEH-ttoh)
MARIO **c'è il petto,**

and here in front...

is the chest,

GINO **e lì dietro c'è...**

(seh-DEH-reh)
MARIO **il sedere.**

and there in back is...

the fanny.

GINO **E da qui a qui ci sono due...**

(KOH-sheh)
MARIO **cosce**

GINO **con due...**

MARIO **ginocchia.**

And from here to here you have two...

thighs

with the two...

knees.

GINO **E più in giù ci sono i due...**

(pohl-PAH-chee)
MARIO **polpacci,**

And farther down the two...

calves,

(kah-VEE-lyeh)
GINO **due caviglie e...**

(PYEH-dee)
MARIO **i piedi**

two ankles, are

the feet

GINO **con dieci...**

MARIO **dita.**

with the ten...

toes.

Now try this difficult association exercise. Which part of the human body would you associate with the following?

l'anello _____, lo shampoo _____, il mascara _____,

la sigaretta _____, il profumo _____, gli occhiali _____,
(een-teh-llee-JEHN-tsah)
la radio _____, l'intelligenza _____, il dentifricio _____,

la collana _____, il guanto _____, la scarpa _____,

la camicia _____.

Ricordati
Remember

Remember that the verb *sentirsi* allows you to say that you are not feeling well.

You can also use *fare male a.*

Mi sento male.	I feel bad.

Mi fa male la testa.	My head hurts.

A list of common ailments might come in handy, just in case! Consider this a basic survival list.

(STOH-mah-koh)
Mi fa male lo stomaco.   My stomach hurts.

(GOH-lah)
Mi fa male la gola.   My throat hurts.

Mi fa male un dente.   My tooth hurts.

(rah-ffreh-DDOH-reh)
Ho il raffreddore.   I have a cold.

(FEH-bbreh)
Ho la febbre.   I have a temperature/fever.

(TOH-sseh)
Ho la tosse.   I have a cough.

(voh-mee-TAH-reh)
Mi viene da vomitare.   I feel like vomiting.

(SAHN-gweh)
Mi esce il sangue dal naso.   My nose is bleeding.

Now pretend you are at the doctor's. Write out the suggested parts. When you have finished composing your dialogue, read it out loud several times.

DOCTOR   **Buon giorno. Si sente male?**   Good day. Are you not feeling well?

YOU   _____ , **dottore.**   Good day, doctor. I feel bad.

       _____ **male.**

DOCTOR   **Che problema c'è?**   What's the problem?

YOU   _____   I have a cough. My throat hurts, and I have

      _____   a fever.

      _____

DOCTOR   **Forse ha il raffreddore. Ha altri**   Maybe you have a cold. Do you have any
      (SEEN-toh-mee)
      sintomi?   other symptoms?

YOU   _____   Yes. My stomach hurts. I feel like vomiting,

      _____   and my nose is bleeding.

      _____

DOCTOR   **Lei ha probabilmente**   You probably have the flu.
      (een-floo-EHN-tsah)
      l'influenza.

YOU   **Che cosa devo fare?**   What should I do?

DOCTOR   **Deve andare a letto e riposarsi.**   You have to go to bed and relax.

YOU   _____ ?   Really?
      (KOO-rah) (mee-LLYOH-reh)
DOCTOR   **Sì. È la cura   migliore.**   Yes. It's the best cure.

Splendid! We knew you could do it!

APRA LA BOCCA!

Open Wide!

You might, of course, need to go to a dentist. If so the following list may prove useful to you.

Mi fa male un dente.	My tooth hurts.
(kah-VAH-reh)	
Mi deve cavare un dente?	Do you have to take a tooth out?
(eem-pyohm-bah-TOO-rah)	
Ho bisogno di un'impiombatura?	Do I need a filling?
(dehn-TYEH-rah)	
Ho bisogno di una dentiera nuova.	I need new dentures.

You did so well with the last assignment—let's try another.

YOU _____.	Doctor, my tooth hurts.
DENTISTA **Non si preoccupi. Apra**	Don't worry. Open your mouth.
(kah-REE-eh)	
la bocca. Lei ha una carie.	You have a cavity.
YOU _____?	Do you have to take a tooth out?
DENTISTA **No. Non è male.**	No. It's not bad.
YOU _____?	Do I need a filling?
DENTISTA **Sì. Prima le faccio un'iniezione.**	Yes. First I'll give you a shot.
YOU _____.	No thanks, doctor. I'll come tomorrow.

DENTISTA **Lei ha paura delle iniezioni? Non si preoccupi. Signore/Signora, dove va?**	You're afraid of needles? Don't worry. Sir/Madam, where are you going?
YOU _____, **dottore.** _____ **volo** _____ **tra** _____!	Good day, doctor. My flight is leaving in two hours!

APRA LA BOCCA E FACCIA AAAAAAH . . .
Say Aaaaaah . . .

You probably won't need to use these terms, but see if you can translate them.

(MEH-dee-kah)
la tessera medica

(preh-SSYOH-neh)
la pressione
(sahn-GWEE-nyah)
sanguigna

(tehr-MOH-meh-troh)
il termometro

la sigla del
(MEH-dee-koh)
dottore/medico

(Mark Smith is not feeling well, so he goes to the doctor.)

MARK **Buon giorno, dottore. Mi sento molto male.**	Hello, doctor. I feel really bad.
DOTTORE **Dove le fa male?**	Where does it hurt?
MARK **In gola.**	In my throat.
DOTTORE **Apra la bocca e faccia aaaaaah.**	Open your mouth and say aaaaaah.
MARK **Che c'è di male, dottore?**	What's wrong, doctor?
DOTTORE *(tohn-SEE lleh)* **Lei ha le tonsille** *(een-fyah-MMAH-teh)* **infiammate.**	Your tonsils are inflamed.

(The doctor takes out his surgical instruments.)

MARK	**Che cosa fa, dottore?**		What are you doing, doctor?
	(TOH-lyehr-leh)		
DOTTORE	**Dobbiamo toglierle adesso.**		We should take them out now.
	È il metodo più sicuro.		It's the best way.
MARK	*(as he is running out of the office)*		
	Mamma mia, quel dottore è pazzo!		Heavens, that doctor is crazy!

Now wasn't that easy? You're nearly there!

1. Mark si sente molto bene. ☐ Vero ☐ Falso

4. Mark ha il raffreddore. ☐ Vero ☐ Falso

2. Gli fa male la gola. ☐ Vero ☐ Falso

5. Mark si fa togliere le tonsille. ☐ Vero ☐ Falso

3. Il dottore gli dice di aprire la bocca. ☐ Vero ☐ Falso

(proh-toh-KOH-lloh)   *(ohs-peh-DAH-leh)*

PROTOCOLLO D'OSPEDALE
Hospital Protocol

(proh-feh-SSOH-reh)

In Italy the head physician of a hospital is called: **il professore.**

(ah-ssees-TEHN-tee)

The other doctors are called: **gli assistenti.**

Then come the nurses (male and female):

(een-fehr-MYEH-reh)   *(een-fehr-MYEH-rah)*

l'infermiere (m) / **l'infermiera** (f).

Try this paragraph—bet you get it the first time!

(een-FAHR-toh) (kahr-DEE-ah-koh)   *(SOO-bee-toh)*

Al signor Dini prende un infarto   cardiaco. Sua moglie chiama subito
heart attack   right away

(ah-oo-toh-ahm-boo-LAHN-tsah)

un' autoambulanza. Per strada l'autoambulanza si ferma. Non ha più benzina!
ambulance   On the way   stops

(fohr-TOO-nah)

Per fortuna passa un'altra autoambulanza che porta il signor Dini all'ospedale.
Fortunately   comes by

ANSWERS
True/False 1. Falso 2. Vero 3. Vero 4. Falso 5. Falso

242

And now the questions:

Che cosa prende al signor Dini?
☐ Un infarto cardiaco.
☐ Il raffreddore.

Che cosa chiama subito
sua moglie?
☐ Un medico.
☐ Un'autoambulanza.

Che cosa fa l'autoambulanza
per strada?
☐ Va velocemente.
☐ Si ferma.

Perché si ferma?
☐ Perché non ha più benzina.
☐ Perché c'è troppo traffico.

Come arriva all'ospedale
il signor Dini?
☐ A piedi.
☐ Con un'altra autoambulanza.

Terrific!

(buhr-tseh-LLEH-ttah)
UNA BARZELLETTA
A Joke

(JOH-vah-neh)
Un giovane va dal dottore. Il giovane dice, «Dottore, vorrei . . .»
young man

(SPOH-llyee)
«Si spogli!» dice subito il dottore.
undress

«Ma dottore . . .» dice ancora il giovane.

«Si spogli!» insiste il dottore. Il giovane si spoglia.
insists

(eh-zah-mee-NAHR-loh)
Quando il dottore va per esaminarlo, il giovane ripete,
goes to examine him

(KYEH-dehr-leh)
«Dottore, io non mi sento male! Io sono qui per chiederle,
I am here to ask you

(ah-bboh-NAHR-see)
se vuole abbonarsi alla rivista *L'Espresso*!»
subscribe

243

Do you remember the parts of the body? See how many words and expressions you can match. Don't look back until you have finished—then review those you missed.

1. il piede	a. face
2. la gamba	b. hair
3. il dito	c. eyes
4. la mano	d. mouth
5. il braccio	e. foot
6. il collo	f. leg
7. la faccia	g. finger
8. la bocca	h. ears
9. gli occhi	i. neck
10. i capelli	j. arm
11. gli orecchi	k. hand
12. Mi fa male lo stomaco.	l. I feel like vomiting.
13. Mi fa male la gola.	m. My stomach hurts.
14. Ho la febbre.	n. My head hurts.
15. Ho la tosse.	o. My throat hurts.
16. Mi viene da vomitare.	p. I have a cough.
17. Mi fa male la testa.	q. I have a fever.
18. cavare un dente	r. nurse
19. l'impiombatura	s. to take out a tooth
20. la carie	t. needle
21. la puntura	u. thermometer
22. il termometro	v. head physician
23. il professore	w. cavity
24. l'infermiere	x. ambulance
25. l'autoambulanza	y. heart attack
26. l'infarto cardiaco	z. filling

UNA BARZELLETTA

A Joke

(ROH-ttoh)

GIUDICE **Allora, signora, ha rotto**

l'ombrello sulla testa di suo marito?

DONNA **Un errore!**

GIUDICE **Un errore?**

(voh-LEH-voh) *(ROHM-peh-reh)*

DONNA **Non volevo rompere**

l'ombrello!

So, madam, you broke your umbrella

over your husband's head?

It was an accident! (*literally*, an error)

An accident (error)?

I didn't want to break the umbrella!

SE HAI BISOGNO DI UN'AUTOAMBULANZA . . .

If You Need an Ambulance . . .

(Mark has fallen down the stairs.
In the foyer of the hotel, Mary seeks help.)

MARY **Signore, aiuto! Mio marito ha**

rotto una gamba. Che devo fare?

IMPIEGATO **È grave, signora?**

Help, sir! My husband has broken a leg.

What am I to do?

Is it serious, madam?

245

MARY **Sì, penso di sì. E a pensare che la nostra partenza per l'America è domani.**	Yes, I think so. And to think that tomorrow is our departure for America.
IMPIEGATO **Non si preoccupi. Chiami l'autoambulanza.**	Don't worry. Call the ambulance.
MARY **Come si fa?**	What does one do?
IMPIEGATO **Si chiama il centralinista e si chiede aiuto.**	You call the operator and ask for help.

(At this point, Mark walks into the room.)

MARY **Mark, che fai?**	Mark, what are you doing?
MARK *(to the clerk)* **Non è necessario telefonare all'autoambulanza. Non ho niente. Scherzavo. Ora so che mia moglie mi ama ancora!**	It is not necessary to call the ambulance. I'm okay. (*literally*, I have nothing.) I was joking. Now I know that my wife still loves me.

No cheating now—complete the missing parts from memory. Afterwards, check your answers in the dialogue.

Signore, a_____! Mio marito ha rotto una g_____.

Che d_____ fare?

È g_____, signora?

Sì, penso di sì. E a pensare che la nostra p _____ per l'America è domani.

Non si preoccupi. Chiami l'a _____ .

Come si fa?

Si chiama il c_____ e si chiede aiuto.

Mark, che fai?

Non è necessario t _____ all'autoambulanza. Non ho niente. Scherzavo.

Ora so che mia moglie mi ama a_____!

(poh-lee-TSEE-ah)
CHIAMA LA POLIZIA!
Call the Police!

One last dialogue—with a few questions following it.

(The Smiths are packing their bags.)

MARK	**Mary! Non trovo il mio portafoglio!**	Mary! I can't find my wallet!
MARY	**Forse è in una valigia.**	Maybe it's in a suitcase.
	(koo-SHEE-noh)	
MARK	**No, non è sotto il cuscino dove lo**	No, it is not under the pillow where I
	metto ogni sera. Chiama la polizia!	put it every night. Call the police!
MARY	**Come devo fare?**	What should I do?
	(teh-LEH-foh-nah)	
MARK	**Telefona al centralinista!**	Phone the operator!

(A policeman arrives.)

MARK	**Signore, qualcuno**	Sir, someone stole my wallet!
	(roo-BAH-toh)	
	ha rubato il mio portafoglio!	
POLIZIA	**Si calmi, signore!**	Calm down, sir!
MARK	**Io lo metto sempre sotto il cuscino!**	I always put it under the pillow!
	E adesso non c'è!	And now it's not there!
POLIZIA	**C'è in una valigia?**	Is it in a suitcase?
MARK	**No.**	No.
POLIZIA	**Nella borsa di sua moglie?**	In your wife's purse?
MARY	**No, non c'è.**	No, it's not there.
	(TAS-kah)	
POLIZIA	**Guardi nella sua tasca.**	Look in your pocket.
	(EH-kkoh-loh)	
MARK	**Ah, eccolo! Meno male!**	Ah, here it is! Thank heavens!

247

POLIZIA (to himself)	*(oo-GWAH-lee)* **I turisti sono tutti uguali!**	Tourists are all alike!
MARK	**Grazie e arrivederla.**	Good-bye and thank you.
POLIZIA	**Arrivederla.**	Good-bye.

(later at the airport)

| THE SMITHS | **Arrivederci, Italia, e grazie per una bella vacanza!** | Good-bye, Italy, and thanks for a great vacation! |

Chi non trova il portafoglio?
☐ Mary.
☐ Mark.
☐ Anne.

È in una valigia, il portafoglio?
☐ Sì.
☐ No.

Dove mette il portafoglio Mark ogni sera?
☐ Nella valigia.
☐ Nella borsa.
☐ Sotto il cuscino.

Per chiedere l'aiuto della polizia, chi si **può chiamare?**
☐ Il centralinista.
☐ **L'impiegato**
☐ Il direttore dell'albergo.

Dov'è il portafoglio?
☐ Sotto il cuscino.
☐ In una valigia.
☐ Nella tasca di Mark.

Aren't you pleased with yourself?

IN CASO DI UN INCIDENTE/UNA DISGRAZIA
(dees-GRAH-tsyah)

Handling an Accident

Here are some common accidents.

Aiuto! Ho ricevuto una scossa elettrica!
electrical charge

Fuoco!
fire

(tah-LLYAH-tah)
Ahi! Mi sono tagliata il dito!   **Attenzione ai bambini!**   **Ahi! C'è troppa acqua!**
cut

If you have an accident follow the normal procedures for any emergency situation. Take care of first-aid needs right away. Then call for the appropriate help. Always have a phone card with you in order to be able to use the public phones in Italy. You will find Italians extremely helpful in emergency situations. So ask for anybody's help and remember the key word:

AIUTO!
Help!

Here are the expressions you might need in an emergency:

Chiam ← **a** (familiar)
      ← **i** (polite)   **la polizia!**   Call the police!
      ← **ate** (plural)

Chiama/Chiami/Chiamate   **il soccorso medico!**   Call for medical help!

(FWOH-koh)
     Chiama/Chiami/Chiamate   **i vigili del fuoco!**   Call the fire department!

     Chiama/Chiami/Chiamate   **il medico!**   Call the doctor!

Chiama/Chiami/Chiamate   **l'autoambulanza!**   Call the ambulance!

BEFORE YOU LEAVE

Prima di partire

Now we come to the final step in the learning process, and the most important one. You might view it as a final exam. What will you do and say in the following situations? You may want to look over the sections of the book that correspond to each of the following seven situations, before you get started. Ready? Then let's go!

Situazione 1: Fare la conoscenza della gente

Situation 1: Getting to Know People

A. It is daytime and you meet someone.

What do you say in order to start a conversation?

1. ☐ Buon giorno.
2. ☐ Arrivederci.
3. ☐ Prego.

B. You have just run into a friend.

What do you say?

1. ☐ Grazie.
2. ☐ Ciao.
3. ☐ Buona sera.

C. It is evening. How do you greet a stranger?

1. ☐ Ciao.
2. ☐ Buon giorno.
3. ☐ Buona sera.

D. How do you say good-bye to a stranger?

1. ☐ Arrivederci.
2. ☐ Arrivederla.
3. ☐ Ciao.

E. How do you say good-bye to a friend?

1. ☐ Arrivederci/Ciao.
2. ☐ Arrivederla.

F. Someone asks you how you are. Which of the following is *not* possible as an answer?

1. ☐ Non c'è male, grazie.
2. ☐ Molto bene, grazie.
3. ☐ Buon giorno, grazie.

G. How would you ask a friend how he/she feels?

1. ☐ Come stai?
2. ☐ Come sta?
3. ☐ Dove vai?

H. How would you ask a stranger how he/she feels?

1. ☐ Come stai?
2. ☐ Come sta?
3. ☐ Dove vai?

I. Someone has just said "grazie." As a possible answer, you might say . . .

1. ☐ Bene.
2. ☐ Prego.
3. ☐ Arrivederci.

ANSWERS

Multiple choice **Situation 1:** A-1, B-2, C-3, D-2, E-1, F-3, G-1, H-2, I-2.

Situazione 2: L'arrivo

Situation 2: Arrival

You do not have a reservation at the hotel. What do you say?
1. ☐ Come sta, signore?
2. ☐ Scusi, signore, non ho la prenotazione.
3. ☐ Buon giorno, signore, come si chiama?

You want to say you really need a room. You might say . . .
1. ☐ Per favore, ho bisogno urgente di una camera.
2. ☐ Per favore, mi dia il passaporto.

You want to inquire about price and what is included. So you might say . . .
1. ☐ Mi può dire come si chiama, lei?
2. ☐ Mi può dire dov'è il bagno?
3. ☐ Mi può dire quanto costa la camera e quali sono i servizi?

Under ''Nome'' one might find:
1. ☐ Duecentomila lire al giorno.
2. ☐ Mark Smith.
3. ☐ Tre.

Under ''Indirizzo'' one might find:
1. ☐ Duecentomila lire al giorno.
2. ☐ Tre.
3. ☐ Via Washington, 25, Washington, D.C., U.S.A.

Under ''Numero di camera'' one might find:
1. ☐ Duecentomila lire al giorno.
2. ☐ Tre.
3. ☐ Via Verdi, 3, Roma.

Under ''Data'' one might find:
1. ☐ Duecentomila lire al giorno.
2. ☐ Via Verdi, 3, Roma.
3. ☐ (Il) 30 luglio.

Under ''Prezzo'' one might find:
1. ☐ Duecentomila lire al giorno.
2. ☐ Mark Smith.
3. ☐ (Il) 3 agosto.

Under ''Firma'' one might find:
1. ☐ Ventidue.
2. ☐ Mark Smith.
3. ☐ (Il) 5 agosto.

Situazione 3: I punti d'interesse

Situation 3: Seeing the Sights

You are on foot and want to find a certain street. You might ask a passerby:
1. ☐ Scusi, come sta?
2. ☐ Scusi, dove si trova Via . . .?
3. ☐ Scusi, lei abita in Via . . .?

The passerby might say:
1. ☐ **A sinistra, a destra, diritto . . .**
2. ☐ Domani, ieri, oggi . . .
3. ☐ Il semaforo, l'ufficio postale, la banca . . .

You have boarded a bus. You want to ask where to get off. You might say:
1. ☐ Scusi, quanto costa il biglietto?
2. ☐ Scusi, dove devo scendere per Via Verdi?
3. ☐ Scusi, come si chiama lei?

You have flagged down a taxi; but before getting in you want to know how much it would cost to get to Via Verdi. You might say:
1. ☐ Scusi, quanto è lontana Via Verdi?
2. ☐ Scusi, lei sa dov'è Via Verdi?
3. ☐ **Scusi, quanto è per andare fino a Via Verdi?**

You have forgotten your watch. You stop a passerby to ask what time it is. You might say:
1. ☐ Scusi, mi sa dire che ora è?
2. ☐ Scusi, ha un orologio?
3. ☐ Scusi, che tempo fa?

The passerby would *not* answer:
1. ☐ Sono le due e venticinque.
2. ☐ È domani.
3. ☐ È l'una e mezzo.

You are at a train station and want to buy a ticket. You might say:
1. ☐ **Scusi, quanto è un biglietto per Firenze?**
2. ☐ Scusi, dov'è Firenze?
3. ☐ Scusi, che ore sono?

The clerk answers that there is no room left on the train. He/She might say something like:
1. ☐ Mi dispiace, ma lei è pazzo.
2. ☐ Mi dispiace, ma lei non parla italiano.
3. ☐ **Mi dispiace, ma non ci sono più posti.**

You want to say that you are an American and that you speak only a little Italian. You might say:

1. ☐ Sono americano(a) e parlo solo un po' d'italiano.
2. ☐ Parlo americano e non sono italiano(a).
3. ☐ Non sono italiano(a); sono americano(a).

ANSWERS

Situation 3: 2, 1, 2, 3, 1, 2, 1, 3, 1

252

If someone were to ask what nationality you are, he/she would *not* say:
1. ☐ Lei è canadese?
2. ☐ Lei è intelligente?
3. ☐ Lei è americano(a)?

You want to rent a car cheaply. You might ask the clerk:
1. ☐ Vorrei noleggiare una macchina economica.
2. ☐ Vorrei noleggiare una macchina di lusso.
3. ☐ Vorrei noleggiare una macchina nuova.

You want to fill up your car. You might say to the attendant:
1. ☐ Per favore, pulisca il parabrezza.
2. ☐ Per favore, il pieno.
3. ☐ Per favore, controlli l'olio.

You have just been in a car accident and wish to ask how the other motorist is. You might say:
1. ☐ Buon giorno, come sta?
2. ☐ Come si sente?
3. ☐ Come si chiama?

A service station attendant might tell you that your car needs repairs. He would *not* say:
1. ☐ La sua macchina è bella
2. ☐ La sua macchina ha bisogno di freni nuovi.
3. ☐ La sua macchina ha bisogno di un motore nuovo.

You ask an employee at a camping site if there are certain services. You would *not* say:
1. ☐ C'è l'acqua?
2. ☐ Ci sono posti per far giocare i bambini?
3. ☐ C'è il cinema?

When asked how much the charges are, a clerk might respond:
1. ☐ Duecentomila lire.
2. ☐ Duecento soldi.
3. ☐ Duecento ore.

If someone were to ask you about the weather, you would *not* say:
1. ☐ Fa bel tempo.
2. ☐ Piove sempre.
3. ☐ Nevica.
4. ☐ È vicino.

As an answer to "Che giorno è oggi?" you would *not* hear:
1. ☐ È il quindici settembre.
2. ☐ È il secondo giorno.
3. ☐ È il tre maggio.

At the airport you might hear this over the loudspeaker.
1. ☐ Il volo numero 303 per New York è interessante.
2. ☐ Il volo numero 303 per New York non arriva.
3. ☐ Il volo numero 303 per New York parte alle sedici e venti.

ANSWERS

2, 1, 2, 2, 1, 3, 1, 4, 2, 3

253

To ask an airline employee at what time your flight leaves, you might say:

1. ☐ Scusi, a che ora parte il mio volo?
2. ☐ Scusi, quando arriva il mio volo?
3. ☐ Scusi, dov'è l'aeroporto?

Where would you find this sign?

1. ☐ All'aeroporto.
   (kah-poh-LEE-neh-ah)
2. ☐ Al capolinea.
   bus terminal
3. ☐ Alla stazione ferroviaria.

Where would you find this sign?

1. ☐ All'aeroporto.
2. ☐ Al capolinea.
3. ☐ Alla stazione ferroviaria.

Look at this plan of the city.

1. To which spot would you go to buy *aspirine*? _____

2. To which spot would you go to buy *francobolli*? _____

3. To which spot would you go to exchange *denaro*? _____

4. To which spot would you go to buy *un anello*? _____

5. To which spot would you go to buy *le sigarette*? _____

6. To which spot would you go to buy *il burro*? _____

7. To which spot would you go to get *la tua barba* shaved off? _____

8. To which spot would you go to get *una permanente*? _____

9. To which spot would you go to buy *una camicia*? _____

10. To which spot would you go to buy *un quadro*? _____

11. To which spot would you go to buy *un giornale*? _____

12. To which spot would you go to buy *delle buste*? _____

13. To which spot would you go to get *il tuo vestito* cleaned? _____

Situazione 4: I divertimenti

Situation 4: Entertainment

You are at a ticket agency. The clerk would *not* ask you:

1. ☐ Lei vuole un biglietto per l'opera?
2. ☐ Lei vuole un biglietto per il cinema?
3. ☐ Lei vuole un biglietto per l'aereo?

If someone were to ask you what your favorite sport is, you would *not* say:

1. ☐ Mi piace il tennis.
2. ☐ Mi piace il nuoto.
3. ☐ Mi piace il calcio.
4. ☐ Mi piace l'italiano.

Situazione 5: Ordiniamo da mangiare

Situation 5: Ordering Food

Use this menu to answer some of the questions.

MENÙ			
Antipasto:	Prosciutto e melone.	**Dessert:**	Gelato Torta
Primo piatto:	Minestra al brodo Spaghetti Risotto alla milanese Tortellini alla bolognese	**Bevande:**	Vino rosso Vino bianco Acqua minerale Caffè
Secondo piatto:	Cotoletta Bistecca alla fiorentina Pesce		

A. You want to ask someone what kinds of restaurants are available. You might say:

1. ☐ Si mangia bene in Italia?
2. ☐ Come sono i ristoranti qui?
3. ☐ Che tipo di ristoranti ci sono?

B. As a possible answer you would *not* hear:

1. ☐ Ci sono ristoranti locali.
2. ☐ Ci sono i bar.
3. ☐ Ci sono trattorie.
4. ☐ Ci sono forchette.

C. When a waiter asks you to order he might say:
1. ☐ Mangia?
2. ☐ Desidera?
3. ☐ Paga?

D. To see the menu you would say:
1. ☐ Posso vedere il cucchiaio?
2. ☐ Posso vedere il menù?
3. ☐ Posso vedere il direttore?

E. Which of the following is not connected with eating?
1. ☐ La colazione.
2. ☐ Il pranzo.
3. ☐ La benzina.
4. ☐ La cena.

F. If you chose *Prosicutto e melone* you would *not* need:
1. ☐ Una forchetta.
2. ☐ Un bicchiere.
3. ☐ Un coltello.

G. If you chose *minestra al brodo* you would need:
1. ☐ Un cucchiaio.
2. ☐ Un coltello.
3. ☐ Una tazza.

H. Spaghetti, risotto, and tortellini are all types of:
1. ☐ Zucchero.
2. ☐ Pasta.
3. ☐ Carne.

I. If you want to order something from the *secondo piatto* section you might say:
1. ☐ Vorrei della frutta.
2. ☐ Vorrei un po' di sale e pepe.
3. ☐ Vorrei della carne o un po' di pesce.

J. To eat *torta* you would need:
1. ☐ Un bicchiere.
2. ☐ Una tazza.
3. ☐ Un piatto.

K. You drink *vino* or *acqua minerale* in:
1. ☐ Un bicchiere.
2. ☐ Una tazza.
3. ☐ Una bottiglia.

L. You drink *caffè* in:
1. ☐ Un bicchiere.
2. ☐ Una tazza.
3. ☐ Una bottiglia.

Situazione 6: Entriamo nei negozi

Situation 6: At the Store

Which of the following would you *not* say in a clothing store?
1. ☐ Scusi, quanto costa questa camicia?
2. ☐ Scusi, quanto costa la benzina?
3. ☐ Vorrei dei calzini e delle cravatte.

Which of the following lists has nothing to do with clothing?
1. ☐ Un vestito azzurro, una giacca rossa, una camicia bianca.
2. ☐ Due calzini, tre cravatte, un paio di mutande.
3. ☐ L'italiano, il tedesco, lo spagnolo.

You would *not* hear which of the following in a supermarket?
1. ☐ Quanto costa la frutta?
2. ☐ Dove sono le ciliege?
3. ☐ Quanto costa la carta?
4. ☐ La carne costa molto oggi.
5. ☐ Il pesce è fresco.
6. ☐ Non abbiamo più pasta.

You would *not* say this at a pharmacy.
1. ☐ **Quanto costa la medicina?**
2. ☐ Dov'è la garza?
3. ☐ Dove sono i francobolli?

You are at the laundry. You would *not* see this there.
1. ☐ Il ferro da stiro.
2. ☐ Il casco.
3. ☐ Il sapone in polvere.

You are at a barbershop. You might say:
1. ☐ **Per favore, mi dia un compact disc.**
2. ☐ Per favore, mi tagli i capelli.
3. ☐ Per favore, mi dia un biglietto.

The hairdresser would *not* ask you.
1. ☐ Vuole la messa in piega?
2. ☐ Vuole un biscotto?
3. ☐ Vuole una permanente?
4. ☐ Vuole uno shampoo?

ANSWERS

Match up the following:

1. Quanto costa un tacco per questa scarpa?
2. Ho bisogno di un orologio nuovo.
3. Quanto costa questa rivista?
4. Quanto costano queste foto?
5. Quanto costano queste cartoline?
6. Lei ha dei ricordi d'Italia?
7. Quanto costa questo compact disc?

a. Negozio di articoli da regalo
b. Calzolaio
c. Orologiaio
d. Negozio di musica
e. Chiosco
f. Negozio di fotografic
g. Ufficio postale

Situazione 7: Servizi essenziali
Situation 7: Essential Services

You are at a bank and wish to exchange a traveler's check. You might say . . .
1. ☐ Scusi, che ore sono?
2. ☐ Scusi, mi può cambiare questo assegno turistico?
3. ☐ Scusi, devo compilare questo modulo?

Now you want to deposit some money. You might say . . .
1. ☐ Vorrei versare questo denaro.
2. ☐ Vorrei pagare il biglietto.
3. ☐ Vorrei firmare il modulo.

A bank employee would *not* ask . . .
1. ☐ Per favore, firmi questo modulo.
2. ☐ Per favore, mangi la pizza.
3. ☐ Per favore, compili questo modulo.

You want to buy stamps at a post office. You might say . . .
1. ☐ Per favore, vorrei comprare delle cartoline.
2. ☐ Per favore, vorrei comprare delle buste.
3. ☐ Per favore, vorrei comprare dei francobolli.

Which of the following would you *not* say in a post office?
1. ☐ Vorrei spedire la lettera per via aerea.
2. ☐ Vorrei spedire la lettera per via raccomandata.
3. ☐ Vorrei spedire la lettera nella valigia.

You answer a phone call with . . .
    1. ☐ Pronto.
    2. ☐ Buon giorno.
    3. ☐ Ciao.

If you want to say "Who is it?" you would say . . .
    1. ☐ Come si chiama?
    2. ☐ Chi parla?
    3. ☐ Perché chiama, lei?

You want to make a long distance call. You would say . . .
    1. ☐ Vorrei fare una telefonata locale.
    2. ☐ Vorrei fare una telefonata interurbana.
    3. ☐ Vorrei il suo numero di telefono.

You want to ask someone how to dial a number. You would say . . .
    1. ☐ Scusi, come si forma il numero?
    2. ☐ Scusi, come si fa la telefonata?
    3. ☐ Scusi, dov'è il telefono?

Which of the following would *not* be used to seek help?
    1. ☐ Chiama l'autoambulanza!
    2. ☐ Chiama la polizia!
    3. ☐ Chiama i vigili del fuoco!
    4. ☐ Chiama il soccorso medico!
    5. ☐ Chiama il gatto!

You would *not* say one of the following to a doctor.
    1. ☐ Dottore, mi sento male.
    2. ☐ Dottore, lei è pazzo.
    3. ☐ Dottore mi fa male lo stomaco.
    4. ☐ Dottore, ho la febbre.

Choose the appropriate box for each of the pictures.

    A.   1. ☐ È un telegramma.
            2. ☐ È una cartolina.
            3. ☐ È una lettera.

B. 1. ☐ Si chiama per i dolori di stomaco.
    2. ☐ Si chiama per un incidente stradale.
    3. ☐ Si chiama per comprare biglietti.

C. 1. ☐ Si beve con il latte.
    2. ☐ Si beve con lo zucchero.
    3. ☐ Non si beve perché è pericoloso (dangerous).

D. 1. ☐ Si trova presso (at) un negozio di generi alimentari.
    2. ☐ Si trova nella camera dell'albergo.
    3. ☐ Si trova presso una libreria (bookstore)

E. 1. ☐ Si prende per il raffreddore.
    2. ☐ Si prende per la colazione.
    3. ☐ Si prende per la cena.

to stay, to feel

How are you?
How do you feel?
I'm well/bad
not bad

to present

A pleasure!
Delighted (to know you)!
Let me introduce you to...

to eat

I eat too much!
What is there to eat?

to come

At what time are they coming?
When is he/she coming?

to live, dwell

dwelling
I live on...Street
Where do you live?

to have

I have a lot of patience!
I haven't got any time!

to go

to go away
to go out
to return, come back

to drink

alcohlclic beverage
beverage
soft drink

to be

I'm American
I'm Italian
Where are you from?

stare

Come stai (fam)?
Come sta (pol)?
Sto bene/male
non c'è male

presentare

Piacere!
Molto lieto (m)!/Molto lieta (f)!
Ti presento (fam)/Le presento (pol)...

mangiare

Mangio troppo!
Che cosa c'è da mangiare?

venire

A che ora vengono?
Quando viene?

abitare

l'abitazione
Abito in via...
Dove abiti (fam)?/Dove abita (pol)?

avere

Ho tanta pazienza!
Non ho tempo!

andare

andare via, andarsene
uscire
tornare, ritornare

bere

la bevanda alcolica
la bevanda
la bibita

essere

Sono americano (m)
Sono americana (f)
Sono italiano (m)
Sono italiana (f)
Di dove sei (fam)?
Di dov'è (pol)?

to sit (down)

armchair
chair
Where are you sitting?
sofa

to understand

I don't understand!
I understand a little!

to see

I can't see
I'll see you!
See you again!/Good-bye!

to want

I would like
May I help you?

to change (money)

change
exchange
to keep

to walk

to drive
to go for a walk
to go by bicycle
to go on foot
to jog
to run

to leave

departure
to go away
to go out
to leave behind

to send

to mail (to put in a mail box)
to mail off

to fly

airplane   airport
boarding pass   by air
flight   ticket

vedere

Non ci vedo
Ci vediamo!
Arrivederci!

capire

Non capisco!
Capisco un po'!

sedersi

la poltrona
la sedia
Dove ti siedi *(fam)* ?/Dove si siede *(pol)*?
il divano

camminare

guidare
fare una camminata/passeggiata
andare in bicicletta
andare a piedi
fare il footing/fare il jogging
correre

cambiare

il cambiamento
il cambio
tenere

volere

Vorrei
Desidera *(sing)* ?/Desiderano *(pl)* ?

volare

l'aeroplano
la carta d'imbarco
il volo
l'aeroporto
con l'aereo
il biglietto

mandare

imbucare
spedire

partire

la partenza
andare via, andarsene
uscire
lasciare

to speak

to speak poorly
to speak slowly
to speak well
to speak too fast

to know (someone)

to know something, how to
to make one's acquaintance

to sell

on sale
for sale

to give

to be on familiar speaking terms
to be on formal speaking terms

to pay

bill
debt
payment

to ask (for)

question   to request

to cost

cost
How much do they cost?/How
much are they?
How much does it cost?/How
much is it?

to buy

purchase
to acquire
to spend (money)

to look for

What are you looking for?
Who are you looking for?

parlare

parlare male
parlare lentamente
parlare bene
parlare troppo svelto (m) / svelta (f)

conoscere

sapere   fare (la) conoscenza

vendere

in svendita, in saldo
in vendita

dare

dare del tu   dare del Lei

pagare

il conto, la fattura
il debito
il pagamento

chiedere

la domanda   richiedere

costare

il costo
Quanto costano?/Quanto sono?
Quanto costa?/Quant'è?

comprare

l'acquisto
acquistare
spendere (soldi)

cercare

Che cosa cerchi (fam) / cerca (pol) ?
Chi cerchi (fam) / Chi cerca (pol) ?

to receive

receipt   to send

to bring, carry

portable

to sign

first name
signature
surname, family name

to take

to have something to drink
to have something to eat

to please, to like

I like it
I like them
pleasant
please
With pleasure!

to sleep

to fall asleep
to go to sleep/to go to bed
to wake up

to be able to

Can you do it?
I can't!

to put

to put on   to take off

to say, tell

Tell me everything!
to tell the truth

ricevere

la ricevuta   mandare

prendere

prendere qualcosa da bere
prendere qualcosa da mangiare

potere

Puoi farlo? (fam) / Può farlo? (pol)
Non posso!

portare

portatile

piacere

Mi piace
Mi piacciono
piacevole
per piacere, per favore
Con piacere!

mettere

mettersi   togliersi, levarsi

firmare

il nome
la firma
il cognome

dormire

addormentarsi
andare a dormire/andare a letto
svegliarsi

dire

Dimmi tutto! (fam) /Mi dica tutto! (pol)
dire la verità

little, few

a little, a bit
several

that, which, who(m)

if
what
when
where
which (one)
who
why, because

preposition

at, to
between, among
for
from
in, to
of
on
with
without

how, as

How come?
What's your name *(fam)*?
What's your name *(pol)*?

much, a lot

enough   too much

to open

closed
open
to close

more

More than ever!   Never again!

how much

How much do they cost?
How much does it cost?

to answer

answer
question
to ask

poco

un poco/un po'
alcuni (m) / alcune (f)

che

se
che, che cosa, cosa
quando
dove
quale
chi
perché

la preposizione

a
tra/fra
per
da
in
di
su
con
senza

come

Come mai?
Come ti chiami (fam) ?
Come si chiama (pol) ?

molto (m) / molta (f)

abbastanza   troppo

aprire

chiuso
aperto
chiudere

più

Più che mai!   Mai più!

quanto

Quanto costano?
Quanto costa?

rispondere

la risposta
la domanda
chiedere, domandare

small

short
tall

new

again, anew

hi, hello

good morning
good afternoon, evening
good night
good-bye

better

I'm feeling better
I'm well

old

old age

all

each one
each, every
everyone
no one, nobody
nothing

easy

difficult

young

adolescent, teenager
adult
to grow up

less, minus

at least
at the very least

piccolo *(m) /* **piccola** *(f)*

basso (m) / bassa (f)
alto (m) / alta (f)

nuovo *(m)/* **nuova** *(f)*

di nuovo

ciao, pronto (on the phone)

buon giorno
buona sera
buona notte
arrivederci

meglio

Sto meglio
Sto bene

vecchio *(m) /* **vecchia** *(f)*

la vecchiaia

tutto

ciascuno
ogni
tutti, ognuno
nessuno
niente

facile

difficile

giovane

l'adolescente
l'adulto
crescere

meno

almeno
per lo meno

left

left hand
to the left

good

good at something
better
best

cold

I am cold
It (an object) is cold
It's cold

beautiful, handsome

ugly

bad

worse
the worst

expensive

cheap
costly

very, quite

very full
very tired

hot, warm

I am hot
It (an object) is hot
It's hot

big

fat
huge
skinny, thin
wide

sinistro

la mano sinistra
a sinistra

buono (m) / buona (f)

bravo (m) / brava (f)
migliore
il migliore

freddo (m) / fredda (f)

Ho freddo
E' freddo (m) / fredda (f)
Fa freddo

bello (m)/ bella (f)

brutto (m) / brutta (f)

cattivo (m) / cattiva (f)

peggiore
il peggiore

caro (m) / cara (f)

a buon mercato, economico
costoso (m) / costosa (f)

assai, molto

assai/molto pieno (m) / piena (f)
assai/molto stanco (m) / stanca (f)

caldo (m) / calda (f)

Ho caldo
E' caldo (m) / calda (f)
Fa caldo

grande

grasso (m) / grassa (f)
grosso (m) / grossa (f)
magro (m) / magra (f)
largo (m) / larga (f)

city

building
city hall
downtown
movie theater
museum
office
skyscraper
square
theater

address

apartment   house, home

right

right hand
to the right

country

farm
field
flower
grass
landscape, countryside
plant
tree
village

to travel

excursion, tour
map
to arrive
to leave
travel agency
trip

date

then
yesterday
after
already
always
before   never
now   often
today   tomorrow
What's the date?

shop

to shop (in general)
to shop (for food)

street

block (of a city)
corner
highway
sidewalk
traffic lights

place

behind   far
here   near
on top   under
up   there
down   where
in front

la bottega
fare delle spese
fare la spesa

la strada, la via
l'isolato
l'angolo
l'autostrada
il marciapiede
il semaforo

il luogo

dietro   lontano
qui/qua   vicino
sopra   sotto
su   lì/là
giù   dove
davanti

il paese
la fattoria
il prato
il fiore
l'erba
il paesaggio
la pianta
l'albero
il paese, il villaggio

viaggiare
il giro
la cartina geografica
arrivare
partire
l'agenzia di viaggi
il viaggio

la data, il giorno

poi
ieri
dopo
già
sempre
prima
adesso, ora   mai
oggi   spesso
               domani
Che giorno è/Quanti ne abbiamo?

la città
l'edificio
il municipio
il centro
il cinema
il museo
l'ufficio
il grattacielo
la piazza
il teatro

l'indirizzo
l'appartamento   la casa

destro (m) / **destra** (f)
la mano destra
a destra

ticket

round-trip ticket
to purchase a ticket

train

first class
seat
train station
schedule
track

porter

elevator
stairs
tip

hotel

boarding house
front/registration desk
key
reservation
room

church

cross
mosque
synagogue
temple

castle

bridge
tower

store

clothing store
food store
hardware store
stationery store
bookstore
department store
drugstore
music store
shoe store
smoke shop

market

merchandise
merchant
stand (of merchandise)

bank

account
bank book
check
bank employee
deposit
form (to fill out)
to deposit
travelers' checks
to withdraw
withdrawal

il facchino

l'ascensore
le scale
la mancia

il castello

il ponte
la torre

la banca

il conto
il libretto di banca
l'assegno
l'impiegato (m) /l'impiegata (f)
il deposito, il versamento
il modulo (da compilare)
depositare, versare
gli assegni turistici
prelevare
il prelevamento

il treno

la prima classe   l'orario
il posto   il binario
la stazione ferroviaria

la chiesa

la croce
la moschea
la sinagoga
il tempio

il mercato

la merce
il mercante/ la mercante
la bancarella

il biglietto

il biglietto di andata e ritorno
fare il biglietto

l'albergo

la pensione
il banco d'accettazione
la chiave
la prenotazione
la camera

il negozio

il negozio di abbigliamento
il negozio di alimentari
il negozio di ferramenta
la cartoleria
la libreria
il magazzino
la farmacia
la discografia
la calzoleria, il calzolaio
la tabaccheria, il tabaccaio

clothes

blouse
boot
coat
jacket
pants
shoe
stocking
sock
shirt
skirt
sweater
tie

door

car door
front door (to a building)
handle

hotel room

bathroom
bed
floor
TV set
wake-up call

house

bathroom
bedroom
entrance
garage
living room
exit
kitchen
roof

price

cheap
expensive
fixed price
How much does it cost?
sale
What's the price?

customs

border
customs officer
identification (paper)
passport
to declare

money

bill
credit card
lira
cash money
dollar
small change

suitcase

carry-on bag
lost suitcase
luggage
to pack one's suitcases

baggage

heavy
light
weight

i vestiti, i capi di abbigliamento

la camicetta
lo stivale
il cappotto
la giacca
i pantaloni
la scarpa
la calza
il calzino

la camicia
la gonna
la maglia
la cravatta

la casa

il bagno
la camera da letto
l'ingresso
l'autorimessa, il garage
il soggiorno, il salotto

l'uscita
la cucina
il tetto

il denaro

la banconota
la carta di credito
la lira

i contanti
il dollaro
gli spiccioli

la porta

lo sportello
il portone
la maniglia

il prezzo

a buon mercato, a buon prezzo
caro (m) / cara (f)
il prezzo fisso
Quanto costa?
il saldo
Qual è il prezzo?

la valigia

la borsa a mano
la valigia smarrita
i bagagli
fare le valigie

la camera

il bagno
il letto
il piano
il televisore
la sveglia

la dogana

la frontiera
il doganiere
la carta d'identità
il passaporto
dichiarare

il bagaglio

pesante
leggero (m) / leggera (f)
il peso

vegetables

bean
cabbage
carrot
cauliflower
eggplant
olive
pea
string bean

mushroom
onion
potato
tomato

fish

clam
lobster
salmon
shrimp

cod
mussels
seafood
trout   tuna

to be hungry

I'm not very hungry
I'm very hungry

bread

baker
bun

bakery
sandwich (flat)

meat

bacon
beef
chicken
cold cuts
ham
pork
turkey

lamb
sausage
veal

to be thirsty

I'm not very thirsty
I'm very thirsty

water

alcoholic beverage
coffee
mineral water
tea

beer
juice
soft drink
wine

meal

breakfast
lunch
dinner
snack
to have breakfast
to have lunch
to have dinner

purse

briefcase
handbag
knapsack, schoolbag
wallet

la verdura

il fagiolo
il cavolo
la carota
il cavolfiore
la melanzana
l'oliva
il pisello
il fagiolino

il fungo
la cipolla
la patata
il pomodoro

il pesce

la vongola   il merluzzo
l'aragosta   le cozze
il salmone   i frutti di mare
il gambero   la trota   il tonno

avere fame

Ho poca fame
Ho molta fame

il pane

il panettiere   il panificio
il panino   il tramezzino

la carne

la pancetta
il manzo
il pollo
gli affettati
il prosciutto
il maiale
il tacchino

l'agnello
la salsiccia
il vitello

avere sete

Ho poca sete
Ho molta sete

l'acqua

la bevanda alcolica   la birra
il caffè   il succo
l'acqua minerale   la bibita
il tè   il vino

il pasto

la (prima) colazione
il pranzo
la cena
la merenda/lo spuntino
fare la colazione
pranzare
cenare

la borsa

la cartella
la borsa a mano
lo zaino
il portafoglio

time

What time is it?
It's one o'clock
It's two ten
It's six thirty
It's noon
It's midnight
It's five minutes to nine

weather

It's cold
It's cool
It's hot, warm
It's sunny
It's raining
It's snowing
It's windy
It's beautiful (weather)
It's awful (weather)

season

spring   summer
autumn, fall   winter

week

Monday
Tuesday
Wednesday
Thursday   Friday
Saturday   Sunday

day

morning   afternoon
evening   night

month

January   July
February   August
March   September
April   October
May   November
June   December

fruit

apple
apricot
banana
cherry
grapefruit
grapes
lemon   orange
pear   pineapple
peach   strawberry

food

cheese   drinks, beverages
condiments   pasta
egg   vegetables
sugar

kitchen

cup   fork
glass   knife
plate   spoon
table

la stagione

la primavera   l'estate
l'autunno   l'inverno

il mese

gennaio   luglio
febbraio   agosto
marzo   settembre
aprile   ottobre
maggio   novembre
giugno   dicembre

la cucina

la tazza
il bicchiere
il piatto
il tavolo, la tavola

la forchetta
il coltello
il cucchiaio

il tempo

Fa freddo
Fa fresco
Fa caldo
C'è il sole
Piove
Nevica
Tira vento
Fa bel tempo
Fa cattivo/brutto tempo

il giorno, la giornata

la mattina, il mattino   il pomeriggio
la sera, la serata   la notte

il cibo

il formaggio
i condimenti
l'uovo
lo zucchero

le bevande
la pasta
la verdura

l'ora

Che ora è?/Che ore sono?
E' l'una
Sono le due e dieci
Sono le sei e mezzo
E' mezzogiorno
E' mezzanotte
Sono le nove meno cinque

la settimana

lunedì
martedì
mercoledì
giovedì   venerdì
sabato   domenica

la frutta

la mela
l'albicocca
la banana
la ciliegia
il pompelmo
l'uva
il limone   l'arancia
la pera   l'ananas
la pesca   la fragola

color

orange
black
blue
brown
green
red
white
yellow
gray

hand

finger
fingernail
thumb
index
ring finger
middle finger
little finger

titles

Mr.
Mrs.
Miss
Dr.
Prof.

body

arm
chest
knee
neck
foot
leg
shoulder

child

boy
girl
teenager, adolescent

family - 2

aunt
uncle
cousin
grandfather
grandmother
relative
parents

head

ear
eye
face
hair
lip
mouth
nose
tongue
tooth

friend

enemy
friendly
friendship

family - 1

brother
daughter
father
mother
sister
son

il colore

arancione
nero (m) / nera (f)
azzurro (m) / azzurra (f)
marrone
verde
rosso (m) / rossa (f)
bianco (m) / bianca (f)
giallo (m) / gialla (f)
grigio (m) / grigia (f)

la mano

il dito
l'unghia
il pollice
l'indice
l'anulare

il dito medio
il mignolo

titoli

Signore
Signora
Signorina
Dottore (m) / Dottoressa (f)
Professore (m) / Professoressa (f)

il corpo

il braccio
il petto
il ginocchio
il collo

il piede
la gamba
la spalla

il bambino (m) / la bambina (f)

il ragazzo
la ragazza
l'adolescente

la famiglia - 2

la zia
il zio
cugino (m) / la cugina (f)
il nonno
la nonna
il parente (m) / la parente (f)
i genitori

la testa

l'orecchio
l'occhio
la faccia
i capelli
il labbro
la bocca
il naso
la lingua
il dente

l'amico (m) / l'amica (f)

il nemico
amichevole
l'amicizia

la famiglia - 1

il fratello
la figlia
il padre
la madre
la sorella
il figlio